BEYOND TIPPING POINT

ANDREW DYHIN

ABOUT THE AUTHOR

Andrew Dyhin is an author, engineer, project manager and innovator based in Melbourne. Day to day news, cross-referenced and viewed from outside the square, provides him with exciting material to formulate into eco-thrillers designed to entertain and at the same time generate discussion about alternatives to every day scientific, economic and political news.

The fictional media empire created in his first novel is on the verge of breaking the news on several more topics of world importance over the next few years.

By Derialle Pty Ltd
ABN 34912749342
11 Mulsanne Way Donvale Victoria 3111 Australia
Telephone: +61412501987 Email: andrew@andrewdyhin.com

Copyright © Derialle Pty Ltd

First published in Australia August 2015
This edition published August 2015
Copyright © Andrew Dyhin 2015
Cover design, typesetting: Working Type Studio (www.workingtype.com.au)

The right of Andrew Dyhin to be identified as the Author of the Work has been asserted in accordance with the Copyright, Designs and Patents Act 1988.

This book is a work of fiction. Any similarities to that of people living or dead are purely coincidental.

All rights reserved. No part of this publication may be reproduced, stored in a retrieval system, or transmitted, in any form or by any means without the prior written permission of the publisher, nor be otherwise circulated in any form of binding or cover other than that in which it is published and without a similar condition being imposed on the subsequent purchaser.

Dyhin, Andrew
Beyond Tipping Point
ISBN 978-0-9944107-0-2
352pp

This one's for James

CHAPTER 1

Halley Research Station, Brunt Ice Shelf, Antarctic

15 March 2015

Halley Research Station is run by the British Antarctic Survey, and is located on the Brunt Ice Shelf along the Weddell Sea in Antarctica. On 15 March the station appeared deserted; it had been battened down for the onset of winter. Two weeks ago, forty of the fifty scientists at the station went back to England. That left a core team of ten to man the station for the bleak winter ahead.

The six months of the Antarctic endless day was coming to an end. Over the next month, the base would gradually fall into perpetual darkness, as the Antarctic entered its long night. The winds created and demolished the continually changing ice and snowfields. The ice shelf had changed dramatically since the establishment of the station in 1956. The bay that the station was originally named after has since disappeared as the elements reshaped the coastline. The scenery was littered with ice mounds and snow drifts in every direction. To the south, the mountains were barely visible. To the north, you could not distinguish the interface between windswept clouds and the ice field.

The wind in the morning was a light easterly. As the day progressed, gusts of up to 15 kilometres per hour caused flurries in the deep powdery snow as the temperature hovered around -20 degrees Celsius. Occasionally there was a bright flash of sunlight as gaps appeared in the cloud cover. The gaps in the cloud were relatively small, magnifying the intense brightness of the sunlight that appeared as an explosion of light as it hit the snow and ice.

Mark Peters had been running the Halley Station for the past five years. He was tall with brown eyes, receding brown hair, a well-toned muscular body and a very cheerful disposition. He had a military background, and a few weeks ago he'd met John Newbury, the Secretary of State for Energy and Climate Change in London before he flew to the base for this winter assignment.

This morning at 8 am, Mark got a call from the minister.

'Minister, Station Manager Mark Peters here.'

'Mark, good to talk to you again. How's the weather holding down there?'

'Not too bad thanks Minister, although it's going to get pretty nasty in the next twenty-four hours.'

'Mark, I'll get to the point. The reason for the call is that I have an urgent request from Downing Street. It appears that they're in a bit of a dither about all the global warming stuff. What you may not know is that we've been cutting back on support for alternative energy projects, due to a growing uncertainty as to its necessity. We bit off more than we could chew when we started the cutbacks by the looks of it. The sector started shedding jobs so fast that we now have a labour crisis.

'Downing Street wants to confirm that the underlying premise of the Stern Report is correct. To do that, the people advising them want the other theories confirmed, validated or checked. Your team is best placed to do that.'

'That could be correct, Minister. I assume that they gave you a list of tests they want us to carry out?'

'There's an email being sent as we talk.'

'Minister, you're new to the position, so you may not be aware that the staff at one of the earlier Halley stations had been instrumental in discovering the ozone layer hole. We're maintaining that research amongst numerous other projects, so the scientific capabilities of the team are extensive.'

'Spot on Mark, I still have a lot of reading to do. Especially on what your team does down there. Are you near your computer? We should go through that list.'

Mark sensed anxiety in the minister's voice. 'I'm just opening the email.'

'As you will see, we need to confirm the extent of the ozone hole, get current cloud reflectivity readings and check the ice build-up on the shelf.'

Mark, a little perplexed, considered his next words carefully, not wanting to embarrass or aggravate the minister. 'That data is being collected by the satellites daily.'

The minister paused then continued, sounding aggravated. 'Therein lies the problem. Downing Street has sound intelligence to suggest that the data has been hacked. We need to do a manual check of the readings being taken by the satellites to be sure that decisions are being made on factual information.'

Mark was astounded but he couldn't stop to think about the implications of the satellite information being incorrect. 'Sounds serious, Minister. Understanding the nature of the request makes a quick response possible. Is it only verification of reading values as opposed to confirming the theories that is required?'

'Can I have an example please?'

'Of course. If the satellites are reporting that there's a build-up of one metre of snow and ice per annum, then we find 2 metres of ice at the marker poles-that would prove a data fault or tampering with the satellites. Is that the sort of comparison you're looking for?'

'Precisely.'

'How soon do you need the results?'

'Mark, it's a very high priority task, so what is the best you can do?'

'We can turn verification around in twenty-four hours, subject to the usual weather and communication constraints. Minister, if you're not aware, the southern lights and storms can impact on communications when they occur in unison. They could stop communications for up to ten weeks or right through winter if it gets intense.'

The minister was silent.

'Are you there, Minister?'

'Yes, I'm here. No delays please Mark, you had better get started.'

Mark heard the increased strain in the minister's voice. The minister had a hard job; the honeymoon period in his new job was definitely over. A delay in providing the information would look very bad for the department and the responsible minister. The Halley team needed to perform, and to get him the results today.

'We'll be straight onto it,' said Mark. 'Expect results inside twenty-four hours, Sir.'

Mark reflected on the conversation for a few minutes before printing the orders and calling a team leaders meeting. The concept of the brief was unbelievable. Hacking of satellite data – why would anyone do that?

Mark was firm with the delivery of the orders from London. The staff generally didn't like last minute changes to their plans; he anticipated resistance and would have to deal with it as it arose. Tony Grey, one of the team leaders, became particularly agitated.

'Mark, why the particular urgency? We have a whole program of tests and works to be completed this winter. This work is unplanned. The satellites do the same tests every day!'

Mark had anticipated Tony in particular being difficult – Tony didn't like change. 'Tony, the minister delivered the orders himself. His orders came from Downing Street and he was not prepared to accept no for an answer, or even consider delays. I know it's a bit harsh, but we don't have time to debate the matter. The weather maps show a front closing in. I'm ordering you to get on with the work right now, please.'

Tony threw up his hands then exclaimed, in utter exasperation, 'Yes Minister!'

After carrying out safety reviews and making a risk assessment, the management team approved a six-hour window for tests to be carried out. The teams were to be back at base by 1500 hours to avoid the incoming severe weather conditions. The approaching weather was expected to cause a total whiteout, with temperatures as low as -40 degrees Celsius and winds gusting to 110 kilometres per hour. At this location without the appropriate survival equipment, those conditions were lethal.

CHAPTER 2

Tony Grey and Peter Smith had spent the last three hours verifying satellite readings of the ice thickness 10 kilometres from the Halley research station. The shelf was up to 150 metres thick and moving toward the ocean at over half a kilometre per year. Up to one and a half metres of snow and ice accumulation buried everything on the surface annually. This barren environment experienced temperatures of 0 to -55 degrees Celsius and 105 days of darkness per year.

Tony was short and heavily bearded; he almost looked like a bowling ball in his bright orange survival gear. Peter, on the other hand, was considerably taller and made an impressive figure in his.

The work that Tony and Peter were doing involved inspecting stakes driven into the ice at one hundred metre intervals. Each stake had graduations on it, measuring the depth of the build-up of snow and ice above a reference point.

Ice had encrusted Tony's beard, his eyes straining through his sunglasses from the occasional brilliant light on the ice field. The light flash created by breaks in the cloud was making progress slow; it took Tony's eyes one to two minutes to adjust after each flash. Welding goggles would have been more appropriate in these climatic conditions; sunglasses did not have the ability to screen out the intense flash of light.

Tony watched Peter check the measuring pole. He had worked with Peter for the last ten years. Peter was a likeable character with a calm demeanour which is important for working in isolated regions. He never lost his temper, even in the most tense and frustrating situations. Peter completed a computer log, photographed the pole markings and location designator, and then moved with Tony to the next pole.

When Peter finished the next set of readings, Tony motioned to him for the camera. Tony inspected the photographs and the computer logs several times and then checked the results against the satellite data. He sat down on the ice, his confusion showing clearly on his face. He needed to shout to be heard above the increasing noise of the wind. 'Peter, can you check this information for me please?'

Peter sat down with his back into the wind to perform the checks. A small snow mound began to form against his back from the wind-driven snow and ice as he checked the data. 'This is amazing.' Peter had a deep frown on his forehead. He continued. 'The satellite readings indicate that we have an increase of 1.05 metres of ice cover in the last twelve months. We haven't been manually checking these poles because of the satellites – everybody assumed that the information from them was correct and accurate. The poles are indicating that the satellites are out by up to 950 millimetres. The reality is the shelf thickness is growing at almost twice the rate that we have believed from the satellite readings.'

Tony moved closer to Peter, analysing the data again. When he completed the check, he looked at Peter. 'I'm not sure what this means. Comparing results back at base with the other teams will give us some idea as to what is going on … I hope. If London suspected this, it certainly gives us some reason for being asked to do these tests.'

'You don't think there's any chance that Andy might have played a practical joke and hammered these pegs down, do you?'

Peter laughed. 'Now that would be a great way to get yourself kicked off the base. But it's a good point. We'll need to add tamper checking to all our results from now on. But these posts don't look to have been disturbed for some time.'

Tony and Peter continued taking their readings, checking information along the pole line until it was time to head back to the station.

The wind speed had intensified to 30 kilometres per hour. With the increase came a much higher volume of airborne snow – the conditions were starting to get unpleasant. Tony and Peter concentrated on stowing their gear and didn't hear the skidoo approaching them. They both felt an impact on their right buttock.

At first Peter began to turn, then he realised that he no longer had control of his arms or legs, and could not draw a breath. He fell face down into the snow, unable to struggle anymore. His lungs and brain screamed for oxygen; he felt no pain as the blackness of death crept over him.

Beside him Tony remained upright, as if frozen in time. The skidoo driver tied a rope around Tony's legs and pulled him 150 metres away from the pole line. He then returned and dragged Peter in the other direction. After a few days, it would be almost impossible to find the bodies; they would have been frozen into the shifting landscape.

———

Michael Bates and Sarah English were out on the ice a kilometre from the station; they, like their colleagues, had their faces encrusted in ice. They were setting up a shelter to hold back the wind and snow, while they launched a helium balloon to photograph the clouds from above.

They worked in silence until the shelter was in place. Michael looked at Sarah. Her face was white, her lips blue, her visible blonde hair encrusted in ice and snow. Sarah looked like an orange Michelin man in her bulky thermal suit; there was not a hint of the curvaceous young blonde woman that was inside it. Michael was pleased to be working with Sarah – she was witty, intelligent and never left anything to chance.

'Cuppa Sarah?'

Sarah flashed a delighted smile. 'Love one.'

Sarah found Michael a little over-caring, but an excellent scientist. He loved research and often surprised her with his depth of knowledge on the environment and anything to do with the weather. She chuckled to herself as she watched Michael head back to their snow cat. He was such a gentle giant, a tall solid man in his early fifties. He walked with a slight limp, the product of a skiing accident in his thirties.

The wind was unrelenting; they would be launching the balloons in winds of up to 30 kilometres per hour. It was not ideal but they needed the information. Michael finally returned from the snow cat with hot tea and toasted muffins coated in apricot jam.

Sarah stared at the muffins; she was delighted. 'Michael, where did the muffins come from?'

Michael shrugged his shoulders. 'If you don't want them, then all the more for me,' he teased.

Without a word, Sarah took the muffins and her tea and went back to the shelter to enjoy them. *He's always thinking ahead*, she thought. *These do look yummy though.*

The experiment they were to conduct tied together several theories, and was to test the reflectivity of the Antarctic cloud cover. Higher reflective cloud meant that less of the sun's energy was able to penetrate the clouds and warm the Antarctic continent. Without the reflected heat, there was the potential for more ice formation and less thawing. This could counter any local global warming effect. The experiment involved sending a balloon above the cloud mass and measuring the amount of light it reflected back into the sky.

After the tea break, Sarah inflated the balloon, which they were able to successfully launch. Within half an hour the balloon was streaming data back to their instruments. Over the next three hours they were able to launch two more balloons. Each launch was as successful as the first and again the data streams were collected and logged, ready for analysis when they returned to base. But it appeared the cloud cover was more reflective than normal.

It took Sarah and Michael over one hour to pack the equipment away and disassemble the shelter. By then the wind speed had reached 40 kilometres per hour; they were both very happy to be ready to return to the station. Just as they were entering the snow cat, about to leave for the station, a skidoo approached from the south and pulled up beside them. Neither Sarah nor Michael saw the dart pistol that the rider drew on them and fired in rapid succession. They both struggled mentally at first, then succumbed to the effects of the powerful paralysing agents.

The Halley station stood out in the environment. Like its predecessor stations, this one had gradually been surrounded by a wall of snow and ice – a product of the massive build-up on the ice shelf. Due to the hive of activity around the station and the compacting and clearing of snow, the station appeared to sit in a narrow valley. Unless the station was moved during the next summer, the walls of the valley would gradually move in and encase the station, in time crushing it.

The current Halley Station was modular and could be moved to avoid burial in the ice and snow. This new station was a marvel of engineering and science. It took four years to construct – extensive environmental and material issues needed to be overcome before the final design was complete. Its predecessor stations were buried and crushed by the relentless onslaught of the elements. The station rose out of ice and snow; its brightly coloured modules standing out against the harsh white light of the environment. The legs on the modules made them look similar to armoured troop carriers out of a sci-fi movie.

Andy Burns and Sean Haynes steadied their large balloon. They were working beside the station because of the size of their instrument package. The package was too large to easily transport to a more suitable launch site. A few more adjustments and they were able to release the balloon and its valuable cargo. At first the balloon did not rise, dragging the instrument package along the ice. Gradually the balloon gained stability – half a kilometre from the base it began to soar, and seconds later, it passed through the cloud layer and was out of sight. Andy and Sean collected their equipment and headed for the laboratory in the fifth module.

Andy and Sean had been the caretakers of the ozone layer hole research since 2005. They had been given the task of confirming the current extent of the ozone hole. Usually this sort of request came in to be quoted, checked against the station schedule and then planned into the workload if required.

Andy and Sean had attended Cambridge together and since 2007 had volunteered to do the winter shift at Halley Station. Both were Londoners; Andy had a tendency to play practical jokes and was an extrovert by nature. He had a slight build and a forever smiling face. Sean, on the other hand, was the quiet nerdy type who took his work very seriously. He was taller than Andy and tended to be much more serious.

Their lab had an enclosed porch where they were able to remove their outer protective clothing and boots before entering the lab.

As soon as he got inside Andy rushed across the lab to the monitors. He flung his hands in the air and shouted, 'Did you turn the instrument package on, Sean?'

Sean sank to the floor on his knees. He had a feeling of utter despair; then he remembered who he was dealing with and launched himself across the room towards Andy at the monitors.

Andy came running at him. 'Wrong way dummy; we have to launch another balloon,' he yelled at Sean.

Sean met Andy halfway and tackled him to the floor. Fortunately their lab was large and had a lot of open space. They both crashed to the floor heavily.

Andy began to laugh. 'Okay, okay you caught me out.' He sighed and extracted himself from Sean's tackle. He reflected on the moment; Sean was getting too good at calling his bluff. He was definitely going to have to change his tactics around him.

Sean sat up on the floor. 'Andy, do you have any idea why we're doing these experiments?'

'Wish I knew. But I suspect something wrong with the satellite data or something like that, because what we're doing is manual checks and you would use that to verify the satellite stuff, so that's my best guess.'

'That sounds fair enough to me.' Sean headed across the room to the instrument panel. He called back to Andy, 'At 4 kilometres and rising at 10 kilometres per hour, we'll get into the bottom layer of the stratosphere in about 70 minutes. Time for a coffee.'

The stratosphere contained the ozone layer that protected the earth from harmful radiation from the sun. This was the altitude at which their instruments started streaming data back to them.

'Might as well head back to the accommodation module. The balloon will take an hour to get to the target zone,' said Andy.

Sean nodded. 'Sounds like a great idea, let's go.'

Andy and Sean headed back to the first module by the interlocking corridors that linked the modules together. It took them no more than five minutes to get to the accommodation module and the mess hall. Both of them were surprised to find Mary Anderson, an environmental scientist, alone in the module.

Andy grinned; he was in a flirtatious mood. Mary was always a good sport. 'How's my gorgeous Mary on this fine autumn day?'

Mary shook her head. Her brown eyes flashed as she attempted to work out Andy's next move. Her light frame tensed; she brushed her long brown hair back from her face as she watched Andy intently. 'Just wonderful Andy, and how are you this fine day?'

'Not bad at all, thanks. Where is everybody?'

'The boss, Frank and Ed are doing a lockdown inspection on the modules before the storm. I expect them back in two hours. Tony and Peter are out measuring the ice poles; Michael and Sarah are launching a cloud photography package. That's all ten of us.'

'A whole hour to kill; no bosses. Do we play up?' Andy said while leering at Mary.

Mary sidestepped Andy's playful lunge at her. 'You saw that, Sean-harassment if I ever saw it.'

Sean nodded. 'You're right – definitely harassment. Should be on video on camera three.'

Mary smiled gleefully. 'Gotcha Andy.'

Andy felt a surge of anger when he realised that the tables had turned – Sean the nerd had out-fooled him. The cameras in the common area were turned off for privacy reasons three years ago. He racked his brain, but he had no smart response. As Andy grappled with his dilemma, he went ashen. Was he losing his touch?

Sean looked at Mary. 'Have we gone too far?' he asked her.

Mary shrugged. 'Good for the old fart.' She beamed with delight. 'You're getting good at this,' she gushed. She had a soft spot for Sean but he always appeared to be in Andy's shadow or the butt of his jokes; this new twist was something to enjoy and promote.

'Let me buy you a drink, Sean.' She almost swept him off his feet as she steered him into the mess and pushed him into a chair. 'Tea, coffee?' She was loving every moment of this; it wasn't every day someone got the better of Andy.

'Coffee please,' came the reply as Sean settled in his chair.

Mary returned shortly with two Danishes and two coffees. 'Need to keep the energy up,' she said, motioning to the Danishes. Then she turned serious; she was two years his senior and felt something needed to be said. 'You keep that up, Sean. It's good for you and we'll all love it. Andy's a bit over the top at times.'

There was a noise in the doorway to the mess. Andy had fallen over a table and lay motionless on the floor.

'Ignore him,' Mary said with a flurry of her hand.

Sean smirked and took a big bite of his sour cherry Danish.

After a good minute Mary became irritable. She shouted, 'Enough Andy, a joke is a joke, but that is too much.'

Andy didn't move.

'Andy, enough,' she shouted again as she rose to her feet. 'Shit, if this is a joke I swear I'll kill you.'

As Mary and Sean approached Andy, they noticed the red dart sticking out of Andy's buttock. The significance of the dart didn't register quickly enough, clouded by their concern for Andy's wellbeing.

A figure wearing full outdoor protective clothing appeared in the doorway. Mary's dart struck her in the left thigh, Sean's in the right thigh. The effects were almost instantaneous.

Mary's feet stopped moving, and her momentum took her under the tables. She came to rest crumpled against Andy. Her last image was the look of shock on Andy's face before darkness fell over her.

Sean propelled his body toward his attacker. Even though the distance was only four paces, the potent drugs stopped him in his tracks – he crumpled at his attacker's feet like a sack of potatoes, lifeless.

Ed Chew put his pistol back in his parka pocket. He pulled back the hood of his jacket, exposing his closely cropped black hair, roundish face and warm oriental features. After surveying the scene, he took each body out onto the ice as he had done with the others. When the summer crew arrive in early spring, there will be no trace of the bodies. The terrain will be flat with snow flurries and the occasional lump but not a trace of what lay beneath.

It took Ed two hours to dispose of the bodies. When he finally returned to the mess, the wind speed outside was exceeding 40 kilometres per hour; he was covered in icicles and he was cold and hungry. He noticed a glimmer of the southern lights through the clouds as he entered the station, noting that communications would be broken. Ed was relieved; no communications removed the need to try to contact London or answer enquiring incoming calls.

Ed surveyed the scene in front of him. Apart from a few upturned chairs and moved tables, everything was 'normal'.

He moved slowly amongst the tables and chairs to place them back in their places before going to the kitchen. Ed felt broken and sad; he had no choice in this horrible matter. Mark, Frank and Eddie had been disposed of within minutes of the others leaving to conduct their experiments. They, like the others, had been dragged out onto the ice and left to be covered in the swirling ice and snow of the ever-increasing storm.

As an agent, Ed had been part of the British Antarctic team for fifteen years, diligently relaying information to his superiors in Beijing. His assignment ensured a comfortable life for his wife, parents and son. The state would look after all of them as part of his contract and sacrifice.

Part of his report earlier in the morning, with the details about the urgent testing, had caused his activation. As he made himself a meal, he continued to ponder the meaning of his instructions. Slowly it began to dawn on him: he was alone and facing 105 days of darkness, and there would be no mission to extract him …

Any thoughts about the reason for the activation no longer mattered. The last line of the instructions now became clear: leave no trace.

CHAPTER 3

Port-aux-Français, Kerguelen Islands, Southern Ocean

16 March 2015

At the French research station on the Kerguelen Islands, Tony Lee was doing routine maintenance on the base helicopter. Tony had been recruited by the Chinese while studying in Paris. His study in Paris was part of an exchange program; his scholarship, part of a large scheme to infiltrate key areas in defence and science within the French military. He had been part of the Antarctic scientific community for five years.

His activation call this morning had been a surprise. The orders he received were even more surprising. His mission, to deactivate the helicopter 'as inconspicuously as possible', was a hard call. He toiled with the planning of the task for several hours. Finally he devised a 'gradual degradation' of the hydraulics associated with the flight controls. The pilot should get enough warning to return to base. The parts for repair should take six months to arrive on the summer resupply ship – just what Beijing ordered. Tony was pleased with his plan.

In Beijing, the political and labour scene was in turmoil. Suntech, the world's largest manufacturer of solar panels, had collapsed under a billion-dollar debt. The four other largest global manufacturers of solar panels were Chinese companies, each one burdened by massive debts. Layoffs in the alternative power industry were forcing thousands of workers onto the street as demand continued to fall. Globally, other green energy products were suffering the same fate. Demand fell dramatically, driven by uncertainty. The British government's slashing of expenditure and support for that sector was causing global instability. Up to now, the Stern Report had been held high as one of the cornerstones of green energy. With the British government appearing to abandon its commitment and funding, confidence in the market was tumbling.

A secretive intelligence unit of the military in China was monitoring developments around the world in the energy sector and environmental sciences. Twenty-four hours earlier, the team had activated a containment policy aimed at protecting Chinese interests. This unit had infiltrated all levels of research and energy business groups around the world. The group was well-trained in containment and information management. Their current operation focused on the Southern Ocean; significant concerns had been raised about a report requested from the British Halley base in response to a directive from London.

The containment policy had as its objectives: shut down the Halley base, restrict flights out of the French Kerguelen base for the next ninety days and monitor all activities in the Southern Ocean.

Within the intelligence arm, other groups were involved with managing social unrest, and placing orders on the factories. The orders would ensure that there were no new job losses for at least ninety days.

CHAPTER 3

In London, John Newbery and several advisers stood, silently watching a large weather map of the Antarctic. There was a massive weather system moving onto the Halley station. Another wall board mapped the electrical disruption caused by the southern lights' activity being experienced in Antarctica in real time.

The chief scientist shook his head and addressed the minister. 'Sorry Sir, when these weather patterns close in and are accompanied by the southern lights, we can expect to lose communication with the station for eight to ten weeks.'

'Damn it. Damn it all.'

The minister left the room at a brisk pace. He walked head-down, talking to himself. In half an hour he had a meeting in the Prime Minister's office, a meeting where he had nothing to report.

CHAPTER 4

Nice Côte d'Azur Airport, France

23 May 2015

Arriving at Nice mid-morning, Timothy Wiley was not shocked to find the airport utterly packed with tourists for the Monaco Grand Prix but was still taken aback by how many people there were. He wove his way through the crowds to the rental car counters where he was recognised and escorted into a VIP lounge. The attendant was very polite and efficient; a slightly-built young man with an engaging face and smile.

'Monsieur, please wait in the lounge. Just ask if you would like tea or coffee.'

Timothy flashed a brief smile. 'Thank you, I'll do that.'

A few minutes later the attendant brought around a Mercedes sports car. 'I see from your file, Monsieur, that you have driven this car before. There are no changes from the previous car you drove. Would like me to take you through any of the features before you take the car out?'

'No, I think that'll be just fine. Thank you very much.'

The attendant packed his luggage in the boot and waved at Timothy as he drove off.

CHAPTER 4

Behind the wheel Timothy began to relax. He set the GPS for Monaco, retracted the roof and drove out of the security car park.

It was a bright sunny day, and Timothy enjoyed the forty-minute drive through the hills to Monaco. It only took a slight movement of his wrists for the car to change direction, and a squeeze on the accelerator to produce numbing acceleration. The traffic was heavy but he enjoyed the power and precision of the sports car, moving smoothly through the traffic along the mountainous roads. As he approached Monaco, the ocean glimpses became more and more spectacular.

He enjoyed the time he got away from the office – no minders to crowd him, and no chauffeurs to deprive him the joy of driving. He was well aware that once he arrived in Monaco he would be surrounded by an advanced security and communication team, briefed to ensure that carefully controlled photographs and newsreels beamed around the world through Timothy's media empire, him being with Penelope providing both page one and three news. In the press, Penelope and Timothy appeared oblivious of the watching eyes and envy of millions of people, as their fairy tale relationship unfolded in the playground of the rich and famous. Timothy directed his staff to be unobtrusive. He was the business owner; who he was seen with was news. His relationship, however, was private – the business could have its photographs, but that's where he drew the line. Articles about the couple were carefully edited to deliver an image of them living life in the fast lane, surrounded by the rich and famous. The images were always of glamour and opulence with very little about the couple themselves. Content always drew the reader into following the upcoming events at which Timothy and Penelope would be present.

Timothy felt excited as he wound into the streets of Monaco but his excitement was tempered a little as he moved into streets packed with thousands of ardent Formula One fans. The air was full of the smell of high octane fuel, tyre smoke and the high-pitched whine of high performance engines. The harbor was packed with sailboats and cruisers of the rich and famous from around the world. Champagne and laughter flowed freely across the still waters of the magnificent harbor.

The car crawled through the crowds to the Monte-Carlo Beach hotel. Timothy handed the car over to the valet and checked in at reception.

He had just completed unpacking in his room when his mobile phone rang.

'It's Penelope.'

'Sweetheart, where are you?'

'I'm just outside the hotel – it's so glorious out here!'

Timothy looked out the window – 'outside the hotel' likely meant she was on the water. She was excited and almost shouting over the distant whir of the cars. Timothy sensed her anticipation.

'I don't have a boat, sweetheart, and I'm not that good a swimmer. Do you have any ideas on how I can get out to you?' he teased.

He heard Penelope take a sharp breath, then she exclaimed, 'I'm sure you can convince one of the porters to bring you out in their tender. I'll take you for a short trip on the *Ocean Odyssey* before dinner.'

'Sounds wonderful. Give me ten minutes to get changed and down to the beach. Shall we book dinner for eight o'clock?'

Penelope hesitated, her tone becoming mischievous. 'Let's decide on that a little later. See you in ten.'

Timothy casually got changed, walked to reception and arranged with the porters to be taken out to the *Ocean Odyssey*.

CHAPTER 4

As the *Ocean Odyssey* came into view Timothy again marvelled at her sleek lines. He felt pride well up in his chest. She was a forty foot marvel of high-tech engineering and materials, a fusion of Cherubini and Farr technology, carbon fibre, kevlar and titanium. The latest in computer controlled sail technology took all the physical work away from the sailor. The sailor focused on monitoring the myriad sensors provided to assist in obtaining the maximum boat speed for a given condition. Because of her narrow design and sharp bow, the *Ocean Odyssey* could sustain speeds 70 per cent above her theoretical hull speed. Timothy had secured all the IP for the design changes and believed his boat to be unbeatable. Her livery of red hull, black masts and white deck, like professionally applied make up, accentuated the beauty and masked some of the inner strength of this magnificent racing ketch.

Five minutes later, the porter brought the tender alongside, where Penelope was waiting to assist Timothy aboard.

Penelope was wearing immaculate white shorts and boat shoes, topped with a short-sleeved white blouse neatly knotted at the waist, her nipples firm against the blouse and teased by the cool offshore wind that had risen slightly as night approached. Timothy took Penelope's outstretched hand and swung aboard – he tried to pull Penelope towards him, but she released her grasp and he stumbled slightly.

Penelope's eyes flashed as she scolded him. 'Now, now, Timothy, you have to be polite. You must say hello to the lady and inspect this beautiful boat.'

Timothy shook his head, his eyes flashing mock anger as he gestured with a wave of the hand to Penelope. 'Okay, Penelope. Start the guided tour.'

Penelope moved slowly towards the bow, just out of his reach this time. Timothy tried to get closer to her; she swung around the main mast and changed direction quickly with a short giggle. Penelope took great pains to point out every trivial detail of the ketch's rigging and electronic fittings, delighting in the chase and sensing Timothy's rising passion and frustration. As they approached the stern, Timothy felt that he had her cornered, but again Penelope deftly moved past him and headed towards the cabin. She slid down the rails, barely touching the stairs on the way down. She moved quickly about the cabin, again pointing out trivial details. She moved into the galley where two glasses of champagne had been poured. She took each glass by the stem and turned to face Timothy, his frame now blocking the exit from the galley.

'Drink?' She felt Timothy's passionate gaze unabashedly undressing her as she leaned back against the galley wall. 'Didn't you like the tour, Timothy?'

'Loved it, sweetheart. You should have seen the view from where I was; that is one gorgeous arse!'

Penelope managed a bemused smile. 'And I always thought you were a breasts man. I get to learn something new about you every day. Now take your champagne and try keep your hands off me for a few minutes.'

Timothy moved into the galley and placed his hand on Penelope's as he pressed against her. She transferred the stem of his glass deftly into his hand and moved her free hand around his arm. They both raised their glasses to drink, their eyes locked in a blissful, playful gaze. They stayed locked in this position, breathing heavily and sipping champagne for what seemed like an eternity.

Only when the glasses were empty did their gaze began to wander. They both placed their glasses out of harm's way, anticipation flashing in their eyes. Timothy's hands unravelled the knot on Penelope's gorgeous white blouse. Only a single button now lay between Penelope's heaving breasts and their release from her blouse. Timothy laboured over the last button and Penelope sighed. Their lips met in a frantic, searching kiss and the button released Penelope's gorgeous breasts that Timothy's hands cupped and fondled. The kiss lasted for an eternity, both of them having to break away to catch their breath just long enough to grab a breath of air before they embraced again.

Timothy's mind raced, as he realised that there was no bed on the *Ocean Odyssey*. She was fitted with a single hammock for a single sailor. His imagination began to fly, and as they embraced he gently turned and slowly walked Penelope out of the galley and towards the hammock, until it was tight against her back. Their eyes were locked as he removed her blouse. Penelope's hands were rapidly undoing Timothy's shirt buttons; she removed his shirt and threw it across the cabin. She released his belt and slid his zipper down. Her thumbs slid beneath the belt at his hips and she pushed the slacks and briefs down to his ankles, placing her right foot between his legs and pushing his slacks and briefs to the floor. Timothy stepped out of his slacks and in the same motion unzipped Penelope's shorts, sliding her shorts and panties down her gorgeous legs. They were both breathing heavily, their gaze still locked on one another's eyes.

Timothy lifted Penelope into the centre of the hammock. She entwined her legs around his thighs, her arms around his neck. Timothy gently rocked the hammock. Penelope groaned and began to thrust. The motion was steady and controlled at first – as their passion rose, so too did the frantic rocking and thrusting. After what seemed like an eternity they both climaxed in one another's arms. They stayed locked, motionless, for two or three minutes before they gradually began to move. Timothy lifted Penelope onto the hammock and slid in next to her. They settled into a tender embrace and were asleep within minutes.

Timothy was woken by the sound of fireworks over the harbor. A party was underway, a prelude to the big race tomorrow. He tenderly looked at Penelope entwined in his arms. She was absolutely gorgeous, with light brown sun-kissed shoulder-length hair hanging gently around her face. Her eyelashes were long and fine against her golden tanned skin, her nose small and cheeky, her lips full and sensuous. She was such a joy to be around, making every moment count as if there was no tomorrow. He woke her gently and they dressed while waiting for the tender from the hotel to pick them up. They would shower in the hotel suite and enjoy dinner in the hotel's restaurant.

Twenty minutes later, Timothy and Penelope were in the hotel suite. They undressed and headed for the shower. No sooner had Timothy adjusted the water temperature than they were once again locked in an intimate embrace. Their passion was electrifying, but neither of them was fully comfortable with a tiled shower recess. Timothy picked up Penelope, who grabbed all the towels in sight. Timothy carried Penelope to the bed, towels flying to cover the sheets, and they continued their passionate lovemaking long into the evening.

Paparazzi had been waiting all evening; word of Timothy's arrival had leaked out within an hour of his arrival at the hotel. They had not been aware of Timothy taking the tender out to the *Ocean Odyssey* or his return with Penelope by the beach and pool complex.

Timothy was aware that the paparazzi were waiting in the foyer, so they used the tower lifts to get to the suite. The paparazzi constantly found Timothy and Penelope a difficult couple to track down and photograph. Penelope had the advantage of access to most of the private mooring berths and wharfs in ports around the world. Coupled with Timothy's own media team and security, and his passion for privacy, they were a very elusive couple. As a result, non-official photographs of the couple had been securing a very high premium, making the paparazzi very persistent and invasive in their attempts to secure photographs.

It was ten o'clock when Timothy and Penelope approached the restaurant. Penelope was dressed in a body-hugging, backless, ankle-length silver silk gown with a plunging neckline, accentuated by a single string of perfect natural pearls. Her shoes were white with pearlescent sheen. Her hair framed her perfect face which hardened a little as they were confronted by a wall of paparazzi. Timothy was dressed in an immaculate black suit with an open neck white shirt.

The paparazzi were still 40 metres away. Timothy pressed the button on a security beeper in his pocket and continued to walk towards the restaurant with his arm around Penelope's waist. He quietly whispered, 'The knights are on their way, gorgeous, just keep walking.'

With no less than 10 metres separating them from the paparazzi, they heard rapid footsteps behind them. Timothy quietly said, 'Just keep looking straight ahead darling,' as six security people filed past Penelope and Timothy. They ushered the waiting paparazzi away from the restaurant door, a restraining tape barrier appearing from nowhere, and Timothy led Penelope past the security men, entering the restaurant in a blaze of light from camera flashes.

They walked into the arms of the maître d', who took Penelope's hand, planted a kiss on it and exclaimed, 'Mademoiselle Penelope, Monsieur Wiley, it's such a pleasure to have you with us again. Our apologies for the photographers outside. Please, this way – your favourite table is waiting.'

Many of the other diners stopped to look at the couple – the young woman was absolutely gorgeous and radiant and the gentleman accompanying her had a face familiar to at least half the people in the restaurant. He was self-assured with a dignified presence about him; many of the diners were simply delighted by their presence. Some continued to stare awkwardly, as if in the presence of royalty. Timothy and Penelope spent the next two hours enjoying their time together and the fine food, wine and service of this delightful restaurant.

One of their admirers in the restaurant was Caroline Murray, the communications coordinator of the around-the-world race that Penelope would soon be racing in. She was with the executive of the race coordination committee, who was hosting a dinner for several large backers of the race. Caroline was a long-time admirer of Timothy, following both his business and yacht racing exploits around the world. She stared at the gorgeous woman on his arm, a twinge of envy making her feel self-conscious. She reluctantly returned her gaze back to her table. The image of Penelope in that gorgeous silver dress played on her mind. What she would do to have that lifestyle. All she could do was hope.

Caroline was currently in a relationship with James White, the race safety coordinator – however, she remained excited at the prospect of contriving a meeting with Timothy in Cape Town after the race commenced, where she was to present him with a submission from the race organisers.

Timothy and Penelope were escorted out of the restaurant by their security team at around midnight. They stepped into a waiting limousine.

'Which club?' Timothy whispered as he gently nudged Penelope's neck.

Penelope looked into Timothy's eyes. 'I'll go anywhere where you take me tonight.'

Timothy was prepared. 'Jimmi'z please, driver.'

He looked back at Penelope. Timothy remembered the first

time he set eyes on her; she had just won the last of her eight international boat races. The media loved her and the public was captivated by her stunning beauty and seemingly endless winning streak. What he really liked about her was her ability to captivate people with her smile – and when you talked to her, you felt you had her undivided attention. She worked a crowd well, enjoying the attention and making an impact on everyone in the room.

A gentle nudge brought Timothy back from his thoughts. Penelope had a broad smile on her face. 'A penny for your thoughts? We're here.' she gently pushed him toward the car door.

They danced and partied until very late in the evening. After they got back to their suite, they collapsed in each other's arms and slept well into the morning. They took a long shower together, enjoying the luxury of a back scrub and the occasional lingering kiss.

At breakfast the hotel manager joined them. 'Monsieur, the hotel would like to invite both of you to the hotel's corporate cruiser during the race in the afternoon. The cruiser is moored just beyond the tunnel, midway down the Formula One race straight. It has a magnificent view of the race. We can assure you, this will be a gala occasion with an A-list of guests.' The manager focused his attention on Timothy.

Penelope was squeezing Timothy's hand as hard as she could to get him to accept the generous offer. After a few seconds delay Timothy conceded to Penelope's pressure. 'We would both love to attend, thank you.'

The hotel manager beamed; getting Timothy as a guest was a major coup. He knew Timothy as a forty-two year old self-made media mogul who ran a billion-dollar enterprise out of the United Kingdom. Timothy and Penelope were valued regulars to their hotel.

Timothy always had special security requirements to ensure that he was not hassled by the paparazzi or autograph hunters. This time they had a large security team who also stayed in the hotel – Penelope was going to have celebrity status at the function.

'Wonderful, wonderful, Monsieur. The hotel tender will pick you up on the beach at 3 pm.'

Penelope and Timothy spent the hours between breakfast and the race browsing in and out of the many shops lining the streets of Monaco. They were both oblivious to the large crowds, only seeing one another, totally engrossed in their time together.

Penelope headed into a small boutique, with Timothy just a step behind her. 'I just realised I don't have a cocktail dress for this afternoon.'

'That's not good. Let's get you a dress,' Timothy said, settling into a comfortable chair against the wall.

After several fittings behind closed doors, Penelope emerged in a body-hugging strapless black dress. The dress accentuated her curvaceous five foot seven body, her light brown hair and golden tan. Timothy beamed.

'Do you like it Timothy? What do you think?'

'You look delicious. I'd …'

Penelope cut him short. 'Not in public please – you could make me blush!'

With Penelope wearing matching shoes and carrying a small black bag, they slowly wandered back to their hotel. Both were oblivious to the efforts of Timothy's security people in keeping the paparazzi at bay. Arriving at the hotel, they entered via a side entrance. They walked back to their suite after stopping for a few moments to gaze out at the spectacular ocean view.

Penelope's thoughts drifted away as she looked at the ocean. Her time on land with Timothy always felt like a fairy tale. Her feelings were confusing her; she didn't want a permanent land-locked existence. She was in a battle with herself, passion against desire – she lived for the ocean, its solitude, the intense rivalry of the competitors and the ecstatic thrill of winning. That was her greatest high.

A gentle nudge from Timothy brought her back to the beach. 'Time to get ready,' he whispered.

They arrived at the beach and were whisked away to the cruiser in the Monaco harbour. The maître d' welcomed them on board, then escorted them around the deck. It was a delightful crowd, intrigued by Penelope's up and coming exploit to single-handedly circumnavigate the world in a boat race. Timothy stood back a little from the limelight, savouring every moment of Penelope's animated description of her exploits. With her delicious personality, she was able to draw out even the most timid person she talked to. She was perfect beyond his wildest dreams – to be his wife, business partner and lover. He had begun planning his proposal for the end of the round-the-world race. Hopefully she would be exhausted with her dream of continuing to race and not in the mood for leading him on a merry chase. The car race seemed secondary to the social and business networking that held the attention of those enjoying the hospitality of the hotel under a cloudless blue sky.

The food and wine flowed all afternoon, and it was early evening before Timothy and Penelope caught the tender back to the beach. They lingered beside the bar at the sea lounge, taking in the glass-smooth ocean and the large sinking orange disc of the setting sun. They held hands in silence as the sun appeared below the horizon and the orange glow gradually faded, replaced by a darkening night sky.

Back at their suite, Timothy and Penelope teased one another about the afternoon. The laughter and skirmishes died down and conversation turned from the afternoon to one another and why they were still wearing clothes. The latter sent them into a frenzy; there was no longer any time for teasing. Their hands moved with serious intent as each piece of clothing was removed. The last few items disappeared at a frantic pace and their naked bodies met in the middle of the lounge room. Penelope pushed Timothy onto the sofa, straddling him like a motorcycle. She maintained that position, gyrating on his muscular body until they both climaxed. Timothy pulled Penelope against his body and rolled onto the sofa until he lay on top of her. Penelope protested, but to no avail – her cries were muffled in a passionate kiss, which changed to squeals as he nibbled her ear and neck. They remained embraced in each other's arms until well into the evening, deciding that dinner was unnecessary after hours grazing on the cruiser.

Their conversation gradually drifted to their feelings toward each other, work and the future. Penelope held Timothy's face while she spoke to him.

'I love you, but that can't mean that I can't sail anymore. Sailing to me is like breathing. It's something you do to stay alive, do you understand me?'

Timothy stiffened. He looked at Penelope; her eyes were wide open and she didn't blink. He felt confronted. He decided the truth was his only option, for better or worse. 'Penelope …' He hesitated. 'You know that I've been working on getting you to have more of a land-based lifestyle ever since I met you. I feel that it's important for us to spend more time together.'

Penelope's eyes flashed with momentary anger. She steadied herself then began to speak quietly. 'I'm not a butterfly that you can pin to a board. Pinning me would make me lifeless … if you want to enjoy this butterfly, it has to be free – that's what you love about me.' She nuzzled into his neck. 'Don't be so difficult. I miss you when I'm at sea … isn't it exciting when I get back?'

Sensing an impasse, Timothy steered the conversation to the news stories of the last couple of days, in particular those that she shared an interest in. They shared a growing sense of intrigue at how there were such differing opinions on the environment and global warming being canvassed in the media.

'What are the scientists saying?' Penelope asked, rolling out of his arms. She propped her head up on her hands and looked inquisitively at him.

'Oddly enough, no-one wants to speak about it. It's an unpopular topic. Maybe it doesn't support the current theories, and nobody wants to discuss that possibility yet. All we seem to get is news about how various theories, ideas or events are occurring ... but nobody seems to have a holistic view.'

The change of topic quickly dulled the conversation – they fell asleep in one other's arms.

In the morning Timothy had an early flight back to London. Penelope was to continue her trials on the *Ocean Odyssey* and was then to return the ketch to Marseilles. At Marseilles it would be packed and shipped to London for the commencement of the race in two weeks' time. Penelope had tried to insist on sailing to London. Timothy and the team manager had convinced her that two weeks' rest and landlocked preparation was a better proposition. They argued that the risk of arriving in London tired and rundown would not be a good start to such a long race. In the morning, Timothy slipped away quietly, leaving the gorgeous Penelope enveloped in white sheets looking like a princess. His princess.

CHAPTER 5

London

6 June 2015

It was a bright sunny day, four days before the race commenced. Timothy had just picked up Penelope from their London hotel, and the race team was now doing final checks on all the equipment, race plans and provisions. Penelope, having finished her checks mid-afternoon the day before, was taking two days' rest before commencing her round-the-world race on Tuesday. She could now see why Timothy had insisted she pack light; the Porsche cabriolet he was driving didn't have very much luggage space. The porters looked at her luggage and the car; Timothy popped the bonnet, and sat looking straight ahead with a smirk on his face. Penelope and the porter managed to shoehorn her frugal luggage into the bonnet space. The porter closed the bonnet, stepped back and opened the door for Penelope. She slid into the passenger seat and playfully punched Timothy in the ribs. 'You said pack light, but that boot is ridiculous!'

Timothy reached over and drew Penelope to him, planting a long kiss on her lips and then whispering in her ear, 'I said pack light.' With that he gunned the engine with gusto, drew it out to the curb and merged into the early morning London traffic. They were driving to Brighton to spend the last two days before the race on the coast.

The paparazzi took one long look at the turbocharged Porsche, snapped a few photographs and went back to their vehicles. Timothy had pulled out the big guns and there was no point in following him on the road. His score to date on road pursuits: all wins, no losses. They would have to find another way to learn where Timothy and Penelope were going. It was a great start to the day for Penelope, as she had an intense dislike for the paparazzi and to see them surrender like this made her very happy.

'Did you pay them off?'

'No, they just know when they're beaten.' Timothy chuckled as they weaved through the light traffic towards the A23.

Conversation was light and cheerful as they drove out of the city into the country. Once out of the city, Timothy took the roof down and they continued with the wind blowing in their hair. With light conversation and laughter, the ninety minute trip seemed more like fifteen. They checked into the Hilton Brighton Metropole, and soon stood surveying the ocean view from their suite windows.

Timothy wound his arms around Penelope's waist. She leaned back into him, moaning gently. 'Mmmm,' she murmured, 'I can see why you said pack light. You feel like you're hinting two days in bed.'

She rubbed herself seductively against him. Timothy tensed as he moved his hands intently over her body. Penelope responded to his every touch; she bumped, gyrated, moaned and sighed. She turned to face him, his hands cupping her gorgeous face. Their lips met and their probing, passionate kisses grew in intensity as their hands groped at one another's clothes. Buttons came undone; a blouse and a shirt lay on the floor. Timothy marvelled at how Penelope never wore a bra in his presence; her breasts were gorgeous, with slightly erect nipples. He sank to his knees, gently teasing her nipples with his tongue. He pulled down her panties from beneath her short skirt. Passions were running high.

Penelope pushed Timothy over onto his back and she gently fell on top of him, her hands undoing his belt and zipper as they rolled on the floor. Penelope knelt and removed Timothy's slacks and briefs. It was then that she noticed that he had left champagne and flowers by the door. She chuckled to herself; either he was getting very smooth or she just wasn't observant enough. Regardless, it delighted her. *He's going to a lot of trouble to spring small surprises.*

Penelope sat forward on top of Timothy and they continued to tease one another for what seemed like an eternity. Lost in the passion of the moment Penelope, with eyes closed, hadn't noticed that Timothy was gently positioning her. With a gentle thrust, Timothy moved Penelope into a sitting position and entered her with a smooth, gentle motion. Penelope gasped and groaned, her eyes flying open. Their exploits were bathed in sunlight streaming through the windows.

After three quarters of an hour, their motions slowed. They lay intertwined in the sunlight on the floor, exhausted, with their eyes closed. Over the next two days they barely left their suite. A quick dip in the pool, a snack in the hotel café, and the rest of the time, it was room service and being alone, enjoying one another's company intensely.

CHAPTER 5

On Monday morning, they drove back to London and checked into their hotel to prepare for the race on Tuesday. They had dinner with team management at the restaurant in the hotel. The teams were checking into the hotel during the day and race briefings would commence Tuesday morning at 8.00 am for the *Ocean Odyssey* team. That would be followed by a briefing from the race organisers at ten o'clock, before the race started at midday.

After arriving back in London, Penelope spent the rest of the day shopping for those last few personal items and packing the few items that she hadn't already stowed on the boat. She was getting tense and Timothy was starting to get to her. She wanted to win this race badly but she also wanted Timothy beside her all the time. She had never felt this way before about anybody; he was so much fun to be around. When she was in his arms, she felt the world stopped and it was just the two of them and she felt wonderful.

Penelope struggled with her feelings into the evening and soon it was time to dress for dinner. She now had to decide: How would she dress for the business at hand? She decided to dress to seduce Timothy one more time before she left for her long voyage. The press were likely to be around tonight, so whatever she wore would be on the front pages of the paper in the morning. Did she care? Would Timothy mind? Probably not. That was all that mattered to her.

Penelope planned ahead. If this dress was going to have maximum impact, then Timothy would have to be right in front of her all night. She rang the restaurant and insisted on an oval table. She then allocated seating, ensuring that Timothy sat directly opposite her. She was certain after two or three hours, he'd cut the night short, just to be with her again.

At dinner, Timothy was seated at the head of the table. Miles Henderson, the team manager, was on his left; Gary Smith, the communication manager, on his right. The restaurant was packed as various media organisations had booked tables for their writers and cameramen. Several other teams were also having their final dinner with their sailors prior to the race tomorrow. The hum in the room stopped and chairs creaked as every male in the room stopped to watch the elegant young woman who had entered the restaurant. She was walking towards the table at the back of the room. Her features were exquisite, her hair framing her gorgeous face. Her lips were bright red and parted in a gentle smile, her eyes flashing gentle acknowledgement to those she knew or that acknowledged her. The breathtaking dress was antique lace, backless with a plunging neck line. The lace was superfine; there was no tell-tale bump or line hinting to anything underneath.

Miles and Gary rose out of their chairs as she approached; Timothy rose last, mesmerised, just as she expected. Penelope greeted Miles and Gary with a kiss on the cheek and shook Timothy's hand with a cheeky smile. 'Hi Boss.'

Timothy stayed composed and responded casually, 'Good evening, Miss Jones.' He then proposed a toast. 'Miss Jones, a toast to yours and the team's success.'

Penelope graciously accepted the toast, clinking glasses with Miles, Gary and Timothy, and savoured the fine French champagne.

Timothy then looked at Miles and asked, 'Are there any changes to our plans or items that we need to cover before dinner?'

Miles looked at Gary, then Penelope, then smiled at Timothy. 'Nothing else to do but win the race. We have the best sailor, the best boat, the best team, and the best owner.'

Timothy looked pleased, ignoring Penelope's gaze. He continued to discuss the race with Miles and Gary after suggesting that they choose from the menu. Timothy became engrossed in discussions with Miles and Gary, deliberately drawing the conversation away from Penelope. He had sensed her intentions and decided to draw the dinner out as long as possible. The relationship had become much more exciting from both of them as he learned to understand her feelings, tensions and motivations. The dress was meant to entice him into keeping the dinner as short as possible. Playing the game would drive the sexual tension between them to electrifying levels. If he could last under the pressure, this would be a memorable evening.

The conversation between Timothy, Miles and Gary flowed smoothly. Timothy deliberately continued to edge Penelope out of the conversation. Gary and Miles failed to notice her growing frustration. The tension defused momentarily as the waiter took their orders and delivered a new round of drinks. 'Penelope, are you all packed?' he said.

'Yes, all packed and ready to go,' Penelope answered flippantly.

Timothy again focused his conversation on Miles and Gary, systematically going through all the details of provisions, fit-out and safety equipment on the *Ocean Odyssey*. Entrées arrived, just in time to diffuse the growing tension. They dwelled on the food for a few minutes and Timothy again engaged Gary and Miles in more details relating to the race and the *Ocean Odyssey*. Suspecting a game of tension, Penelope excused herself and spent the next fifteen minutes greeting fellow competitors at their tables and wishing them all the luck in the race. She returned as the main course was served. She sat with a jubilant smile, searching each of their faces for a response.

Only Timothy appeared to understand the game. He made a supportive comment, as if to ignore her taunt. 'Did you get a chance to wish them all well?'

'I did. They're all such delightful, attentive and talkative guys.' She gave him a wicked look and transferred her attention to her main course.

The tense banter continued between Timothy and Penelope throughout the main course and dessert. Timothy insisted that they have cheese and dessert wines; Gary and Miles obliged and time dragged on. They finished dinner with a coffee and a cognac at around 11.30, by which time Penelope had become very agitated. They rose and left the almost-empty restaurant; Gary and Miles said their good nights and disappeared towards the lifts.

'Were those two having an argument?' said Miles.

'Hard to tell with those two. Personally I put it down to a really big tease.'

'Oh, to be young again!' Miles laughed.

In the hallway, Timothy turned towards Penelope with a smile on his face. 'Lovely evening, wasn't it Penelope?'

'Absolutely lovely, Timothy.'

She took him by the arm and pushed him into the nearest lift – the door had barely closed before her lips clamped onto his and her arms wrapped around his neck, her body oozing sexuality. There was no inhibition; her intent was seduction at all cost. She took his hand and directed it under her dress onto her erect nipple. The lift door opened and without disengaging their embrace they managed to get to their suite, unlock the door and enter. Penelope's dress vanished, the sudden attention making her dizzy. She had never felt this way before. She thrust her naked body against Timothy, and whispered in his ear, 'You've got three seconds to get your clothes off!'

Timothy had his clothes off in record time. Penelope pushed him into the bedroom, throwing back the sheets and pushing Timothy onto the bed. She slid onto the bed beside him; propped up on her elbow, she looked into his face with enquiring eyes. She whispered, 'Didn't you know how badly I wanted you all night?'

Timothy slipped on top of her, staring into that beautiful face, and drew her into a long, deep passionate kiss. Penelope slid her body beneath his and drew Timothy into her. She locked her ankles around his back and her wrists around his neck, drawing Timothy into a breathtaking period of intense lovemaking.

They woke at 7.30 am to the sound of Timothy's alarm; there was a mad scramble for the bathroom. They dressed quickly, made a dash down to breakfast, and then to the foyer just in time to meet with Gary and Miles and take a cab to the wharf.

Gary was in a jovial mood. 'Late night, kiddies?'

They commenced their on-board briefing at 8.00 am and were in the clubhouse by nine, with time for a coffee before the 10.00 am race briefing. The tension of the night before had vanished, and Timothy and Penelope smiled and joked with Gary and Miles while they had their coffees and watched the other teams arriving at the briefing.

At 10.00 am Caroline Murray, the race communications coor- dinator, brought the room to order and commenced briefing the sailors and their teams for the long trip ahead. Caroline method- ically covered the anticipated weather for the trip, potential hazards, and all the necessary safety procedures. She highlighted the route on a world map and what was involved in each leg of the race. She emphasised that failure to follow the prescribed route would result in disqualification. As she progressed around the globe with the race she described various festivals and events that would coincide with their arrivals. Caroline emphasised the importance of exemplary behaviour on the part of the sailors and their teams to ensure the world held the race in great esteem and secured its place in the global race calendar.

Caroline continued with her details until 11.30 am, when she made a final announcement. 'Ladies and gentlemen, the race will commence in thirty minutes. I wish you the best of luck and fine sailing ... and may the best sailor win.'

The euphoria of the race filled the room and the teams became animated, with many rounds of hugs and kisses for the sailors before they headed out to their boats. Timothy and Penelope, for the first time, showed off their relationship and emotions in public, embracing in a long passionate kiss before Penelope joined the other sailors on the tender to head out to the boats. Penelope spent a long time at the stern of the tender, watching Timothy slip further and further away through tear-filled eyes. Slowly she drew on her inner strength, and then turned to be with her fellow competitors. The mood on the tender rapidly engulfed her; she was in her element and the smell of competition intoxicated her. She began to mingle and share jokes. This would be her competitive family for the next sixty to eighty days.

The race started under London Bridge. The crowds were enormous; they lined every vantage from the bridge to the ocean. The race started without incident. There was a brisk westerly allowing for a dramatic spinnaker run down the river. Penelope reached Margate ninety seconds ahead of the pack, having steered a course down the centre of the river. At Margate, she set a course for Calais to take maximum advantage of the wind. Spectator craft made the exit from the Thames difficult and Penelope was forced to tack several times to avoid a collision.

She made a quick call to the race coordinators. '*Ocean Odyssey* to Race Control.'

'Receiving you, *Ocean Odyssey*.'

'I've been forced to tack to avoid spectators four times in the last ten minutes. Can I get a police escort please?'

'They're on their way, *Ocean Odyssey*. ETA, five minutes. Their first boat appears to have run a spectator craft down.'

How predictable, thought Penelope, *there's such a large crowd of spectator boats and too few police boats. I hope no-one got hurt.* 'Thank you control.'

The start of the race had been spectacular. There had been thousands of spectator craft and clippers. The water was churning into a confused mix of wakes from craft and the ocean's swells. The clippers played havoc with the wind and Penelope had to work hard to keep her line in the difficult conditions. Ninety minutes into the race, she was clear of the spectator fleet, with only open water ahead of her. She was now three minutes ahead of her closest rivals. Penelope kept an eye on the wind speed. That had been an incredible start to the race. A helicopter appeared to her north, flying to intersect her course. It was one of Timothy's film crews, taking footage of the race. The film crew got their footage, did a flyby at a respectful distance and headed back to London. The quiet after they left was a relief for Penelope. Now it was just the ocean, and the *Ocean Odyssey*. Penelope could now enjoy the race.

The coast of Calais came up sooner than expected. The westerly had increased in power and Penelope was keeping to the centre of the channel to gain as much power from the wind as possible while it lasted. The weather report before the race had predicted that the wind should start to ease several hours into the race. She scanned the surface behind her and detected a wind shift five miles out. It was time to use the full force of the wind and head towards the French coast. The direction change proved to be a stroke of genius. Behind her, the fleet was becalmed while she approached 15 knots ahead of the westerly.

Penelope watched the horizon as she tidied the deck of the *Ocean Odyssey*. It was going to take several days to make landfall in Cape Town, and it was important to keep the decks clear and safe at all times. Her passion in adhering to these important routines had made her a world champion, feared by all male and female competitors. Her attention to detail made reacting to change effortless – everything was in its place, always ready to be used. An albatross appeared to be stationary off to her port as it rode the wind effortlessly, and two dolphins swam ahead of the bow wave as if in a race with the boat. The sun was high in the sky; Penelope soaked in the warmth. She knew the Southern Ocean and its bitter cold was only days away to the south.

With the decks cleared and the course set, the steady wind and stable conditions provided Penelope time to think. She had been thinking about the hectic pace in the lead-up to the race. From the time she met up with Timothy in Monaco to now, the pace had been frantic. Timothy had been placing enormous pressure on her to give up the sea and begin a life on shore with him. She had been lulled by his passion and attention. Away from his wonderful warmth and passion, there was a creeping feeling of uneasiness about giving up her sailor's life. A life of constant wonder, the beauty of new ports, the changing faces of the people around her and the exhilaration of conquering the greatest challenges. Out here, she was free and in total control. Could she change to a life in the limelight? Always on the lookout for the paparazzi, never being able to be herself?

She responded to a sudden wind shift without losing her train of thought. A five-degree change in wind direction kept her sails full and the *Ocean Odyssey* moving at maximum speed for the conditions.

Her time in Monaco and London was disturbing her. She had realised that in front of the media, she had to rely on Timothy. He provided her with the protection and planning to avoid her life being at the media's mercy. Sailing was so different. Out on the ocean, the media tended to leave her alone. Approaching and departing ports, she was under scrutiny, but on her own boat, she had control. Landfall was usually in private marinas where she could easily avoid the media and only appear when she was comfortable to deal with them. Did life with Timothy mean that she would need to live behind closed doors?

With the boat and wind stable, she eased herself into her deck hammock and caught a few hours' sleep. The weather report was indicating increasing winds; the night could get rough and she hadn't had much sleep the night before, so she needed to sleep while she could.

Penelope slept fitfully. Was she overreacting? Could she adjust to life in the media's constant gaze? What did it mean if she couldn't? Would she lose Timothy? What would her life be like without him?

As she woke she slowly took in her surrounds. The wind had picked up a few knots, but no clouds had eventuated in front of her. Could this be another lucky break? As she turned to the north, a line of dark, low cloud confronted her. The change had moved in behind her. Her opponents would have less favourable winds, aggravated by rain and rough seas. This could give her an additional lead of up to twelve hours. This weather pattern was predicted to last up to two days, giving her a vital edge over her competitors. Penelope carefully scanned the weather charts. This latest break could get her all the way to Cape Town without much change in conditions. Her support team were miracle makers and she had steered a course within one kilometre of the plan. Weeks spent pouring over old weather maps and looking at forward forecasts had given them the edge over the opposition. She felt in command – this was her race.

Penelope's report to the team that night was going to be a glowing commendation to the planners. Her lead continued to grow. One more glance at the weather map and she was back to pondering her relationship. What would it be like if her life could be planned out as well as this race? Her attention moved back to the race – another minor course correction and she could settle in for the night.

Penelope went back to her earlier thoughts. What would life be like without Timothy at each port – the high life, the fast cars and laughter? Before Timothy, life had been simple. No fixed relationship, a carefree lifestyle going from race to race, groups of friends at each port and no media to worry about. Money was never an issue for her. She had a small amount put away; she was able to live from race to race. But Timothy wanted a land-based commitment.

After another restless night, Penelope made a promise to herself to not dwell on the issue until after the race. The strain from lack of sleep was dangerous and reckless, considering the long race ahead of her. The dawn was glorious; a golden disk rising in the east and warming the air. Penelope's spirits began to soar; the morning race reports had her competitors falling further behind in foul weather.

CHAPTER 6

Cape Town

23 June 2015

The Royal Cape Yacht Club was the Cape Town Host for the race. Penelope was startled to be woken by a motor launch while still 150 kilometres out from Cape Town. The locals had sent out a thirty metre yacht to escort her into port. The yacht's decks were awash with media and well-wishers – Penelope's mood changed instantly. This was her world; lots of excitement and the world at arm's length, under her control. She appeared on deck in shorts and a tight white blouse, acting up to the captive media; the wind was holding so the yacht was in no need of her attention. She started a conversation with the passengers through a loud hailer, keeping all the captivating adventures and tensions of the west coast trip for her formal interview later in the morning.

Ten kilometres from landfall, the escort grew rapidly and Penelope had to take the helm to be able to react to amateur sailors not following the requested race protocol for right of way to the race yachts.

As Robben Island came into view, Penelope's radio came to life. '*Ocean Odyssey*, come in.'

'This is *Ocean Odyssey*.'

'Penelope, Race Control here. There's a message from Timothy. He is running late and will not be able to come out and meet you. He will meet you at the yacht club.'

'Understood, Race Control.' *That's odd*, Penelope thought. *The plan was to meet at the yacht club – I guess he's under pressure.* Penelope caught herself being concerned about Timothy. Was there too much pressure in his life with the media empire, as well as chasing her around the world to be in every port of call?

The last 2 kilometres were very fast, with escort vessels clearing the spectators. The dock loomed and she was assisted in mooring the yacht by her attentive team.

Due to several favourable wind shifts, Penelope arrived in Cape Town around three days ahead of the nearest competitor. At the yacht club, formalities were brief. There was a formal welcome dinner that evening, after which there would be two days of rest before Penelope sailed out 24 hours before her nearest rival arrived. The city was abuzz with the celebrity sailor and her wealthy team owner. A media frenzy began 2 kilometres from the port, following them to the yacht club and then to their hotel. In their hotel room, Penelope threw herself into Timothy's arms and held on tight. Neither of them said a word; the separation had been too long and the time away from each other was becoming unbearable.

Penelope spent half an hour in the shower, warming her bones from the long chill of the race. The temperature had begun to drop the last few days, only reaching 10 degrees with the wind chill. Timothy brought her formal clothes for the dinner. She chose a three-quarter white wool crepe wraparound dress with matching pearlescent high heels and clutch bag. The crepe hugged her shape and Penelope loved its warmth and style. The dress floated like a sail as she walked, giving brief glimpses of her shapely legs.

Timothy stopped to stare as she entered the room. 'Who are you out to get the attention of tonight, gorgeous?'

'Why Timothy, I was hoping to get the attention of a different yacht owner for the race next year, since you don't want me racing anymore.' She pouted with a diabolical look in her eyes.

'Win the race and the let's consider a new job offer.' Timothy moved toward Penelope.

She sidestepped his advance, her lips parted in a mischievous smile. 'A new job offer? That's the first I've heard of that! Tell me more …' She moved again to keep him at arm's length.

'Can't tell, unless you retire from the race or win. Sorry.'

'First one isn't going to happen, and if you wait until the second one, I could end up committed to another team.' Penelope was momentarily distracted as she pondered life on another team. *Not a good thought*, she decided, but she couldn't afford to let Timothy know and spoil the fun.

Timothy had his arms around her and she struggled, but his strength overpowered her. His lips pressed firmly onto hers. She resisted him then went limp in his arms. Timothy responded in fear that Penelope had fainted; he swept her off her feet and gently placed her on the sofa, kneeling beside her with his eyes locked on her gorgeous face. Her eyes were closed, and her long lashes looked as if they were painted onto her tanned skin. Her eyes flashed open. 'What's the time?' she asked.

'7.45,' he replied.

Penelope brushed past him as she bounced to her feet. 'We can't be late!' she exclaimed. 'Guest of honour, and all that stuff! Need to put on a good show for the sponsors!' She headed for the door. 'Come on, Timothy!'

Penelope was out the door before he reacted. He found himself sprinting down the corridor to catch her. They travelled to the dinner in silence. Timothy couldn't work out if Penelope was serious about the other team or if she was just playing hard to get. He glanced at her from the corner of his eye but Penelope was looking out the window as the car moved toward the yacht club. There were paparazzi on motorbikes around their car and for the first time she appeared unfazed by their presence. Maybe she really was looking at a move. He would definitely need to make up his mind before Perth.

Penelope's anger was rising. Why wouldn't Timothy just come out and say it? They'd been together a long time! She was threatening to leave the team and he wasn't budging. She got furious with him when he was so pig headed, blind or whatever it is. Men!

The dinner was a very happy, boisterous affair. The big screen had a looped news reel with footage of the race start and sections for the race down the coast of France and the final leg into Cape Town.

Penelope did the rounds of the tables and the sponsors were keen to spend time with the race leader – and to be seen with her. Timothy circulated in the opposite direction, casting a glance in her direction from time to time. She looked radiant, but he never caught her giving him a glance throughout the evening.

Their table-hopping had them meet at a yacht manufacturer's table. Penelope was engaged in an animated discussion with the company principal when Timothy approached the table.

'Timothy, good to see you. You must be very proud of your fine sailor! That's almost a winning lead. Three days in the Roaring Forties could put her in an unbeatable lead by Perth.'

'Let's hope so Eric. The investment is huge and a great outcome is what Penelope deserves for her genius sailing. She is an asset to the sport.'

Eric turned his attention to Penelope. 'So Penelope, what's after this race?'

Timothy sensed no tension in Penelope's body as she responded to the question. Eric was a bit of a father figure to her. This was beginning to feel like a setup. 'Well Eric, I've been on Timothy's team for a while now. This race would be a mountain climbed. I could be looking for another mountain to climb.'

Yes, thought Timothy, *definitely a setup. Don't dwell on it, better move on.* 'Let's win the race first, Penelope. I'm happy to discuss all options when your race is finished.' He turned his attention to Eric. 'Let's catch up after Penelope sails. There's some business I need to discuss with you.' With that Timothy made his exit from the table.

Why is she lining up old friends? he wondered. *Is she really contemplating leaving?*

Timothy and Penelope met back at their table just as the evening was drawing to a close.

They joined a group of local sailors at the bar and shared stories of the ocean for the next two hours. Their ride back to their hotel room was again in silence.

Once inside their hotel room, Penelope exploded. 'I can't take it anymore! I think about you day and night but we need to make some decisions about us. It needs to be before the end of the race!'

Timothy felt confused. Wasn't he the one saying that this needed to be Penelope's last race? That he wanted her around him? What did he need to say or do, to put her mind at ease? Penelope's face was ashen and she appeared to be on the edge of tears. Timothy hated doing anything by the seat of his pants. This needed a lot more planning, and it wasn't something he wanted to just blurt out.

'Penelope, I've been asking you to join me on shore for a while now and I acknowledge that you want to finish this race. I suggest that we both have a long think about what we want between here and Perth. That's where we can start some serious planning. What do you think?'

'Give me a minute!' Penelope was stunned by Timothy's response. Perth, instead of London, was progress. She felt that it was probably all the progress she was going to make at this stage. Eric warned her not to push too hard. He had witnessed other women in Timothy's life push too hard, and he had walked away. 'Okay, a discussion about us in Perth. Does that mean we get there prepared to make some decisions?'

'That's the plan.'

A little colour came back into Penelope's face and a small smile touched her lips momentarily. She wasn't going to show him that she sensed victory. Not just yet. 'Okay. I'm going to have a long bath and go to bed.'

'Good night.'

Two days later, Timothy watched Penelope edge the *Ocean Odyssey* away from the wharf. The media loved her all the more for the amazing lead she had developed over the rest of the crews coming down the African coast – that lead had shrunk to just over two days while she was in port.

As the *Ocean Odyssey* slowly moved out of sight, Timothy's thoughts drifted away from Penelope back to the next phase of the race. The other teams were two days behind Penelope. There was some possibility that they could catch some of that lead up on the leg to Perth. The race committee hadn't placed the Kerguelen Plateau off limits, which did pose a risk that they could use the strength of the winds further south to catch her – but the risk in those waters was very high. The seas across the plateau were notoriously treacherous and no sailors in their right mind ventured there. Timothy's plan was for the fastest safe route to win the race and up until now the plan was working. He could not judge the risks the other teams might take to claw back two days. The legs to Perth and South America were the only ones that had a constant wind advantage available by heading further south and everything else was up to chance and good planning. There were to be no course changes for his team to pick up the constant wind advantages of the Fifties and Sixties in the race to Perth. His team would keep a close eye on the progress of their opponents and hope they didn't head south. Timothy knew the risks of his actions; he had wondered if he was needlessly putting Penelope's safety above the team effort.

His thoughts shifted. He was pleased that his business fortunes were increasing as the race progressed. The attention that his team was getting as race leader was phenomenal. There were plans to add additional sponsorship to the boat in Perth. On top of the sponsorship to date, his income from selling advertising on his media outlets had risen eighty per cent since the start of the race. Advertisers were flocking to the company; all the live TV race coverage and his internet channels were experiencing a boom in sales as the public watched the race unfold.

Timothy focused on the race again. The next strategy meeting for the team was in Perth. If Penelope wasn't race leader, would that be an opportunity to get her to give up the race? If he insisted that for safety reasons he wasn't going to let her course drop below the 40th parallel, could he lose her? Or would she give up the race and join him? The big question was: Would she forgive him if he insisted that it was too dangerous to go south of the 40th? Was that a good way to start a committed relationship? Would the regrets catch up with them one day? He continued to gaze out to sea long after the *Ocean Odyssey* disappeared across the horizon.

He was brought back to the pier by a tug on his sleeve. Caroline Murray was beside him. 'Hello Timothy. I don't believe we've had the opportunity to meet properly. I'm Caroline Murray, communications coordinator for the race.'

'Of course! Caroline, lovely to meet you.' Timothy stepped back and took in her relaxed form. He had admired Caroline's delivery at the race presentations and had placed her on his watch list as a possible presenter on his networks in the future.

'I hope you don't mind me asking, but I was wondering, are you going to be in Perth when the *Ocean Odyssey* arrives?'

Timothy was intrigued by the question – this was leading somewhere. 'Yes, at this stage I'll definitely be there. Why do you ask?'

'Well, thanks to your marvellous race coverage and the amazing lead Penelope has, the race is proving to be a major marketing and communications coup. May I invite you to lunch? There is a massive opportunity for both our teams to leverage this race to the maximum, if we can keep the drama high enough.'

Caroline had his attention. 'Lead the way.'

'I'm staying at the Pepper Club. I have a conference room there that is at my disposal for the rest of the day so the meeting will be private.'

Timothy was impressed by her efficiency. This was obviously a planned approach, pretty meticulous by the sound of it. Caroline made a brief phone call then brought her attention back to Timothy. 'This way. I have a club car waiting.'

They exited the Yacht Club to Berrio Road as the club Rolls-Royce pulled up at the curb. Timothy made a mental note: *This lady likes the high life and does it in style.*

The club was five minutes from the wharf and they spent the time in a light analysis of the way the yacht club had handled the events and the world media coverage that was increasing daily.

The Pepper Club was a beautiful complex. The boardroom they were escorted to was private, well appointed, and had a spectacular view of Cape Town. Timothy took a seat facing Caroline.

Caroline had felt Timothy's mood change back at the wharf when she mentioned the opportunity that was before them. She had watched him carefully on numerous occasions – he normally paid attention and was always courteous, but now he had become very attentive and inquisitive. The change excited her. This could be a very productive meeting. Caroline produced a folder from her bag and slid it across the table to Timothy, who was now feeling cautious.

'Caroline, is this sanctioned by the committee?'

Caroline blushed slightly then glared intently at Timothy. She smiled. 'Timothy, how could you even suggest that I would do this unsanctioned? The committee has asked me to present this paper to you for your consideration. Pending the outcome of this meeting, they may or may not choose to be involved in this process.'

Timothy started thumbing through the document. He paused at page three and looked at it intently for a good minute. He found the page had been signed off by Dave Michaelson, the race coordinator. The document signed off on an initiative, instigated by Caroline, to leverage the opportunity in the current communications portfolio to maximise the organiser's profits. Timothy looked up to find Caroline intently staring at him. Once again he admired her initiative. 'Caroline, what is your business background? Just flicking through this report, it's clear this is not the work of a communications coordinator.'

Caroline was enjoying the moment and she could see that she had Timothy captivated. She chose not to answer that question yet. This was one man whose undivided attention she wanted more than anything else. Caroline had charted the growth of the media and public interest against the difficulty of access to Penelope, the intrigue around the other yachting people and the lead that Penelope had over the fleet. The results were graphically obvious. Caroline shifted her chair and looked Timothy squarely in the eyes. 'The cost of Penelope getting to Perth more than a few hours ahead of the pack is upward of two hundred million to the race committee. I would hazard a guess that the impact on your bottom line would be in the same order of magnitude.'

Timothy returned Caroline's gaze without blinking. He then swivelled to be side on to Caroline and looked out the window. He instinctively pulled his right earlobe.

Damn her, he thought, *she has all the numbers and she's right*. The further ahead Penelope got, the less interest the public and advertisers would have in the race after Perth – he had seen it all before. If they could get the lead changing and create a bit of drama, the interest would go back through the roof!

The problem was that Penelope would lose in that type of race and she didn't lose well. Who could convince her to slow down or lose time? Timothy turned to face Caroline who had been studying his profile intently.

Just as he was about to speak, a waiter entered the room with lunch. Caroline gestured to the waiter. 'Over by the window with the mountain view, please,' she said.

They both waited in silence until the waiter had left the room. Caroline got to her feet. 'Shall we continue over lunch?'

Timothy rose to his feet, nodding. He followed Caroline to the window table that had been laid out for lunch. Caroline removed the cloches to reveal half a lobster and prawn salads. There was a bottle of white wine in the ice bucket. Timothy acknowledged her eye for detail – no dessert or entrée; just as he would order for himself. Caroline had put a lot of work into the presentation and the delivery. He felt exposed, as if someone had been watching him closely and knew a lot about him.

This is very odd, he thought. *Surely people had put this much detail into impressing me before. Why am I just noticing it now?*

Timothy looked up to find Caroline smiling at him.

She chuckled, casting him a seductive glance. 'It's the best the Cape has to offer.'

'Looks like good homework,' he quipped with a wicked smile.

'Now now Timothy, that sounds like a touch of paranoia!' *If only he knew*, she thought to herself.

'Comes with the turf,' he sighed, smiling at her laughing eyes.

Timothy opened the wine. Tokara Director's Reserve White 2008 – now he knew she had done her homework. The wine wasn't easy to find and it was his local favourite. Timothy felt that it was time to feel at ease with Caroline. If she had done this much work, he had better take her very seriously. Her technical assessment of the situation was flawless; her projections and sketch for a strategy going forward were calculated, icy and commercially brilliant. In the distance, he heard Caroline.

'A penny for your thoughts …?'

Timothy realised that he had drifted off into thought, completely ignoring Caroline – and worst of all, her empty glass. He looked into Caroline's eyes; their intensity had him mesmerised. 'I'm terribly sorry, I drifted off. Would you like some more of this exquisite wine?'

'Yes please … thank you.'

'Caroline, your observations of my likes and dislikes are exceptional. I like your presentation and I can't fault the detail.'

Caroline was breathless; she fought hard to keep her poise and managed a dignified reply. 'Thank you,' she said, looking down to compose herself.

Timothy felt a twinge of attraction at the gesture and scolded himself. *Now mister, control yourself. She's a professional doing a great job. Back to the presentation.* He handed her a glass of wine. 'Congratulations, it's a thorough and commendable presentation and a concept that we must implement together immediately. Cheers!'

Caroline was speechless as their glasses met with a crystalline *ting*! She hadn't expected this quick a closure, and certainly not for Timothy to make the close.

Timothy continued. 'The process of managing this media event is going to be very sensitive. On the one hand, we can't appear to be manipulating the outcome of the race, and on the other, we can't get ourselves offside with our teams and crews.'

'How are you going to manage that?'

'Well, Dave has been pretty helpful by letting the teams go as far as the Kerguelen Islands and beyond if they want to take the risk. I've restricted Penelope to above the 40th parallel for safety reasons.'

'I don't understand the connection.'

Timothy was surprised to find that Caroline was not aware of the significance of the Roaring Forties, Furious Fifties and Screaming Sixties. 'A bit of geographic sailing knowledge is needed here. Since the early days of sailboats taking freight around the world, they have used the constant strong winds below the 40th parallel south to do the trip in the shortest time possible. Basically, there's a lot of constant wind below the 40th, because there is no landmass to block its path.'

Caroline learned forward to capture every word Timothy was saying. She studied his face intensely; she loved his intense passion for everything he was saying. 'I never knew that. How does this work for us?'

Timothy felt a twinge of irritation at the question. This was where he was going to have to bare his soul. He was in the racing game to expand his media empire; the gains from the race to date represented about three years' profit and the race had just started. How could he package this so he didn't appear to be a manipulating business mogul?

'Well, the only way the other teams have a chance of catching Penelope, is for them to take the risk and drop below the 40th, using the resulting stronger winds and higher boat speeds to catch her. My team has its orders and they will not disobey those orders. Penelope will not drop below the 40th.'

Caroline's excitement rose. How could he be so calm? His plan from the start was to manipulate the race. Her plan was his plan. This is the outcome he planned from the start. He was just resisting admitting this to her. 'Can you rely on the other teams taking the risk?'

Timothy's attitude to the other teams changed as he sat there thinking. Of course they would take the risk – it was what he was counting on. The extent of Penelope's lead left the other teams in a desperate position. With Penelope so far ahead, the race was all but over if they didn't take the risk.

'I'm certain the *Shanghai Sunrise* and the *Ocean Mist* teams will go further south. If they don't move now, they will lose the race. Their owners probably aren't as concerned about safety as I am. I don't want Penelope taking any risks out there. The directions I have given my team also inadvertently gives me the opportunity to control who wins this leg of the race.'

'Timothy, is there any way we can ensure that your opponents head south?'

'It's a done deal. If they don't catch Penelope before Perth, the next chance is the leg to Cape Horn, and that's cutting it too fine. They need to get ahead now and fight from in front. I know these guys. They'll do that to get ahead of Penelope.'

Caroline was amazed at Timothy's confidence and that he

knew his competitors so well. She had tried to understand all there was to know about Timothy before this meeting, but she was still surprised at every turn. She felt that she had barely scratched the surface in understanding him. 'Okay, if you're happy with that, then there is just the carving up of the advertising and endorsements to deal with. I have the proposal for that in the presentation.'

Timothy reflected on the conversation – yes, he was absolutely sure that the two rival teams most likely to pose a threat to Penelope, would head south to gain an advantage. His mind wandered. It was a shame that Penelope couldn't be more like Caroline. The ability to be on land and still self-assured and confident in everything that she was doing – just like the way Caroline had put together a plan to make sure both companies extracted the maximum benefit from the situation, leveraging the human-interest side to get more paper sales, viewers and web hits.

Caroline had been watching Timothy intently. He had vanished into deep thought again and she pondered calling him back. He seemed troubled about something, so rather than taking the risk of losing him to his thoughts and possibly the deal, she interrupted him again. 'Timothy, are you alright?'

Timothy eased back into the conversation, acknowledging his distraction. 'My apologies, I've done that twice today. I have a lot to consider. In making this deal, I can make a lot of money. But if I'm not careful I could lose a lot that I care for.'

'That's fine; take your time. It's best that we get this right for both companies.' *That's it*, she thought. *Keep it commercial, keep him away from the team and Penelope, and this can be relatively uncomplicated.*

Caroline took Timothy through the proposal to boost revenues, taking advantage of the projected boost in the audience, due to race lead changes and the drama on the high sea. She stressed that the committee had left the Kerguelen Plateau in the race, knowing the advantages available there. The presentation took another two hours. The evening was rapidly approaching before Caroline completed the deal. Timothy had her email the contract to his lawyers. At the start of the final presentation, the lawyers sent their response back and Timothy was able to sign off on the deal.

They both took a break to speak to their respective offices before proceeding. Caroline took a side room and phoned Dave Michaelson.

'Dave, you won't believe it. The deal's done! Signed and delivered.'

There was silence at the other end of the line. After a long pause, Dave began in a stern tone. 'Congratulations Caroline, that's sensational. Now a word of warning miss – no running off to join a corporation as a deal maker, is that clear?'

Caroline laughed quietly on the other end of the line. 'Not today Dave, I'm exhausted.'

'How is Timothy getting to Perth? Most important, you know when he is going?'

'I don't know. Why do you ask?'

'Just thought he could travel with you, or you with him, to keep the deal bubbling over.'

Caroline was bemused by the suggestion. 'Any concerns Dave?'

'No, but if we keep him thinking about the benefits of the deal he won't have time to stray, that's all.'

'Okay, I'll see what I can do.'

Timothy touched base with his race and corporate teams. He put the media sales team on notice with an email without too much detail; they needed to be ready to strike as the race profile started to rise. The race support team was busily packing for the trip to Perth and Timothy chose not to disturb them. He would catch them in Perth – he knew they would follow his plan to the letter as always. His coordination team in London was available, so he contacted them and was pleased to hear that Penelope had reported steady progress throughout the day. The rest of the teams were also reporting steady progress into Cape Town – they were making up a little more of their lost time.

Caroline stepped back into the boardroom to find Timothy sitting at the table, looking out the window at the mountains. He turned to look at Caroline. 'Is Dave happy?'

'Yes very happy, thank you, and he sends his regards. He has suggested that you hitch a ride to Perth with me if you have no other plans.'

Timothy knew his diary intimately; there was no need to check it. He had planned to work from Cape Town or Perth while he waited for Penelope to arrive. Leaving earlier or later would make no difference, as long as he could use a laptop and a phone. He smiled at Caroline. 'When are you leaving?'

Again Caroline was stunned by the quick response from Timothy. He was the most focused and responsive person she had ever worked with. Apart from his lapses into deep thought, he was able to process information and make very rapid decisions. He was much easier to work with than the decisions by committee that she was used to.

'I'm leaving in two days, after the lead group of the pack leaves. Does that suit you?'

'That fits perfectly with my plans. Email me the details and I will make sure the schedule gets managed.'

'Of course. We'll let the teams talk to one another to sort out the plans.'

'Caroline, if any of your team is available, I think a celebratory dinner is in order.'

Caroline was thinking on her feet. Team members could over-complicate things. Dave was entertaining backers, so that meant that she was the only other team member not tied up for the evening. How would she deliver this? She didn't want to seem too forward, and couldn't let her feelings slip. 'I'm the only one free tonight. The others are tied up entertaining backers. I'm happy to accept for the team, if that's alright with you?'

Timothy felt a little uneasy – was this business relationship becoming a little too personal? 'You don't need to check with them?'

Caroline was prepared for that question, but was Timothy suspicious? 'No, I did suggest to Dave that we should take you to dinner to celebrate the agreement. Unfortunately the prior engagement has taken precedence.'

Timothy was back-peddling now. What was he thinking? Caroline was a professional doing her job. 'Sorry Caroline, you're ahead of the game again. Shall I pick you up at eight o'clock?'

Caroline hesitated. Just enough time for hair, eyes, nails, and possibly a new dress. 'Can we make that eight thirty?'

'Done, see you then,' Timothy replied. With that, he took his document folder and proceeded out of the room. Caroline sat back in the chair facing the mountains. Her head was in a spin. That was a multi-million dollar deal that they had just signed. Dave would have the first ten million settled that evening – and after that, the sky was the limit. Her half of a per cent commission was going to be a tidy sum before the end of the race.

On top of that, spending half a day with Timothy had been intoxicating. His decision-making processes were obviously a product of being incredibly well-informed about the topics that the meeting covered. To see someone that confident operate and be part of the process was where she wanted to be, as soon as possible. How was she going to keep her emotions out of the relationship? She found him absolutely gorgeous. What a man – power, intelligence, attentiveness ... and that body! Even in his trousers and open neck shirt she could see the outline of a well-toned and fit body. She had seen him with Penelope. That was a powerful relationship. Caroline remembered the scene at the pre-race dinner when the room had become hushed as Penelope entered the room on Timothy's arm. She remembered wishing like a little girl that she could have been that princess.

'Enough!' she scolded herself. 'You have to go and get ready!'

Rodwell House was a magnificent five star beachfront hotel located a short distance from the centre of Cape Town. Timothy's personal assistant had chosen the location well, with its stunning ocean views, business centre and private dining facility. It was an ideal office away from home.

He arrived at his hotel and was met by the manager enquiring about his stay, if he had any plans to extend his reservation and how the hotel could further offer assistance. Timothy smiled at the manager and contemplated a quiet evening, accompanied by the pounding surf and a quiet dinner without the irritation of the media throng a public dinner would attract. Hopefully Caroline wouldn't mind a private dinner. The manager suggested a small open-front pagoda be erected with torches and a little heating, for great ocean night views and privacy. The suggested menu was a selection of cured bush meats, parmesan and melon, with a seafood selection and an optional dessert for the lady. Timothy nodded his approval but suggested a paved area, anticipating that Caroline may wear high heels.

Timothy arrived at the club at 8.30 pm to pick Caroline up. She appeared at reception just a few minutes later and Timothy was stunned by the transformation. Earlier in the day she had been dressed in a formal navy suit with white blouse and flat shoes; her makeup was professional but not flattering. Now she was radiant; her clothes and makeup reflected her delight with herself after a very successful business day. He felt uncertain about his choice of dinner location, as Caroline appeared to be ready to party. She walked towards him, unbuttoning her coat. Timothy made a mental note – short skirt, long jacket, stiletto shoes, red lips and nails contrasting against her white coat. She looked down, highlighting her gorgeous lashes, then her eyes came into focus as they watched Timothy's with a flashing smile. Several people in the foyer stopped to stare as the two met in the centre of the room.

Timothy took Caroline by the arm and directed her towards the door. 'I've booked a private room. Or would you prefer something more public?'

Caroline was bemused by the brisk exit from the foyer, but she was relaxed. She had realised that she was meeting with a media mogul and photos of him with another woman would be gold in the wrong hands. She needed to be very mindful of that if she was going to make this venture successful.

'I think our business relationship is best kept private, Timothy. We need to protect this relationship. In future, I suggest that we arrive alone to avoid possible issues.'

Timothy gave her arm an involuntary squeeze. 'I should have thought of that. I agree, that's our strategy going forward.' He felt a twinge of uneasiness again. Caroline was ahead of him again – could he trust her? After a few moments' thought he decided that this was a win-win relationship and it was time to relax and enjoy the evening.

Caroline sensed Timothy's relief and felt warmed by the squeeze on her arm. She could sense that it was going to be a wonderful evening. Most of all, it was going to be the beginning of a great business relationship. The drive back to Timothy's hotel was taken up by light conversation. After being ushered through a private entrance, they were driven directly to the torch-lit pagoda that had been erected beside a remote lodge on the hotel grounds.

'Le Privy Club,' whispered Caroline. 'I love it!'

Timothy was impressed that the hotel manager had delivered the goods. A waiter opened the car door when they arrived at the pagoda. 'Sir, Miss, inside the lodge we have a powder room and lounge room if you wish to retire inside at any stage. The kitchen will operate for you from the lodge. This way please.'

The waiter ushered them into the pagoda, taking Caroline's coat. Timothy was again stunned by Caroline and the simplicity of her short black dress, her pearl earrings and the way her necklace accentuated her beautiful features. The waiter poured their champagne into delicate crystal flutes and left the pagoda discretely.

Timothy proposed a toast. 'To a long and successful business relationship!'

After touching glasses with a delightful *ting* they settled back in their chairs to take in the scenery. In front of them, the ocean was framed by two tall palm trees and the surf was visible under the glow of a full moon. The night was still – the only sound, the crash of the distant waves. The flicker of the torches gave the pagoda a soothing warm glow, dappling the white walls with flickers of gold.

Caroline looked at Timothy. 'It's stunning, and so private. I get the feeling this is the way you like your life to be.'

Timothy looked at Caroline, the torches flickering in her eye. 'It's an escape from the very public life I lead on a daily basis. You can imagine the media throng that I attract wherever I go.

In fact, you've seen it at the race functions. This is a regenerative time for me, a time to enjoy the presence of friends and business colleagues without intrusion.'

Caroline felt a twinge of pain in those comments. It certainly felt like work was dominating Timothy's life. His work had invaded every aspect of it, to the point where he needed to create his own privacy to get the peace and quiet he craved.

Time out Timothy, he thought to himself. *No more work tonight. The deal is signed, it's time to celebrate.* Even so, he was very conscious that Caroline and he were thinking alike and that there was an uncanny closeness in their relationship.

With a subtle wave of his arm, Timothy had the meal delivered to the table. The conversation turned away from work and they began to enjoy the relaxing environment and each other's company. Timothy and Caroline found themselves laughing at life's adventures and the trials and tribulations that had gradually drawn their lives together.

At twenty-eight, Caroline had an MBA and a degree in economics, and was starting her business career. Timothy had been through this development stage and he remembered having this type of passion. Caroline's life was very rounded and stable; she was progressing to plan and enjoyed her work intensely. She was living life to the limit. Her position as communications coordinator in the race management team could have amounted to just that, but she had turned it into a stepping-stone to take her to a new level, driving business development for the committee.

'So Caroline, are you getting a slice of the action coming from his venture?'

Caroline looked disapproving. 'Timothy, can we agree that we were not going to talk about business this evening?'

'This is about you,' he said with a wicked smile. 'This isn't about business. Don't avoid the question, out with it!'

Caroline dropped her head again, eyes down and lashes extended, a look of total exasperation. She gave him a steely look. 'Okay, if you insist. I get a small commission on all the new business that this agreement puts into the coffers of the race committee.'

Timothy beamed. 'Caroline, congratulations! I hope the commission is not too small.'

Caroline did not hesitate again. If Timothy thought it was good, it was good. 'Half of one per cent is a reasonable going rate on top of my contract.'

Timothy raised his eyebrows. 'On top of a contract, which is how much?'

Timothy wanted it all, but Caroline was getting a little annoyed. She had gone this far. 'One eighty, all expenses paid for six months work.'

Timothy raised his eyebrows again. 'Wow, that's a great rate. And there's the possibility of at least another two fifty plus on the commission. Will you be in the market after this project?'

Caroline was on the defensive now as she sensed a job offer approaching. How much was she valued at if Timothy thought her current rates were great? 'I'm still on this project but I am planning ahead. Next week I'm reviewing my résumé, including this deal. I hadn't thought about it yet.'

'That's fair enough. Based on this deal I would put your contract market value at upward of five hundred thousand per annum, plus bonuses.'

Caroline relaxed back into her chair. She had not anticipated a value above three hundred and fifty; five hundred plus bonuses was just another league. 'Thank you. I'll keep that in mind during negotiations.'

Timothy looked at his watch for the first time in the evening. It was 1.30 am. 'Look at the time! I can't believe I haven't offered you dessert.'

Caroline smiled politely. She knew that Timothy didn't eat dessert so she hadn't expected him to offer. 'I've been delighted with the company. I didn't notice that we hadn't thought about dessert.'

'That's no excuse. Would you like one now?'

Caroline frowned. Her body needed sleep. She had to be at work at eight thirty in the morning. 'No thank you, I must be going. I have a busy schedule tomorrow … have to work, you know.'

The car arrived a few minutes later and Caroline disappeared into the night.

Timothy ordered a large scotch and settled into his chair facing the beach. He listened to the waves pounding the beach for a while, then sank into a comparison between Penelope and Caroline. Penelope was still fighting his advances on her taking up a land-based lifestyle that was more stable and gave them more time together. But then what? Her whole life had revolved around sailing. He pondered his options. She was a university dropout from an engineering course who had no other driving interest other than being the best sailor in the world. Were there any career opportunities in land-based sailing? Perhaps being a commodore of a Yacht Club? That was an all-male world, which may be a challenge, but maybe she could rise to it? That was a tough one. He felt very unhappy about having to change the topic in Monaco, when he felt that she wouldn't listen to reason about being shore-based. Either Penelope accepted a life with him, not based on the ocean and a boat, or the relationship was over.

If she was to accept his request, then she would not only be a companion but also have business input and give their relationship a more balanced and rounded structure. There was common interest, and challenges to enjoy. There were wins and losses to understand, celebrate and commiserate. Certainly this day with

Caroline had opened his eyes to the opportunities beyond what he saw with Penelope. His previous relationships had been with women who had been happy to be kept as party women. He always became dissatisfied in their inability to share his business ups and downs or support him through the occasional period of anguish and the stress of a difficult business situation.

He sat on the pagoda until dawn, having taken the scotch bottle and let the staff go a few hours earlier. Before going to bed Timothy left a message for the kitchen to prepare a dessert and send it over to Caroline with lunch.

Timothy didn't see Caroline again until he boarded the A380 bound for Perth. The race committee had arranged for a private suite in first class for the trip. Caroline was seated beside him reading a magazine. She looked professional as usual.

'Good morning Caroline, how has the rest of the week been for you?'

'Good morning, and a belated thank you for lunch and dessert. It was delicious. Did you have dessert?'

Timothy smiled; she was teasing him. He figured that she had the whole flight planned and that he was not going to have a dull moment. He ignored the comment graciously. 'Are you looking forward to Perth?'

'Very much so. I haven't been there before, have you?'

'Yes I have, it's a beautiful modern city.'

As Timothy had predicted, Caroline got straight into an extension of the previous business meeting before they had even taken off. She continued almost without break until they landed in Perth. He left the airport for his hotel with a report and an agreed plan for the next leg of the race.

CHAPTER 7

Penelope slept fitfully. Her experience of Cape Town and the time she had spent with Timothy was absolutely wonderful on one hand, depressing on the other. Now she was even more torn about what she wanted for her future. She was in an isolated environment with Timothy – even the press conferences were under his control. She had no freedom at all. She wondered whether that life was really for her.

She rolled out of the hammock onto her feet; the boat was pitching more than she expected. The weather had changed in the last few hours. It was time for her to batten down the hatches and haul out the heavy running gear. She would be able to tap into the strength of the Roaring Forties a few hours earlier than planned. The air temperature was 5 degrees colder than the ten that had been predicted. She still had to go a few hundred kilometres south to get the most out of the winds. It was going to be cold down there – very cold. With somewhere between twelve and sixteen days sailing to Perth in very tough conditions, Penelope double-checked all her rigging and sails. There was no room for error at the speeds and in the tough conditions ahead.

The swells were increasing to 60 metres with a wave height of 5 metres and the wind speed had increased to 60 kilometres per hour. Hopefully the conditions would not get much worse.

She was hoping to get into calmer water 2000 kilometres west of Perth.

Six days out of Perth, as she passed the Kerguelen Islands, Penelope received a disturbing report from her team. Her two main competitors had dropped to the 50th parallel coming out of Cape Town and were reducing her lead at a rate of almost one hour in every two. Their course took them through the unpredictable and dangerous shallows of the Kerguelen Plateau. Penelope had her map out and could see the path that they were taking, but also she knew that the area had numerous unmarked hazards. The race coordinators had considered placing the area off limits but they'd relented at the last minute.

This changed everything! At this rate they would catch her in five to six days. She was now passing the islands, so she could avoid the shallows and still pick up the winds of the Furious Fifties and possibly the Screaming Sixties if needed. Could she cut off the assault on her lead? The weather maps looked positive but the air temperature had dropped to 3 degrees. Heading further south meant the danger of snow and ice, which could slow her down, but the other two boats were closing in by the hour. Her initial strategy was to see if they kept up their pace across the plateau. She should still have enough time to correct her course if needed, in twenty-four hours. Timothy's instructions were in the back of her mind, winning in the front of it.

Back at race headquarters, the team was preparing to head to Perth for the next leg of the race. Miles had his team monitoring the progress of the *Ocean Mist* and the *Shanghai Sunrise*. Both ketches were heading further south, picking up speed and closing in on Penelope's lead. Their teams were abuzz with activity – they could should catch and pass her in the next three to four days.

The *Ocean Odyssey* team was struggling with the situation but had agreed with Penelope that they would wait twenty-four hours before taking any action. Miles was constrained by the plan agreed with Timothy, and any deviation would add risk and likely not be approved. He began to struggle with that thought. All that money and effort could be wasted if they couldn't take the faster route like the other teams. Miles was reluctant to authorise any changes to the race plan, even though the race seemed to be rapidly slipping through their hands. Timothy had been very stern about the safety issues of sailing into the 50th and 60th parallel. There was speed to be gained, but the risks were just too high.

CHAPTER 8

Port-aux-Français, Kerguelen Islands, Southern Ocean

27 June 2015

The French research station on the Kerguelen Islands was a hive of activity. There had been several fleeting radar contacts in the ocean to their east and plans were being made to investigate the contacts. Speculation was rife in the camp about the source of the signals, the most possible cause being a whale breaching, or possibly shipping containers that had fallen off a container vessel in a storm. Their helicopter was fuelled up and was ready to take off, heading for the zone of last contact.

As they headed out over the ocean, the only sign of life was the seal colony on the shoreline and the occasional albatross. The winds were gusting to 60 kilometres an hour, and waves to 5 metres with swells to 70 metres. The swells were being whipped to a frenzy by the wind; the white peaks of each wave were being blown off toward the following wave.

The pilot struggled with the controls of the helicopter – they seemed slightly sluggish. He made a conscious note to have the helicopter checked again on return to base. The controls should not have been that heavy.

The radio operator called out to the pilot. 'Incoming weather Sir, they want us to return to base ASAP.'

As soon as the base issued the warning about an incoming snowstorm, it quickly swept in front of them.

'Tell the base we are coming,' reported the pilot. 'New course please, nav-man.'

The navigator began plotting a course back to the base.

Within seconds of coming about, the pilot was experiencing difficulties with his controls. He was finding it difficult to maintain altitude and bearing. He began to sweat with the exertion of controlling the helicopter.

He advised the crew of the difficulties with a stern note in his voice. 'She's being difficult lads – be prepared for anything. Watch out for your mates.'

His crew watched in white-knuckled silence as the pilot struggled with the controls. A jolt, then a dive of the helicopter saw the crew checking their safety harnesses and reassuring one other. There was tension and uncertainty in their faces.

The crew had flown with this pilot for two years and he was one of the best they had ever had. This was also the first time they had been in a helicopter having difficulties over the ocean in a snowstorm.

The pilot noticed the activity. 'Steady lads, I'm not about to put down just yet, it's too far to walk from here.'

The navigator responded immediately with a sigh of relief. 'Thank you Sir, we weren't looking forward to a swim today.'

The tension in the cabin eased immediately. There were thumbs-up signs from several crewmembers and the odd strained smile. The crew nodded encouragement to one another and eased back into their seats.

The helicopter continued to veer off course and it took the pilot several attempts to redirect it back. Thirty kilometres from base, the chopper dropped to an altitude of 1200 metres; having developed a strategy for maintaining course, the pilot worked on increasing the helicopter's altitude.

'Dump all unnecessary survival equipment,' he called to the crew.

The click of safety harnesses being released filled the air. The crew began jettisoning anything that was not bolted down.

The pilot gradually increased the helicopter's altitude and finally reached 1850 metres.

'Nineteen kilometres to base,' called the navigator.

The pilot had managed to stabilise the helicopter. They crossed the coast and a few minutes later they began dropping again. This time the pilot was unable to maintain altitude.

'Brace yourselves; we're going in,' he called as the altitude fell through 200 metres.

Crew members looked at one another for support, each one bracing for the impending impact.

'Two kilometres to base,' called the navigator, just before the pilot eased the helicopter onto the ice.

'Make the call nav-man,' said the pilot as he eased onto the ice and shut the helicopter down.

The crew looked at one another in stunned silence; the pilot got them down safely. A loud hurrah exploded from the crew.

'Mayday, mayday, base this is Chopper One. We are down 2 kilometres north of the base.'

'Base to Chopper One, received, any injuries?'

'Chopper One to base, no injuries. We have no heating so don't take too long please.'

'First cab available Chopper One.'

The pilot addressed the crew. 'Try to keep warm lads.'

It took the recovery team two hours to mobilise and find the helicopter in the snow. The crew was cold and miserable by the time the rescue team arrived. The salvage of the helicopter would need to be left until the snowstorm cleared.

At the control centre, the base commander was in a quandary. Since the helicopter had been launched, there had been no more fleeting radar contacts. With no merchant traffic in the area and no hazard description to provide, he entered the incident into the base log but did not broadcast a warning or any alerts.

He momentarily looked at the note about the Mercedes Around the World Ketch Race. He pondered the issue for a few moments but the probability of the ketches going that far south, was very remote. He chose not to issue them a warning, but he did put a posting on his website, noting the fleeting radar contacts. A footnote said that they could not be confirmed due to his helicopter being out of service.

CHAPTER 9

29 June 2015
6.00 pm Perth time
Day twenty-nine of the race

'Ocean Odyssey to Team Control.'
'Team Control receiving you, Ocean Odyssey.'
'Hi Miles, radio check time. Making about 10 to 12 knots, driven by a westerly of about 65 kilometres per hour, swells to 70 metres, waves to 6 metres, air temperature zero. It's damn cold out here!'

Miles leant into the microphone. 'Penelope, how's it going?'

'Lousy. The *Shanghai Sunrise* is catching me at about 5 nautical miles every hour. They've taken a course about 100 miles south of me and they're obviously getting a lot more wind. At this rate, they'll be in Perth two to three days ahead of me. We will lose the race if I stay on this course. Miles, I need a new course, otherwise the race is lost. It will all be for nothing!'

Miles was silent on the other end of the radio. Penelope was getting agitated.

'Miles I'm absolutely certain at this rate, we've lost the race.'

'Penelope, Timothy invested a fortune in plotting out the best course for you to follow in this race to win it. I can't change it without going back to Timothy and I just can't see him agreeing to change it.'

Penelope was nearing exasperation. She didn't feel as though she needed to negotiate this point. 'Miles, just give me the new damn course. Without that the race is all over, and trust me – you will be looking for a new job if we lose. You know how important this race is to Timothy and to me. We can't afford not to win this race. Just give me that course, now!'

Miles sensed doom if he didn't agree. Timothy had underwritten the attempt by Penelope to become the first woman to win an around the world ketch race single-handed. He had a very short temper and was very demanding of his employees. Near enough was not good enough – when Timothy laid out a plan, anyone who deviated from it did so at their own peril.

Miles turned to Gary. 'I really don't like it when she's like this! There's no point in calling Timothy because I know his answer. I also know that's not going to change the outcome – she's going to do whatever she wants. Any suggestions, Gary?'

Gary waved his hands and took a backward step. 'Way above my pay grade but you're damned whichever way you go. Sorry mate, it's all up to you, but if it were my call I'd ring Timothy.'

Miles turned reluctantly back to the microphone. 'I don't like this, Penelope.'

Penelope began to sense victory. 'Just do it Miles!'

Miles was now beyond desperation. His feeling of dread was overtaken by one of doom. He calculated the new heading. 'Alright. I don't see that you're leaving me any other options. Head 45 degrees south for a new position, 100 nautical miles south of your current course. You should intersect your new course in the next four to six hours.'

'Thanks Miles, you're all heart. Talk to you in an hour.'

Penelope's calls were uneventful until the eleven o'clock radio check.

'*Ocean Odyssey* to Team Control.'

'Team Control receiving you, *Ocean Odyssey*.'

'Hi Miles, it's radio check time again.' Penelope sounded cheerful. 'We've stopped the gain of the *Shanghai Sunrise* team, making about 15 to 20 knots, driven by a westerly of about 50 kilometres per hour, swell to 8 metres, air temperature zero. One thing, Miles ... I'm getting unusual radar contacts, between 30 and 60 nautical miles south from my current position. I'm not sure what they are. Could have been from the solar flares last week or the southern lights – radar and communications are all a bit weird down here. I will keep an eye on them.'

Miles frowned; the unexpected was always a fear in those deep southern waters. 'Gary, can you check all sources? There must be some information out there on those radar contacts.'

'Right on top of it, Miles.'

'Penelope, I don't like the sound of this. Do you have any idea what those contacts could be?'

'As I said, all I can think of is solar activity.'

'Penelope, I suggest you keep an eye on them. If any of those contacts get within ten nautical miles of you, I need you to take a 90 degree tack and head away from them as fast as possible. Is that clear?'

'Loud and clear. I think if those radar contacts get any closer than 15 nautical miles from me, I'll be making that tack.' Penelope paused. 'Back to the race. I am picking up speed, even on this tack. I really feel we made the right decision. Will report back in an hour.'

'Take care.'

Miles and Gary sat in front of their computers, scanning the web for unusual radar contacts in the southern ocean.

'Gary. I came up with a blank. How are you going?'

'Nothing conclusive here either. The French base at the Kerguelen Islands posted a report but they also said it could just be the sunspots and they are unable to send a chopper to confirm the contacts.'

'I guess we just keep an eye on it then.'

CHAPTER 10

At race headquarters Janice Yew, the *Shanghai Sunrise* team communications coordinator, was sitting in her office reflecting on the proceedings to date. The race had been uneventful for her. She would normally be at the owner's side; however, Lee Chang had been tied up with business in China and was unable to be present at race headquarters or ports along the route.

She had researched Lee's background extensively before approaching him for a position. Lee came from absolute poverty in Baotau in Inner Mongolia, and successfully completed his first property deal at eighteen years old. At thirty-two, he was one of Shanghai's many billionaires. Lee had made a name for himself in being seen in Beijing and Shanghai with the rich and beautiful set, haunting expensive bars and discos until the early hours of the morning. He had strong ties to the Communist Party and its military. She had heard that a specialist was needed to manage intelligence gathering from within Lee's business and had decided to apply for the position. She was intelligent and ambitious; within twelve months she had become Lee's current mistress – until this assignment. She knew about the length of relationships in Lee's life, and she felt they had now entered a purely business phase with this new assignment.

The race was of particular interest to the Chinese Government since it took place in the Southern Ocean. She had been instructed to be on the lookout for any unusual occurrences during that portion of the race.

Lee Chang had been very excited about employing Janice; prior to joining his team, she had been part of the intelligence community working with both the Americans and Chinese. He had found her talents extremely useful in gaining business intelligence and assisting him in furthering his business objectives in China and throughout Asia. She had been a very successful commercial operative, able to infiltrate most companies and obtain commercial information that Lee had traded with his political masters. With this information, Lee was able to obtain commercial concessions in the real estate sector across China.

These talents had made Janice a very valuable part of his team. Her efforts had added almost a billion to his net wealth and while he valued business acumen, he was beginning to tire of their romantic relationship. He had put Janice in charge of his team on the round-the-world race, to give him time to work out what to assign her to next.

It was 2 am Beijing time. Lee and his date Wendy had just returned to Lee's fortieth floor penthouse in downtown Beijing. Lee had found Wendy too attractive to stay out any longer. There was no resistance to the suggestion of going back to his place, even though it was still early.

Lee dropped his keys, quietly closed the door and followed closely behind Wendy as she moved like a moth to a flame towards the floor-to-ceiling windows. As they approached the windows, Lee quietly uttered the words, 'Music, six,' and an interactive sound system slowly came to life with an erotic soundtrack. The lights came on, low and sensual.

Wendy pressed against the window, mesmerised by the bejewelled city below and she uttered a quiet sigh. Lee pressed against her gorgeous body from behind, his hands pressed firmly on her hips. He felt the heat of her body through her sensuously clinging short silk dress. His hands moved firmly around her hips, lingering for a moment and then moving upwards with intent, finally cupping her tight full breasts under the thin sheath of fine fabric. Her erect nipples teased his palms as their bodies began to gyrate to the intoxicating music filling the room. Wendy smoothly broke from Lee's embrace, turned to face him and pressed her warm body against his like a soft pillow. The intensity of the music rose and the volume slowly crept up, enveloping Wendy and Lee with sensual tones and driving the sense of passion in the room to a frantic level. Slowly, ever so slowly, they began an erotic dance.

Holding Lee tightly as they danced, Wendy bit each button from his immaculate white cotton shirt. He groaned. Wendy wouldn't let his hands stray; she held his right hand firmly and followed his left if he tried to move it. Wendy teased Lee's thighs as they danced in a clinging sexual embrace. Wendy's petite frame was no match for Lee's muscular body and he deftly manoeuvred her through the doorway into the bedroom. Her groan sparked a flurry of activity that in seconds found them in each other's embrace, but now totally naked.

As Wendy danced backwards, she found herself up against the wall. Lee was pressed up against her; his hands firmly clasped her naked buttocks and as their lips met, he gently lifted her up the wall, sliding beneath her. She wrapped her legs around him tightly. As their kiss intensified, she slipped gently down the wall and impaled herself on his manhood. Lee's rhythmic motion intensified with the music as Wendy clung to him and pressed back against the wall. Wendy and Lee climaxed spontaneously and Lee carried Wendy to the bed, where they both lay curled in a tight embrace, breathing heavily.

CHAPTER 10

Lee turned to Wendy and was about to speak as his mobile phone rang.

'Have to take that call, I'm sorry. I'll be right back. Don't go away.'

Lee broke from Wendy's embrace and moved hesitantly back into the lounge room.

CHAPTER 11

Sanjay Singh, the *Ocean Mist*'s team manager, was in his mid-thirties. He'd worked for VJ Gupter, an IT outsourcing genius, for the last ten years.

Sanjay has risen up through the ranks, firstly as an IT project manager then as a program director. This assignment was seen in VJ's business as a stepping-stone to managing business units and then joining the board. He was now very focused on risk mitigation – looking to ensure that only praise came his way.

In Mumbai, VJ Gupter had entered the gym with his personal trainer Antara. Antara walked with a slight bounce in her step – she was very happy with her job. Being the personal trainer of a billionaire had its perks. She was petite with waist-length black shiny hair.

'VJ, today we will increase your program slightly. Your heart rate during training was slightly down last week, so we need to increase your workout just a little.'

VJ gave Antara a scornful glance and nudged her. 'You're the only person I employ who gets to push me around. But then again, none of my other employees are quite as good looking as you.'

Antara took the compliment with grace and nudged VJ back. 'Let's keep your mind on your workout, otherwise your heart rate might tell me that you're being overworked when you're not. Please begin your warm-up exercises and I will set the treadmill.'

When VJ had completed his warm up Antara motioned him over to the treadmill. 'Time for walking. I want you to do a good sixty minutes today please.'

VJ made another playful lunge at Antara. 'I will catch you one day,' he said with a grin.

Antara gave him a coy look. 'Maybe when you get fit.'

'It will help me get fit,' protested VJ.

Antara slipped out of reach again.

He donned his headband and wristbands, stepped onto the machine and commenced walking at a slow pace, while observing the television screen in front of him. Antara exited the room, expecting VJ to continue walking for the next sixty minutes.

VJ watched Antara as she left the room. His thoughts wandered – he would like to spend more time with her. She made him feel good. He reluctantly pulled his thoughts back to his exercise and the screen in front of him.

Sometime later, he was startled as Antara briskly entered the gym, carrying his mobile phone in her outstretched hand. She looked concerned, her face was strained her eyes intense.

'VJ, you have to take this call – it's from Michael Amore at the race headquarters.'

CHAPTER 12

Gary Smith, the *Ocean Odyssey* communications coordinator, was at loggerheads with his team manager Miles Henderson over the handling of the route taken by Penelope. Gary was very aware of the pressure that Miles was under and he was in no position to advise Timothy of the change in Penelope's route. He consoled himself with the fact that it was Miles's decision not to advise Timothy of the change, and not his.

Gary normally admired Miles, but this time his decision did not feel right. He had the ability to get the best team outcomes under the most difficult circumstances. Miles was in his mid-forties, and had held a management position with Timothy for six years. Prior to joining Timothy he had held media positions in the USA and Australia. Despite this, Gary felt that Miles may be a little out of his depth having to manage Penelope.

Gary was in the media room of race headquarters. While he checked his communications details, he became aware of the rising tension in the people around him. He had sensed this before; it usually came before a major announcement, a significant strategic change or an unexpected event. He was not sure which had occurred, but he knew it was his role to make sure that all his communication channels were open and working. If this was a new event, then it was up to him to get the news out first. It was 12.04 am and all the attention appeared to be centred on his own radio room. Gary rushed to the radio room to find out why and he was met at the door by Miles.

'Gary, we have a crisis.'

Miles was ashen and he motioned Gary into the room, closing the door behind them.

CHAPTER 13

Perth, Race Control Headquarters for the Mercedes Around the World Yacht Race

July 7, 2015
1.05 am, Perth time

At Race Control Headquarters, organisers and support team members anxiously watched their race monitoring screens. The focus of their attention was the last known contact points for the *Ocean Odyssey*, *Shanghai Sunrise* and *Ocean Mist* – the three frontrunners in the race. In the last hour, all contact had been sequentially lost with all three vessels. There had been no distress messages and no emergency radio beacons activated. The tension in the control rooms was mounting as the minutes ticked by.

Meanwhile, David Michaelson was discussing the race rules with James White.

'James, time is up. The rules require us to instigate a briefing and emergency plan after one hour of lost contact.'

James looked sad and quite miserable – this was not good and looked like it would get even worse over the next hour, with the clock ticking on two other vessels that had not made contact. 'Let's have that briefing soon, David. I'll get the message out.'

CHAPTER 13

James turned to his computer and scheduled the meeting with the team managers.

'Okay, time to get this meeting on the road. We'll update Caroline on the way.'

Ten minutes later, Dave Michaelson addressed the concerned gathering of race officials and team members.

'Ladies and gentlemen, it has now been over one hour since we lost contact with the *Ocean Odyssey*. The *Odyssey* failed to make her midnight radio update. Based on race rules and risk management, we have a clearly defined process to manage this situation. You all know my team by now – on my left we have James White, our safety and rescue coordinator, and on my right we have Caroline Murray, our communications coordinator.'

Mayhem erupted across the teams, with everyone talking at once.

'Dave, have there been any weather events or other disruptions in the area?'

'What about the southern lights – have they blocked out communications?'

'The weather's pretty bad down there; should we leave it another hour?'

'Have our radios and internet connections been checked?'

'Is the power on?'

Dave brought the room back under control with a loud whistle. He steadied the room with calming hand gestures. 'Stay calm everyone, please.'

Caroline took the microphone. She had a captivating and calming presence – the room responded to her with silence. 'Can the *Ocean Odyssey* team please confirm that they have had no contact with their vessel since 11 pm yesterday?'

Miles sprang to his feet. 'We can confirm that the *Ocean Odyssey* team has had no contact with our vessel since 11 pm yesterday, July 6th local time.'

'Thank you, Miles. Please give us an update on the weather conditions at the last location that we have for the *Ocean Odyssey*.'

Miles continued. 'The last communication with the *Ocean Odyssey* was at -49.75098 south, 85.103516 east. The location is approximately 1000 kilometres east of the Kerguelen Islands and 2500 kilometres southwest of Perth. The last weather report from the *Ocean Odyssey* was that she was riding the Furious Fifties in a 65 kilometre per hour westerly; air temperature was zero degrees Celsius, waves to 6 metres with long swells to 80 metres and a boat speed of 15 to 20 knots.'

Conversations erupted around the room. There was a lot of disquiet, particularly about the air temperature.

'That temperature is too low for this time of year!'

'The information must be wrong?'

'Who checked the information?'

Caroline motioned for calm again. 'I will now hand the floor over to James White, who will brief us on the risk assessment for that location and the current situation.'

It was proving to be the most difficult day of James White's career. Not one, but possibly three vessels were now in severe difficulties. In all other races, his position had been one of 'lay back and enjoy the ride'. Now he was under the hammer – he needed to perform, to earn his keep in the most stressful of situations. In the back of his mind, was the time Caroline had spent with Timothy Wiley – it was nagging at him but he couldn't quite work out why. He brought his thoughts back to the room.

'Ladies and gentlemen. Firstly, under the race rules, failure to meet a radio contact requires the racing team to activate alternative communication methods.

'Each boat has been fitted with distress radio beacons. The *Ocean Odyssey* has not activated any of her beacons which suggests she has lost radio communication or encountered severe difficulties. We must presume that a life-threatening situation exists. Before I detail the next level of risk activation, however, I should mention that we have the *Shanghai Sunrise* and *Ocean Mist* teams potentially exhibiting the same communication difficulties. At this point, I call on the *Shanghai Sunrise* and *Ocean Mist* representatives, for the record, to advise us whether they have had any communication from their boats in the last hour.'

The atmosphere in the room was electrifying; conversations again broke out all over the room.

'Who else is in trouble out there?'

'Why we just hearing about this now?'

'Is there any danger to the other boats?'

'Who's in charge here? We're just not getting the information that we need!'

Miles let out a shrill whistle and the conversations rapidly subsided.

Janice rose from her chair as she responded to the question from James. 'Janice Yew for the *Shanghai Sunrise* team. We can confirm that we have not had communication with our vessel in the last hour.' She sat back in her chair, feeling that she had just triggered a series of events that would change her life forever. She had lost several companions over the years in catastrophic events; in this case there was no reports of severe weather from the Southern Ocean. A feeling of dread rose inside her.

Sanjay Singh rose to his feet. He had a lump in his throat as he answered the question. 'We can also confirm that we have not had communication with our vessel, the *Ocean Mist*, in the last hour.'

The room erupted again, and James motioned for calm.

'Considering the high level of risk associated with this lack of communication with the three race leaders,' he said, 'I am taking the decision to treat all three vessels as being in very serious risk. I now declare a race emergency of the highest level, the time being 1.30 am on July 7th 2015. The boats in this emergency are the *Ocean Odyssey*, *Shanghai Sunrise* and *Ocean Mist*.'

James motioned Caroline to the rostrum.

'Caroline will now activate communications with the Australian Rescue Coordination Centre, under whose jurisdiction this section of the Southern Ocean lies. I would ask all three team managers to accompany Caroline to the communication centre.'

Caroline leaned over the rostrum and continued after James. 'For all the teams involved in this emergency, should you have any communication with your vessels, you must bring it to our attention immediately. Thank you for your time and please keep your eyes on the race online notice board and your emails. We will post any developments and will be in constant communication with your team managers. We are scheduling another update on the situation for 2.30 am. For now the race is still a race, so the other teams need to continue racing.'

With that, the impacted teams raced back to their team offices, to transmit the terrible news to their owners. The unaffected teams began working on strategies to win the race.

CHAPTER 14

Gary Smith had the task of advising Timothy that his boat could be missing in the Southern Ocean. He mumbled, pushing back his blonde hair as he dialled the number for Timothy's mobile phone. 'He's not going to like this; he is not going to like this at all. She was too far south; there's going to be hell to pay.'

Gary took a deep breath.

It was just after 1.30 am when the call woke Timothy. He fumbled with the phone. 'Timothy here.'

'Timothy, Gary here, sorry to ring you so early in the morning. Can you talk?'

'Keep going,' replied Timothy gruffly, as he switched the light on and eased himself out of bed.

'A serious situation is escalating in the Southern Ocean. Penelope missed her midnight radio contact and she hasn't activated any of her bacons, which makes it look as if she is in a very serious situation.'

Timothy felt empty and disorientated; a deep feeling of dread enveloped him and he struggled with his emotions. He took a few moments to regain his composure. 'Okay Gary, where did they lose contact with her?'

'-49.75098 south, 85.103516 east.'

As Timothy began to comprehend the location that Penelope

went missing at, he felt his rage growing. His response was to the point. 'What in the hell is she doing so far south?' he shouted. 'Has somebody lost their mind? We had a plan, a good plan!'

Timothy's crisis management kicked in. He took a few deep breaths seated himself at his desk.

'We'll deal with that later!' he said in a quieter tone, before his anger took control again for a moment; he cleared the top of his desk with one angry arc of his right hand. Glasses, stationary, a scotch bottle and document folders flew across the room and lay scattered on the floor. He surveyed the carnage, composed himself and continued. 'Okay Gary, what is happening on your end?'

Gary braced himself, then continued. 'The race organisers are contacting the Australian RCC and we will have an update in about an hour.'

Timothy took a long breath, did some quick mental arithmetic and started writing on a pad he had retrieved from the drawer. 'It's now 1.30 am. Gary, find out what charters I can get out of Perth to be at her last location by dawn. How far from Perth was her last location?'

Gary did a quick search of his notes. 'Approximately 2500 kilometres.'

Timothy again did the sums, looking over his notes. 'With a speed of say, 600 over water, I need four and a half hours of flying time to get to her last location. What time is first light over the location?'

Gary took a moment. 'Approximately 6.00 to 7.00 am depending on cloud cover,' he replied.

'That means I need to be on a flight in the next hour. I'll need a plane with enough fuel to give us at least two hours over the last location. There will need to be a survival raft and rations on board and the ability to drop them if we need to. Make it happen Gary. Keep in touch.'

Gary relaxed a little. That was a lot better than he thought it would be.

On the race circuit, Timothy was seen as a professional. He tended to keep his cool under the most extreme situations. His ability to immediately focus on a problem, find a solution and move forward inspired confidence – a characteristic that was uncommon amongst the owners of the other boats in the race.

Gary stared at his phone. It was 1.35 am. Fortunately his job required him to have contacts here in Perth for just such an occasion. Now he needed those contacts to make things happen, just as Timothy required. He felt this was a big chance to stand out as somebody who could get things done. Gary turned to his computer and began the process of waking his contacts.

Back in Perth, Timothy's phone rang – he had been staring out the window in deep thought.

'Timothy Wiley here.'

'It's Caroline, Timothy. Are you okay?'

'Yes, it's not the sort of drama that we wanted, but it is drama. How do you suggest we manage the external media on this?'

Caroline was taken aback. 'Aren't you concerned about Penelope, Timothy?' She regretted the question as soon as she finished it – it was none of her business.

Timothy felt exasperated by the question. 'Caroline, I have a plane to catch. I'm going to search for her within the hour. Beyond that, we have a business arrangement to manage. Black out the other media outlets; force them to take feed from me. You have my current advertising take; your team gets twenty-five per cent of the increase. Make it happen.'

Caroline had recovered from her earlier mistake and was fast to react. 'Timothy, can you repeat that back for the record, please?'

Timothy repeated the commercial terms back to Caroline for

the record. He noted her calm commercial astuteness. A rookie would have missed that, had no record and lost the deal when the lawyers got to it. 'Okay, I have to go.'

Caroline was lost for words but managed to stammer out a few. 'I hope you find them, I hope you find them all. Godspeed.'

'Thanks Caroline; speak to you later today.'

Timothy then took a quick shower and dressed, waiting for Gary to get back to him on his flight arrangements.

CHAPTER 15

1.35 am, Perth time

Simon Quan was a bespectacled, short dark-haired Harvard trained MBA who had been working with Lee Chang for five years. Simon was relaxed about the call he was about to make to Lee, as he had felt that Lee's interest in the race had slowly been undermined by his growing interest in the wealthy and ambitious young women in Beijing and Shanghai.

'Lee, can you talk?'

'Real bad timing Simon, but go on.'

'Lee, we have a serious problem here in the race. The team coordinators have escalated the risk on the three frontrunners to the most serious level. All three have failed to meet their last radio checks. None of the boats have activated any of their emergency beacons, which means a catastrophic event could have occurred. There's a good chance that we've lost Tim and the boat.'

The silence from Lee's end of the phone was deafening.

'Are you there Lee?'

The silence continued for a while longer.

'Yes, I am here.'

Lee slowly sank to the floor, his head hanging low. His mentors in the Chinese Government were counting on a victory to build prestige for the country's achievements on the world stage.

Wendy slowly entered the room, walked over and sat down beside Lee, putting her arm around his shoulders. No words passed between them as Lee stared at the phone.

'Where is Janice?' said Lee after a few more moments.

'She's with the race coordinators in Perth. They're talking to the Australian RCC who will be organising a search. Lee, do you want to fly down to Perth to be with the coordinating people?'

There was another long pause.

'No, I don't think so. We have a number of big deals on the table at the moment. I'm really torn but the business cannot risk losing these deals. Simon, please prepare a communication from the team for the media. Outline my strong desire to be there but due to pressing business needs, you and Janice will be in charge of our rescue activities.'

Lee paused.

'Please make sure I get updates as soon as they occur. I need to be constantly up to date. As soon as the media gets wind of what is going on, they will be all over me like a rash. Also loop in our corporate communications here in Beijing and Shanghai. I will be directing all media enquiries to them. Simon, I'm going to leave everything in your hands at that end; please keep me informed. Is there anything else you need to tell me?'

'No, that's about it at this point. We have another update in an hour. If there's a development, I will contact you. Apart from that, we will have an update every hour and I will only contact you if things change. That's all for now. I'd better get back to the control room. Call you as soon as there is any additional news.'

'Let's hope for the best, I'll keep my phone with me. I'll talk to you soon.'

Simon hung up the phone and headed back to the

communication centre. 'Yep, all left in my basket,' he mumbled to himself. 'A show of compassion for his sailor with a quick trip to Perth …' He was frustrated and angry – he had obviously expected too much of Lee.

CHAPTER 16

At 1.36 am Michael Amore, the *Ocean Mist* communications coordinator, was pacing nervously. Michael had joined the *Ocean Mist* team a week after the boat was commissioned. At thirty-five years old, with the weatherworn sailor's face and receding hair, he had spent fourteen years moving from one ocean racing team to another as communications coordinator. He had never been confronted with a more difficult situation in his career. He felt the next few minutes would make or break his career.

It was late evening in Mumbai when VJ answered his phone. 'VJ here. Michael, what's up?'

Michael commenced cautiously. 'VJ, you might want to grab a chair.'

There was extreme tension in VJ's voice as his short temper kicked in. 'I'm okay Michael. Why did you call?'

Michael started his delivery with trepidation. 'VJ, we have a serious problem here at the race. Sam failed to make his last radio contact. The other two frontrunners also missed their contact … all three have failed to activate any of their emergency beacons. This is a worst-case scenario. We can now only assume that some catastrophic event has overcome all three vessels.'

'Hang on a moment. You're telling me that not one of the three leading vessels has communicated or activated emergency beacons? How long have they been out of radio contact?'

'It's now close to two and a half hours since the last contact with the first vessel and two hours since last contact with the *Ocean Mist*.'

'So what are the race organisers doing at this stage? What do we need to do?'

Michael was getting frustrated with VJ. Rather than letting him provide all the information, he asked a pile of questions, prolonging the process.

'The race organisers are in control of their situation and it's now a matter of the owners getting into the act and providing support, not questioning the organiser's actions. The race organisers are talking to the Australian RCC who are about to organise a search. We are having an update shortly.'

VJ didn't see the point of getting involved in an unclear situation, as he hated wasting resources. 'Okay Michael. The situation sounds serious. Keep me informed and I will make plans at my end. At this stage, we can only hope the situation improves in the next hour.'

Michael was getting exasperated. 'VJ, I think we are at the serious stage here. The race organisers are clearly saying we're looking down the barrel of a catastrophe, which means there may be no hope of finding the vessel or Sam. If we do find them, there is little chance we will find Sam alive.'

'Michael, please don't be overdramatic,' he said. 'Give the situation one more hour – report back to me after the briefing and I'll decide what my next course of action will be.'

'It's your team, VJ. I'll call you back, bye for now.' Michael hung up the phone, his anger rising rapidly. 'Arrogant sod,' he mumbled. 'It's times like these I really hate working for this guy!'

Michael strode rapidly back towards the briefing room. It was now approaching 2.00 am.

CHAPTER 17

In the race communications room, Caroline Murray and the team managers had been in contact with the Australian RCC for thirty minutes. The regional commander, Phil Seamore of the RCC, was discussing logistics with Caroline.

'Caroline, the only aircraft that we have are Dornier with a range of 1800 kilometres, which isn't suitable for search and rescue beyond 600 kilometres out to sea. We are coordinating with the Royal Australian Air Force to bring an Orion aircraft out of Base Pearce.'

'Philip, we're very concerned about any potential delays in getting an aircraft to the search location. How long will it take to have the Orion prepared and airborne?'

There was a brief pause as Philip consulted with his team.

'The Orion is in the process of being refuelled and prepared for the search mission ... the current estimate is that it will be airborne in forty minutes. Then there will be a flight time of four and a half hours to the target search site.'

'Caroline,' said Janice, 'please ask them how long they will be able to be over the target zone, and if they are carrying supplies that can be dropped should a survivor be located.'

Philip's reply was immediate and to the point. 'The Orion will arrive forty minutes after dawn, at the last known position of the ketches. The timing allows the aircraft to commence searching as soon as it reaches the target site, with a duration of four hours. The aircraft is carrying forward-looking infrared cameras. Should survivors be located, the aircraft will be carrying additional survival gear that can be dropped to the sailors.'

Gary motioned to Caroline. 'Caroline, you want me to update Philip on what we are doing with the second aircraft?'

'Please do.'

'Philip, Gary Smith here – I'm a communication coordinator for the *Ocean Odyssey* team. Just letting you know that we will have an aircraft in the air thirty minutes before the Orion and we will need to coordinate all search activities with them. That aircraft doesn't have the thermal search capability but it is carrying additional supplies for the survivors should they be found.'

'That's great to hear; we'll take the details about setting up a communications off-line after this meeting is complete and will also make sure that all activities are coordinated. Caroline, I think we might have all the information we need at this stage. We should have continuous communication set up with your control room within the next fifteen to twenty minutes, so I believe we can conclude this meeting and commence continuous communications as soon as the links are complete.'

'Okay Philip, look forward to us having communication set up shortly. Thank you, bye for now.'

After the RCC meeting, the team managers returned to their teams and briefed them on the rescue mission. Other information on hand was not good. Satellite information on the weather in the rescue zone was indicating that air temperature was still zero degrees and the ocean waves and swells were rising.

When the link was set up to the RCC, the first communication caused bewilderment amongst the race team management.

Communications between the RCC and the French mission on the Kerguelen Islands revealed that the French mission had experienced anomalous radar contacts in the ocean around the islands in the previous forty-eight hours. At times, the radar contacts appeared to extend for several hundred metres and then disappear over a period of twelve to fourteen hours. The radar contacts had not been reported to the authorities, as they had yet to be confirmed by an actual sighting. The French mission continued to try to confirm what the radar contacts were, but as it stood they continued to list them as anomalous radar contacts and could not confirm them as being a hazard to shipping. The mission did not have a vessel capable of reaching the area where the radar contacts were made. To complicate the process of identifying the contacts, their helicopter was grounded until parts arrived to replace faulty components.

The mission team leader had strongly expressed a view that the radar anomalies were most likely caused by the current sunspot activity having an impact on the radar electronics, thereby giving the unusual contacts. The French team had been running electronic diagnostics on their radar for the last thirty-six hours to ascertain if the contacts were in fact being generated within the electronics of the radar system due to the sunspot activity.

The RCC had alerted the Antarctic division in Hobart and requested their input into any unusual weather activities in the target region. It was anticipated that initial feedback from the Antarctic division would arrive within four to six hours.

NASA had been notified that satellite camera time could possibly be requested in the following six to twelve hours to assist in the search. It was now a waiting game as the race organisers in Perth prepared for the first emergency update at 2.30 am.

The team managers assembled in the control room were embroiled in a set of heated discussions about the RCC communications.

'Why in the hell didn't the French issue a precautionary warning?'

'We've possibly lost sailors because of their arrogance!' 'Why are we still able to communicate to the rest of the fleet?' 'It can't be sunspot activity!'

Dave Michaelson stepped up to the rostrum. 'Ladies and gentlemen, could I have your attention please? As you know, at roughly 1.30 am we broke from our previous meeting. Your team managers and Caroline Murray have been in contact with the RCC. The Australian Air Force has provided an Orion aircraft to assist us with the search, and that aircraft has now been airborne for approximately two minutes.'

Dave paused.

'In the meantime, we have been advised by the *Ocean Odyssey* team that the team owner, Timothy Wiley, has chartered a long-range aircraft out of Perth. His aircraft has been airborne for approximately thirty minutes and is now four hours from the target site. When this aircraft reaches the site, we believe there will be sufficient light to commence an immediate search. Ladies and gentlemen, unless any of the teams have anything to report, we are focusing on testing all our communication with the RCC, the Royal Australian Air Force, the Australian Antarctic Division and NASA. There isn't much more that we can do other than monitor communication channels in case one of the boats makes contact. I do advise, however, that we are now directing the rest of the fleet to chart a course at least 500 kilometres north of the last known position of the three front-runners. This is a precautionary measure and will be taken into account with handicaps in awarding the race winners.'

This news caused a few teams to leave the conference immediately. In the middle of the uncertainty the competitive drive of some of the teams was still alive. They were prepared to use any opportunity to improve their stakes in the race.

Janice raised her hand. 'Dave, the report from the Kerguelen

Islands is very disturbing. Why weren't you advised by the French base that there were radar contacts made in the ocean in the path of our ketches?'

'That's a good question, and it is an important one that will need to be answered. Unfortunately, I am unable to answer at this time, but we will take it on notice and ensure that we do get answers.

'Once again I request that if you have any communication with the boats in question that you bring it to our attention immediately. We do insist at this time that all media communication be made through the team organisers. We anticipate briefing the press at approximately 5.30 am here in Perth after a team briefing at 4.30 am. Ladies and gentlemen, that's all for this meeting unless you have any further questions.'

'Dave.' Janice again. 'These aircraft are taking over four hours to get to the target zone. Is there any chance of getting a jet to the site sooner?'

'Unfortunately, because of the time of morning in the target zone, a jet would only encounter predawn conditions. With the lack of light and the speed of the jet, it would be impossible to make any worthwhile observations.'

Janice nodded. 'Thanks Dave, had to ask.'

Dave scanned the room. 'No further questions. See you back here in just under an hour. Thank you all.'

The mood of the remaining assembled teams was tense and agitated. They reluctantly moved from the conference room back to their own offices in almost total silence.

Michael Amore walked slowly back to his office. He had nothing more to report to VJ. He was reluctant to make the call because in reality, it would be another four hours before VJ would commit to any action.

VJ immediately picked up the phone and Michael gave a

quick summary. 'VJ, I suggest I ring you if there is any change to the current situation, or after the search aircraft reach the target site.'

VJ's impatience was evident as he curtly replied. 'Okay, call me in four hours. I have work to do. Goodbye.'

The next two hours dragged by slowly. The 4.30 meeting was uneventful; however, the news conference scheduled to last for ten minutes dragged on until 6.45.

The media pack was relentless in its pursuit of information, drama and intrigue. Dave insisted that they take all their information from Wiley International as the media communication support group for the race organisers. Dave justified this action in the face of a storm of complaints on the need to keep his communication team focused on the search and rescue mission.

Howls of complaint came from the media pack.

'Censorship – this is stifling our ability to report.'

'How much are you being paid for this Dave?'

'You can't do that Dave, it's not fair.'

Dave knew he would have representations from governments and other interested parties by the end of the day because of his stance on communication. Caroline would have to complete work on that strategy during the day.

Dave took control of the media pack with one of his shrill whistles.

'Ladies and gentlemen, that concludes our first media conference relating to this unfortunate event. You will be able to get current information from Wiley International by the usual communication channels.'

As Dave led the team members from the news conference,

he turned to them with a frown on his face. 'We're well over time,' he said. 'Timothy Wiley's aircraft will be approaching the search zone shortly. I suggest team managers and communication coordinators come with us to the communication centre, so that you can all be updated as Timothy's aircraft reports.'

The team members filed into the communication centre and stood pensively around the radio operator. It was now 6.50 am.

'Rescue Charter to Rescue Control.'

'Rescue Control receiving you, Rescue Charter.'

'Rescue Control, we just entered the search zone, the water surface temperature is ... that doesn't appear right ... it's ... it's, uh, zero degrees.'

There was a pause on the radio.

'We have a westerly of 60 kilometres per hour, waves to 5 metres, long swells of about 90 metres, and air temperature, again ... it doesn't seem right. It's -8 degrees Celsius. Also, 12 kilometres visibility; no vessels or wreckage in sight.

'Rescue Control, we don't have any more to report. I suggest we contact you in approximately fifteen minutes. We are expecting the Australian Air Force Orion in this area in the next thirty minutes and we will be commencing a search grid pattern with them.'

The communication centre was silent. Everyone stood staring at the floor trying to avoid each other's gaze. Dave surveyed the crowd.

Janice caught Dave's gaze. 'Dave, are they normal temperatures for down there?'

Dave turned to James. 'You should have most of that information at your fingertips, can you give us some details please?'

James was caught a little off guard by the question – he was thinking about how desperately tired he was not having slept for over 30 hours. He shuffled through the information in front of him. 'Yes I do have information. Based on all the historical information the air temperature at that part of the Southern Ocean at this time of year should not be falling below zero. Minus eight is incredibly low. As for the water temperature, I can only assume that something is wrong with the equipment that is being used because we were expecting temperatures well above zero – so there is something unusual about those temperatures.'

'James, have you engaged anybody to assist us with understanding the climatic conditions in the area down there?'

James was visibly starting to get agitated by Janice's constant questions. 'Yes, the Hobart Antarctic division has been engaged. We should be hearing from them from time to time as the search parties engage them.'

Dave saw James's agitation and intervened. 'Ladies and gentlemen, I suggest that your team leaders stay in the control centre and the rest of you report back to your teams. We will be in touch as more information comes through. Thank you.'

CHAPTER 18

7 July 2015
7.45 am, Perth time

Timothy Wiley stared anxiously out of the cockpit window as the rescue charter entered the search zone. His mind was going over old ground again. He had been very concerned about Penelope undertaking this particular trip. He was now starting to blame himself for not convincing her to abandon the race. Timothy had hired a group of experts to chart a winning course for Penelope, within commercial constraints and minimising potential risks along the way. Penelope had been told not to deviate from that course. Had she let him down? She certainly had the temperament to get her own way.

Up until now, he had been prepared to do anything to have her as a permanent part of his life. The phone call this morning had shattered his dreams. A sailor in the water in this area without protective gear could not survive thirty minutes. In a properly equipped raft, survival relied on rescue within forty-eight hours. The clock was ticking and no signal from the radio of one of the three distress beacons was a very grim sign. Timothy was not prepared to give up yet. Penelope had to be out there and she had to be alive.

CHAPTER 18

Along with the crew of the rescue charter, Timothy surveyed the constant unbroken carpet of grey white-capped swells. The aircraft had returned to the westernmost limits of the search area, and was now turning to retrace its steps, moving one step further down the search grid. This was the third flight down the grid and there had been no sightings.

The pilot reported, 'We just had a fleeting radar contact, 130 kilometres south-west of here. It was just fleeting – could have been a rogue wave. I will mark the position of that contact and make sure we check it out as we move down the grid.'

'Shouldn't we investigate the radar contact?' Timothy called back.

'Sorry, it's search and rescue protocol to keep to the grid. Unless we have a visual, it's one of those damned if you do, damned if you don't situations. But I have to insist we stick to protocol.'

'You're the boss – it was just a fleeting contact. I can understand that.'

The observer called out in an excited tone. 'Have a visual, 3 kilometres southeast. Lost it now, but we should pass within almost a kilometre of it if we stick to this heading. There it is again; stick to this heading until we are closer. Now, possibly two contacts.'

The pilot called out in response. 'I see the contacts, dropping down to 500 metres and approaching from the north. Turning now … throttling back to 300 kilometres an hour. Flyover in approximately fifteen seconds … ten … five. What in God's name was that?' yelled the pilot. 'Turning for another fly pass.'

The pilot banked the aircraft.

'Jack, can you activate the cameras on my call? Give us sixty frames a second. I couldn't make out what that was. Did anyone else?'

Timothy was struggling with a visual image in his head. He was striving to make sense of what passed beneath him at 300 kilometres per hour as he moved from screen to screen. Struggling with his thoughts, he began rationalising. The camera would make sense of what they were looking at. Nothing was making sense. His thoughts raced backwards and forwards. The image made no sense at all. The blood was draining from his face. He felt unsteady on his feet and he felt terrible. He was jolted from his own personal misery by another call from the pilot.

'Start the camera rolling now, I'm taking her down to 200 metres. Hang on, this could get bumpy!'

The plane shook violently as they nudged 200 metres. The pilot pulled up sharply to avoid damaging the aircraft.

'Wow, that's worse than I expected. I think we might have our photographs though. Jack, can you blow those photos up? Timothy, can you work with Jack and see if you can both make any sense of what we are looking at?'

Timothy was fully focused now having regained his composure. 'Okay, I'm on it!' he said.

Jack worked with the images and brought them up on a computer screen. He scrolled through them while a mesmerised Timothy watched on. 'Seventy-five frames, that's a target zone close to 200 metres.' Frames appeared to show the large object, about the size of a forty-foot ketch in a huge field of debris. Some of the debris was almost transparent, and did not make any visual sense.

The pilot called out. 'A lot of silence back there guys, what do we have?'

Jack responded while continuing to stare at the screens. 'We have a large debris field, one large object close to the size of a forty-footer. The debris field extends over 200 metres. It's very difficult to make sense of it all. It just doesn't look right. I'm seeing what looks to be a boat, but there's no rigging, decks or masts.'

Timothy interrupted; he was visibly shaking. 'Let's have another look at photo thirty, there's something about that image. I'm not certain. Jack, blow up this area here.'

Timothy motioned to a section of the photograph. It appeared to be a forty-footer. The only sound to be heard was the whir of the engines as Timothy poured over the photograph. The blood drained from his face; he clenched his fists, then relaxed them. He started at the screen as the computer software slowly improved the resolution of the image. He spoke, struggling with every word.

'From what I can make out, the object I'm looking at is the inside roof of the *Ocean Odyssey*. She was fitted with buoyancy in the roof to assist in the case of a rollover. It looks as though the whole top of her has been sliced off at just above the water line, and the masts are torn out.'

Silence filled the aircraft. If this was in fact the upper half of the ketch, then where were the hull and keel? The grim reality swept through Timothy's mind: without the upper buoyancy and cover, the hull would have rapidly filled with water. Then the keel would have dragged the hull to the bottom of the ocean like a rock.

'Okay. Let's run with that,' the pilot called back. 'I've had an incoming call from the Orion. It's approaching the edge of the search zone. I'll update them on the debris field. There is a reasonable degree of certainty that the debris field belongs to the *Ocean Odyssey*. We will clear the path for the Orion to make a sweep with their infrared cameras to see if there's any life amongst the debris. Until the Orion makes their sweep and reports back with a result on their infrared cameras, we will continue working the grid pattern to ensure we get maximum search time while we're on-site.

'Jack, can you relay the message to the Orion? Let them know that we're continuing on the search grid, and that there is severe turbulence below 300 metres. Have you got that?'

'No worries mate – onto it right now.'

Timothy continued to pour over the photographs, wringing his hands and shaking his head as he studied them. He had to steady himself against the shock and emotion the images were causing him. Six months of planning the fastest and safest route for the voyage to make sure Penelope came through without a scratch, all destroyed in seventy-five photographs. Photographs of a 400 metre square debris field that once was Penelope and the *Ocean Odyssey*. Was he responsible for the carnage? Was it his planning that forced the other teams to go further south, inadvertently drawing his own team into this horror?

He regained his composure. 'Jack, can I have hardcopies of frames forty through fifty-one please?'

'No worries Timothy. They'll come straight off the printer behind you; grab them as you need them.'

Timothy started working through the photographs as they came off the printer, circling items of interest and passing the marked photographs to Jack to enlarge. Timothy was searching through the jigsaw puzzle, trying to find any indication of the two safety rafts, EPIRBs and other safety and survival equipment that had been fitted to the *Ocean Odyssey*. He had no doubt in his mind that if Penelope was conscious amongst the wreckage, she would have activated a flare as soon as she heard the aircraft approaching. If she were still alive, she would be somewhere out there in a survival raft, waiting to be rescued. He just needed to put the pieces together, to show that there was sufficient survival gear missing for her to have survived. Frantically he kept circling pieces of debris in the debris field.

The pilot called back. 'Timothy, I just informed Race Control and the RCC that we have found a debris field that we believe may be the *Ocean Odyssey*. The Orion is currently assessing their infrared photographs. They indicate that there is some difficulty with the photography due to some abnormalities in the water temperature around the debris field. The Orion is going to make another pass over the area to try to get a better set of photos. In the meantime, we will continue our grid pattern search.'

At 7.59 am back at Race Control, Dave Michaelson had just taken the call from the radio operator on the rescue charter aircraft, prior to the 8.00 am race briefing. He re-entered his office to find James and Caroline busy at work.

'James, Caroline, it looks as though we need to ready ourselves for a worst-case scenario. We just had a report in from the rescue target zone and in the first hour of searching they have found a debris field over 200 metres. At this stage it's unconfirmed, but it could possibly be the *Ocean Odyssey*.'

Caroline shook, her face ashen, and she began to sob. 'That's absolutely terrible,' she whispered.

James put his arm around Caroline's shoulder. 'Come on Caroline, you need to pull yourself together. We're here to support the teams, remember.'

Caroline glared at James. 'Don't be so heartless – I just need a moment to get myself together.'

Dave intervened. 'Okay, give ourselves a minute; it is difficult for all of us. Then we have to guide and support the teams.'

After a short delay, Dave continued.

'For the other teams, we will need to deal with their anguish, particularly of the unknown. So I think we'd better be prepared for some pretty agitated people in this next meeting. I think the best way that we can manage this situation is to only have the team managers come to the briefing – that way, we can brief them one-on-one initially. Then I will give a detailed overview of where we are in the search and what the next steps are.

'Caroline, if you can get that message out to the teams, we can then start preparing for the meeting. I'll get you to take *Ocean Mist*. James, you take the *Shanghai Sunrise* team, and I'll take the *Ocean Odyssey*. Let's get them into our offices – then we will all meet in my office in ten minutes.' Dave gave each of them a supportive squeeze of the shoulder. 'See you back here soon.'

Dave tried to stay calm as Miles Henderson entered the room. Miles looked pensive and drawn, with bags under his eyes. He looked as though he hadn't slept for days. Dave motioned Miles to a seat and they both sat down. Miles's eyes searched Dave's face, but he was not getting a good feeling. Dave looked very drawn and intense.

Dave commenced slowly. 'Miles, we've just had an update from the search zone. The news isn't good, I'm afraid. Timothy's aircraft has detected a debris zone, potentially identified as being what's left of the *Ocean Odyssey*. The Orion has done one infrared camera scan of the area but it's inconclusive and they are doing another one as we speak. We should have results of that within the next fifteen to twenty minutes.'

Dave paused. Miles slumped in his chair and appeared to be in a world of pain. Dave needed to complete Miles's briefing before the others arrived.

'Timothy is pouring over high-resolution photographs of the debris field to try to determine if any survival gear appears to be missing. That would potentially indicate that Penelope could be out there in a survival raft waiting for rescue. Miles, I'm sorry that the news isn't any better. In the next minute or two the other impacted team managers will be coming into this room. We have no news on their vessels but again, because of the lack of communication with their vessels over the last six hours, we can only assume that their fate is similar to that of the *Ocean Odyssey*.'

Miles stumbled over his words. 'I … I … re … really can't say an … anything. I'm so … so *responsible*.'

Dave placed a reassuring hand on Miles's shoulder. 'There's no time for self-pity at the moment. Miles, you're the team manager. You have to carry your team. I suggest you put all the self-pity on the backburner until this is all over. Am I clear on that?'

Miles looks calmly at Dave. 'Very clear. Thanks Dave, I need that,' he said as he turned to face the door. 'The others are coming.'

Caroline and James led Janice Yew and Sanjay Singh into the room. Their faces were drawn, Janice and Sanjay searching Dave's eyes for some reassurance, hope or meaning. Dave motioned them to chairs, gathered his thoughts and addressed them.

'Miles, Janice, Sanjay, this is a very difficult time. We are now facing the worst situation in the history of this race and as teams, we are jointly confronted by the potential grief of the loss of our team members.'

Janice interrupted. 'Dave, so far we have been told that one debris field has been found in the target search zone, and that the field has been tentatively identified as being from the *Ocean Odyssey*.'

Dave hesitated for a moment before answering the question. 'Correct. In the first hour of searching the target area, one debris field has been identified, with a strong indication that it belongs to *Ocean Odyssey*.'

Janice continued. 'So isn't it odd that the *Ocean Odyssey* was the first site found? What is the current strategy at the search site?'

Dave was starting to find Janice very trying. 'In the first instance, the *Ocean Odyssey* was the boat closest to Perth, so it was found first. The strategy is to systematically check the entire target site in a grid pattern. This is standard search procedure and must be followed to avoid potentially missing wreckage or survivors.'

Janice pondered the answer; it seemed reasonable that the *Ocean Odyssey* be found first under those circumstances. Was there any way she could get more information as to what was happening out there in the Southern Ocean?

Her thoughts were interrupted as a radio operator entered the room and handed Dave a message. He read the message and then addressed them.

'I have just had an update from the Royal Australian Air Force Orion on-site. We can now confirm that forward-looking infrared cameras have detected no signs of life in the first wreckage field. This does not mean that there are no survivors; it only means that there are no survivors in the wreckage field. We are continuing our grid pattern search and will report any contacts as they occur.'

Dave paused.

'Okay, that's the status direct to you from the search site. Unless there are any further questions, I'd suggest you go back to your teams and start breaking the bad news.

'At this stage, it is our view that we have lost one vessel, and possibly one sailor. We won't give up hope for the other two sailors, but due to lack of communication from them, the prognosis is grim. It's now approaching 8.30 am and we intend to have another media briefing at 9.00 am. I ask that the team managers and communication managers are present at that meeting. With no further questions, I suggest you go back to your teams and I will see you in the conference room at 9.00 am. Thank you all.'

Dave had a knot in his stomach. He turned to James and Caroline and gestured towards the coffee machine in the corner of his office. Each made a cappuccino in absolute silence and then took a seat around Dave's desk. He looked at them and solemnly shook his head.

'The initial indications from the Air Force and Rescue Charter is that something appears to have sliced the boat in half, stem to stern, just above the waterline. I can only guess that if the sailor were below decks at that time, they had no chance of survival. This information is not to be made public yet – we have a lot more investigating to do to understand what really happened to this boat.' Dave was silent for long time, then again looked at Caroline and James. 'Is that understood?'

They both nodded silently in agreement, both speechless, struggling with the reality of the tragedy and grappling with the possible effect it could have on the race, and the future of any such race.

James headed back to his office, shaking his head as he had headed towards the door.

'Caroline,' said Dave, 'I need you to work with me in preparing a detailed communication to our sponsors. They may want to bring strategic people in to look at how to manage advertising and media going forward … they invested a lot in this venture and stood to make ten times the investment. At the moment it looks as though they will get out with two to three times what they put in. I believe it's time we handed that side of things over to Timothy's team. If you can work on that for the next half hour, we will then have the 9.00 am update meeting. After that, we can review and look at finalising the communication.'

Caroline looked at Dave. 'I'd suggest that after the 9.00

am meeting, we advise the media that there will be a 10.30 am briefing. I believe we need to advise the team managers and communication people to be there. We could start the release of specific information from the search aircraft then.'

Dave nodded. 'Let's do that.'

Caroline left the room and headed back to her office, leaving Dave in a very drained and pensive mood. Caroline's head was aching. She needed sleep and she needed to talk to Timothy about the media situation as soon as possible. There was so much going on.

Dave's head was spinning with ideas. In the last hour, the race had been hit with the most terrible news – the loss of a sailing boat and possibly its sailor, 2500 kilometres from Perth. The RCC was scouring the Southern Ocean for vessels close to Perth to come to their assistance and provide salvage and hopefully rescue for any sailors found. With no freighters closer to the search zone, preparation began on fitting out a vessel in Perth to assist in the search. The search zone was approximately seventy hours away for a rescue vessel. With less than thirty-six hours' survival time left in any raft set afloat when contact was lost, time was running out and Dave knew it.

The RCC was pulling together the rescue effort and Dave felt a little helpless, sitting in Perth with his boats thousands of kilometres away. Timothy Wiley was the only owner who had taken initiative in the search for the missing boats, perhaps driven by the fact that he was the closest owner to the vessels when they got into difficulties. Dave was feeling uneasy about the two other owners and he sensed very difficult questions coming from the media about them not being in transit to Perth.

With no updates on the other two vessels, the 9.00 am meeting was cancelled.

Dave's thoughts turned to the remaining vessels in the race.

Should it be called off? That was certainly not an outcome that the race sponsors would be happy with. However, until there was some clarity as to what exactly had happened to the three frontrunners, there was no justification for cancelling the race. But there were some difficult decisions to be made in the next few hours in relation to whether the race should proceed or not.

Dave checked the time. It was rapidly approaching 10.15 am, at which time Timothy Wiley's aircraft would need to commence the journey back to Perth. The Orion would still have one hour's search time remaining before it also needed to return to Perth. With a ten hour turnaround time, Timothy would not get back to the search zone before nightfall. They would need to plan tomorrow's search to have one aircraft leaving the search as the next one commences. They effectively only got four and a half hours' search time out of a possible six. It had been a rush to commence the search in the hope of finding survivors and being able to provide them with additional safety equipment, allowing them to survive until a vessel arrived to assist them.

As it neared 10.20 am, Dave walked towards the conference room. As he approached the door he was met by the radio operator.

'Dave, the Orion pilot was about to give a briefing on the search, prior to the rescue charter aircraft leaving the grid to return to Perth.'

Dave headed into the conference room and shepherded the waiting team members into the communications room away from the press. They took up chairs just as the Orion pilot called in to make his report.

'This is Orion Rescue to Rescue Control.'

'This is Rescue Control – receiving you Orion Rescue.'

'Rescue Control, I'm going to give you an update on how the search is proceeding in the search zone, prior to the Rescue

Charter aircraft leaving the search and heading back to Perth. At 10.20am Perth time, we report that we have covered approximately 50 per cent of the search grid. We have located one debris zone, believed to be that the *Ocean Odyssey*. That debris zone currently covers an area of approximately 400 square metres and is moving in a westerly direction at approximately 4 kilometres per hour. No signs of life were found in the vicinity of the debris zone. Since the discovery of that debris zone, our search has covered an area 20 kilometres south, 15 kilometres north and 100 kilometres east and west of the zone. No signs of life, debris or a life raft were detected in that area. We are also reporting that we have had no fewer than fifteen fleeting radar contacts that we are unable to explain. We made a calibrating flyover of the debris field to confirm that other debris sites are more than likely not associated with these fleeting radar contacts.

'The air temperature at site is fluctuating from 0 to -5 degrees Celsius, while the water temperature is fluctuating from 0 to -1 degree Celsius. We have confirmed with the Hobart Antarctic Division that those water temperatures are extremely unusual for this location at this time of year. They would have expected temperatures at least 5 degrees higher on all measurements. We have another ninety minutes of search time remaining. In that time, we anticipate being able to complete a full search of the current search grid. A radio operator will give you brief updates every fifteen minutes and unless we have another contact, I do not anticipate a detailed report until we have completed the search.'

The assembled teams broke into animated conversations and comments began to fly as they grappled with the unusual climatic conditions at the site and the fleeting radar contacts. It was a case of more questions than answers.

With no news on the *Ocean Mist*'s predicament, Michael decided to leave updating VJ until the Orion's final report of the day. He was counting on an outcome in the search for the *Ocean Mist* within that time. During the last call, he had sensed VJ's extreme displeasure at there not being substance to act on. To him, talking was a waste of time without substance.

Dave Michaelson conducted a brief media conference, informing the gathered media representatives that the search was continuing. He omitted the fact that the debris field had been located, at the insistence of the race teams. The teams were now busily contacting next of kin, to brief them on the dire situation unfolding in the Southern Ocean. Dave rescheduled the next media briefing for midday, giving the Orion sufficient time to have completed its search grid.

At 10.35, the Orion spotted a second debris field. It was larger than the first and did not contain any debris exceeding 2 metres in length. The Orion's pilot made two infrared camera runs and three high-speed hundred frame a second photo runs and then moved on. Time was running out and the pilot wanted to finish searching the entire grid before he needed to return to Perth.

At 11.15 am, only minutes before the Orion was scheduled to depart the target zone for Perth, they spotted a third debris field. It was the most southerly field found, just below the 50th parallel. The site, like the other two, mesmerised the pilot and crew. Just as the pilot commenced his approach for a photo run, a significant radar contact appeared, 8 kilometres south of the wreckage.

'We're going after that radar contact,' called the pilot. He was doing a north-south photo run – he now climbed sharply away from the wreckage field, levelling the aircraft at 1000 metres and heading towards the radar contact.

Everybody on board the aircraft had been focused on the radar image in the ocean and they failed to notice the weather closing in rapidly from the west. A kilometre out from the radar contact, they entered a snowstorm that reduced visibility to 100 metres.

The pilot calculated the risk as being much too high to proceed. 'Sorry boys, that's too thick to see anything from the air. I have to come around.' He banked sharply and headed back towards the wreckage field. 'Let's see what we can get from the last debris field before we call it a day.'

He had decided that the most useful thing he could do with the remaining few minutes of search time was to outrun the storm and make one more photo run across the third debris field. He successfully dropped to 200 metres as they crossed the debris field, taking photographs that would be crucial in furthering their knowledge of what had happened to that vessel.

The Orion was like a small bird being attacked by a large eagle. A wall of dark clouds and snow swept across behind her as she completed her last run. The Orion climbed steeply and turned to the east just as the snowstorm swept through.

'Time to go home boys. Let's analyse those photographs, get the blow-ups done and be ready for debriefing when we get home.'

At 11.25 am, Dave Michaelson received another update from the Orion at the target zone. The report was devastating. Another two debris fields had been located in an area that corresponded to the last known locations of the *Shanghai Sunrise* and the *Ocean Mist*, allowing for drift in the prevailing ocean currents and winds. This was further confronting news for the teams, whose hopes of finding a vessel intact or perhaps even a sailor alive had been fading rapidly. They now had three vessels missing, three debris fields, no signs of life and near freezing conditions. It was a complete disaster and yet there was still no indication of what had caused this catastrophe.

Dave's report to the team management was met with an outpouring of grief. Several team members had to be helped from the room. Dave, Caroline and James provided as much support as they could to the devastated teams. Race Management decided to cancel any further meetings for the next six hours to allow the teams to grieve. The next meeting was timed to receive feedback from the debriefing after the aircraft had landed.

After an hour of scanning and rescanning the photographs of the debris field, Timothy was trying to piece together all of the objects that he had identified. He had found no evidence of the three EPIRBs, life rafts, survival equipment or any equipment that would assist Penelope to survive in the hostile seas of the southern ocean. However, in analysing the hardcopy photographs with a magnifying glass, he had determined that the *Ocean Odyssey*'s deck was separated from the keel, approximately four hundred millimetres below the deck. Timothy could only assume that the contents below deck had sunk rapidly with the keel. The only chance that Penelope had of survival was to have been on deck, close to the second survival raft, if she had been in a position to launch the raft before the deck and masts crashed into the sea.

As Timothy sat reflecting, he accepted that the possibility of Penelope being above deck at around midnight in freezing conditions was highly improbable. He was looking at the remotest chance that Penelope had survived such a horrific event. What in the ocean had the force capable of slicing the deck off a forty-foot carbon fibre ketch? He closed his eyes as he could not bear to imagine what had happened.

CHAPTER 19

Timothy responded to a firm hand on his shoulder; he had been in a fitful sleep for almost three hours. The navigator smiled at him. 'Time to get the seats upright Sir; we're approaching Perth.'

Fifteen minutes later they were met on the tarmac by an Air Force limousine, which was there to whisk them to the Air Force base for a joint debriefing when the Orion landed.

As they approached the base, the Orion swept in from the west, landed and taxied to the hangar. The limousine entered the base through the security gates and was directed towards a large briefing centre. A large throng of media and paparazzi were left outside at the gates.

In the briefing centre Timothy met the Orion's pilot for the first time. He was a tall, lightly built man with piercing blue eyes. Flight Lieutenant Alan Stewart took Timothy by the hand and shook it firmly. 'A pleasure to meet you Timothy; it's a pity we couldn't meet under more pleasant circumstances.'

Timothy nodded with grim recognition, and was directed towards the front of the room where there were four large screens.

'Timothy, these displays are for analysing the photographs. Four operators with computers are here to assist in data manipulation.'

Crews from the two aircraft settled into their chairs. Flight Lieutenant Stewart took the floor.

'Ladies and gentlemen – we're here with a difficult task in front of us. The photos we're about to review are debris fields that we believe are the remains of three racing ketches – the *Ocean Odyssey*, the *Shanghai Sunrise* and the *Ocean Mist*. Contact was lost with these vessels at approximately 1.00 am this morning. As we will see shortly, there is quite a lot of unidentified material in the ocean amongst the debris. To assist in our deliberations on the photographs, we do need to point out that there were several unexplained, fleeting and very large radar contacts in the search zone. We were forced to abandon inspecting one of these contacts due to a sudden snowstorm that swept in from the west, just before a visual contact.'

He briefly paused and motioned to the image on one of the screens of the massive dark cloud descending on the Orion.

'We also have seventy-five frames to view from the rescue charter aircraft. These photographs were taken using different equipment, at different altitudes and from a different approach. They may assist us in piecing together how these vessels came to grief. We're seeking to determine if the sailors on these vessels have sufficient survival equipment, or if in fact, they could have survived the incident that destroyed their vessels. We need to make these determinations prior to committing resources to go back to the target zone tomorrow. We need to be prepared to either search for survivors or to preserve and track the debris zone for retrieval by recovery vessels. To begin, I will ask the crew of the rescue charter to present their photographs. Over to you, Rescue Charter.' He motioned to Timothy and Jack who took the floor and introduced themselves.

Jack motioned for the first slide. Timothy felt a knot in his stomach; this was going to be difficult.

Jack turned to the aircrew and operators. 'I'll get Timothy to take us through the photographs. He is the owner of the *Ocean*

Odyssey and its team and knows every part of this boat. He has scanned the photographs in detail. We've blown up relevant parts of a large number of photographs that are important in making this assessment.'

Timothy took the floor, looked at his feet and then gestured with his hands. 'Ladies and gentlemen – this is in fact very difficult for me as I was going to propose to the young sailor on this boat when she crossed the finish line.'

Timothy hesitated, then turned to the screen and motioned for the first photograph to be displayed. He then commenced, his voice a little shaky.

'This first frame, twenty-three of seventy-five, is without doubt the deck of the *Ocean Odyssey*. It has been sliced off the hull approximately four hundred millimetres below the deck.' He paused for a moment then continued. 'I can't imagine what could possibly have done this to a forty-foot vessel.'

Timothy swept his arm across the image from stem to stern.

'We can see that the sever line moves away from the deck as we get towards the back of the vessel.' He pointed to an upward movement in the thickness of the object. 'This perhaps indicates that this was not an instantaneous disaster but took several seconds to tear the deck off the vessel. We can imagine this vessel under sail encountering a sword blade coming through the bow and exiting the stern. The keel would be dragging the hull down and the masts and sails pushing the deck up by the bow. The sails, in effect, would be ripping the lid off the hull.' Timothy motioned with two cupped hands, then moved the fingertips apart, flipping the top away to indicate the type of action that could have caused the damage they were looking at.

'As the sword exits the stern, the masts and the sail would flip the deck upside down and then float upside down in the water. The deck was full of buoyancy, to assist in a rollover situation.

Without anchorage, the masts would have broken free of the deck, constrained only by the rigging.'

One of the operators gestured to the frame. 'That's a pretty clean cut – what in the ocean can do that?'

Timothy shook his head then swept his right arm across the room. 'Any ideas? I've never seen anything like this before.'

At this point, Lieutenant Stewart interjected. 'Ladies and gentlemen, we have a lot of work to get through tonight. We will park all questions on a whiteboard and deal with them later in the session. Timothy, continue please.'

'Thanks Lieutenant. We'll now go back to that photograph and look at five areas of interest around the deck. As we scan through those, the key points are further down into the cabin where survival equipment and a below-deck life raft were kept. We can only assume that if this event occurred with speed and the sailor was below deck; then, if they weren't killed by the intruding object, they would have been left in the exposed hull which would have been pulled down into the depths by the keel in seconds. Should the sailor have been on deck, there would have been considerable impact in the first instance, throwing her off her feet. The deck would have flicked over the top, pinning her into the cold sea. She possibly had no warning of the impending impact and therefore, she most probably would have had no chance of grabbing a raft and survival equipment.'

Timothy struggled with the words he had just uttered and the images they threw up in his mind. He braced himself against the table and continued.

'Before we look at the other fifty images or so, I will add one thing. Each of the two scenarios above and below deck are inconclusive until we can inspect the topside of the deck section of the *Ocean Odyssey*. There is still a one in three chance that Penelope could have survived this horrific event and escaped in a survival raft. We need to accept that a below-deck chance of survival was very slim. You will note that there is no trace of the three EPIRBs or any of the survival equipment, in particular the above-deck and below-deck survival rafts.'

Timothy spent an hour taking the assembled group through the photographs of the *Ocean Odyssey* debris field. He was strained and looked to Lieutenant Stewart for some relief.

The lieutenant took the floor. 'Sergeant Harris will now take us through the Orion's photographs and the same debris field. Flight Sergeant Harris, you have the floor.'

Without another word Flight Sergeant Harris commenced to present the analysis of the photographs. 'Moving on from where Timothy left off, when it comes to survival gear and analysis of what we now know to be the deck, we have no more pertinent information to offer.'

He then looked up at the assembled group and motioned in the next frame.

'If we look at this particular frame, and then put frame fifty-seven from the rescue charter beside it, we can see the common areas that are mapped out and the objects in the frame. However, there are now several objects missing. Elapsed time between the rescue charter photo and the Orion photo is less than twenty minutes, and it is highly improbable that the current could move those objects out of a photograph path in such a short time. I believe this observation is the second one we should now put on the whiteboard, to deal with later.' He looked up and continued. 'Unless there is an objection?'

There were no objections.

'It's fair to say at that the Orion photographs have provided no more information in determining whether the sailor could survive this incident. I now hand the floor back to the lieutenant.'

Lieutenant Stewart took the floor. 'Timothy and Flight

Sergeant Harris have made our decisions in this process relatively clear-cut. Without an inspection of the deck of the *Ocean Odyssey*, we can't positively determine whether the sailor has left the vessel with any survival equipment. I suggest we add to the whiteboard, any ideas about how to inspect the surface of the *Ocean Odyssey* deck from the air. Ladies and gentlemen, we have now been working on this task for ninety minutes so I suggest we take a short break and be back here in fifteen minutes.'

During the break Timothy sat silently in his seat, reflecting on the events of the past few weeks. Going through the photographs was striking a nerve. He was angry with himself and Penelope for not having settled the matter of her continuing to sail. They could have found an alternative sailor. For the first time in his life, Timothy had been scared of losing the woman in his life. He had been afraid to pressure her to live his way; it had cost him dearly. It was a hard lesson to accept.

When the teams returned, Flight Sergeant Harris took the floor and re-commenced the review process.

'I am now putting up the four key photographs from the debris field that we're associating with the last position of the *Shanghai Sunrise* vessel. As we can see, the largest debris in this field is only a fraction of the size of that of the *Ocean Odyssey*.'

He stood back, surveying the screens, then turned to face his audience again.

'We can only assume from these images that the *Shanghai Sunrise* was broken up by the event it encountered. We'll now go back to the first photograph and zoom in on the top left hand corner.'

The operator flicked back to the first photograph and blew up the area of interest. The room gasped and two attendants stood in distress as one as the image came into focus. The image showed the first of the life rafts.

'You can see that we have the first of the survival rafts still in the debris field. If we now pan through to the middle of image two ...'

There, underwater on a section of the cabin wall, were the three emergency EPIRBs still held by their retaining brackets.

Flight Sergeant Harris didn't dwell on the image, but instead motioned towards the third image. 'Blow up the bottom left-hand corner please,' he said to the operator.

The focused image revealed torn debris sections of the mast, still attached to the deck portions. It appeared as though the *Shanghai Sunrise* had exploded or been ripped to shreds; debris pieces were no larger than a small car.

'We'll now focus on the top right-hand corner of the fourth image ...'

The image came into focus, revealing the second life raft. The room fell silent. Several people came to their feet and walked to the front of the room staring up at the large screen. The life raft had a large gaping hole in it.

Flight Sergeant Harris motioned everybody back to their seats and continued. 'Having identified the three EPIRBs and two life rafts as being in the debris field associated with the *Shanghai Sunrise*, we can only assume that the sailor of this vessel died during the event that destroyed the vessel or within fifteen to twenty minutes of being thrown into the water. For the record, the evidence is sufficient to confirm that the sailor of the *Shanghai Sunrise* went down with his vessel, or died soon after. Again, we will have another break for fifteen minutes, before we proceed with photographs relating to the *Ocean Mist*.'

The sergeant looked a little shaken as team members dispersed and headed towards the coffee room. Timothy approached him. 'Excuse me, Flight Sergeant Harris.'

'Yes?'

'I wonder if I can ask you a few questions about the *Ocean Mist*?'

'Fire away.'

'From the little I know so far about the *Ocean Mist*'s photographs, it sounds as though we're looking at a situation almost identical to the *Ocean Odyssey*. Would I be correct in saying that?'

'It certainly looks that way. We have one large object resembling an upturned deck in the middle of a large debris field, almost identical to the *Ocean Odyssey*. So it really comes down to whether or not there is a way to get a view below the waterline of the deck and identify if the deck safety raft is still in position. But that doesn't answer the question of the one missing below deck.'

'True, that's a mystery for all of us,' replied Timothy. 'Come on, I'll buy you a coffee.'

Flight Sergeant Harris took the floor after the break. They commenced a review of the slides for the last known position of the *Ocean Mist*. The sergeant took the gathered team members through four photographs where they found wreckage similar to the *Ocean Odyssey*, with no trace of the three EPIRBs or the two survival rafts. Similar to the *Ocean Odyssey*, the deck was clearly visible; it was inverted and had been severed completely from the hull. There was no way of determining if a life raft on the deck had been removed or not.

Sergeant Harris summed up the review of the photographs. 'Firstly, the *Ocean Odyssey*. Until we get some sort of view of the deck, we cannot determine if the life raft from the deck is still in position. Next, the *Shanghai Sunrise*. It is clear from having found both life rafts and three EPIRBs that the sailor on the *Shanghai Sunrise* would have died as a result of the incident. Therefore, the search and rescue mission in relationship to the *Shanghai Sunrise* and its sailor will be terminated. The situation with *Ocean Mist* is almost identical to the *Ocean Odyssey*.

'Now to the probability of survival. It is rapidly approaching twenty-four hours since the sailors may have entered the water. If they have not been found and re-rationed by noon tomorrow, we will be forced to assume that they are deceased, due to current sea and air temperatures. If we consider the physical devastation caused in this incident to all three vessels, we come to the conclusion that the probability of a sailor being able to get into a life raft, either from the deck or from the water, is possible – but improbable.'

He hesitated, briefly consulted his notes and continued.

'I was made aware during the last break that there is a classified surveillance device available that will allow us to see into the ocean and identify items on the inverted decks. As we speak, these items are being fitted to the Orion and will be ready for us when we take off at 0200 hours tomorrow morning. The task for tomorrow, based on this analysis, is to determine if the life rafts are attached to the decks beneath the water. If we determine that they are not attached, we will need to be in a position to estimate drift rates and create new target search areas for the detached life rafts. It's approaching 2000 hours, so it's time for the team to stand down. Be prepared to depart at 0200 tomorrow. Are there any questions?' No-one responded, so he terminated the meeting with a brief command. 'Dismissed.'

As people filed out of the room, Lieutenant Stewart approached Timothy and Sergeant Harris, who were discussing details. 'Gentlemen, do we have a plan for tomorrow?'

'Yes Sir,' said Harris. 'The Orion will depart Perth at 02.00 am, and the rescue charter at 06.00 am. The Orion is due to depart the search zone at 10.30 am, but the rescue charter will have commenced by 10.00 am. That will give us six and a half hours over the search grid. The Orion is being fitted with the equipment required to penetrate the decks of both vessels to determine whether or not there are still life rafts attached. Based on whether or not life rafts are found, we will make a call about continuing the search.'

Lieutenant Stewart nodded. 'That's the call we will jointly make when the time comes,' he said. 'Timothy, before we make that call we will be in touch with you to discuss the next course of action.'

Timothy shook hands with Lieutenant Stewart and Sergeant Harris, gathered his team and headed towards a waiting car. Timothy and the pilot discussed a strategy for the next day in detail as the car whisked them through the suburbs of Perth. Timothy was dropped off at his hotel and the air crew disappeared into the night in the Air Force limousine.

CHAPTER 20

The Orion departed the Air Force base at 2.00 am the next morning. She had a new instrument dome protruding 2 metres back from her nose. The dome housed modified Gorgon technology – cutting-edge surveillance equipment that allowed the military to see through solid objects. The Air Force was relying on the equipment to allow them to survey the submerged decks of the two vessels that could provide clues as to whether or not the sailors from the *Ocean Odyssey* and *Ocean Mist* had survived the incident that completely destroyed their boats.

The flight to the target zone took four and a half hours and as they approached, the weather was unusually calm. Swells had dropped to 90 metres and the waves to 5 metres and the westerly was blowing at 30 kilometres per hour under an overcast sky.

The Orion flew over the *Ocean Odyssey* debris field three times and then returned for a fourth. There had been a dramatic change in the debris field since the day before, with the debris volume being reduced by half. Technicians poured over the photographs, while the Gorgon technologists assessed the data with their sophisticated equipment.

Flight Sergeant Harris called the pilot. 'Lieutenant, we have a dramatic drop in the volume of debris in this field since yesterday.'

'Any ideas, Sergeant?' The lieutenant sounded surprised.

'The only explanation I can give for the decrease in the debris field is that half the debris has sunk. I have no other explanation.'

Flight Sergeant Harris had barely finished speaking when the Gorgon operator commenced his report. 'Lieutenant, we can report that the life raft is still connected to the deck at the exact location that we expected to find it.'

There was a brief silence before the lieutenant replied, 'Okay gentlemen – let's wrap up this site and head to the debris field of the *Ocean Mist*.'

The Orion banked as the navigator locked in the new course. They were positioned over the depleted debris field from the *Ocean Mist* ten minutes later.

The crew was again intrigued by the reduction in debris since the last sighting – how could objects just disappear? There was at least a 50 per cent reduction. It was gone without a trace.

'Note to log at 0645 local time – we need to take meteorological readings back at the *Ocean Odyssey* site before we leave,' said the lieutenant. 'Lock that in navigator.'

The Orion made six passes over the *Ocean Mist*'s debris. Flight Sergeant Harris was the first to report. 'Lieutenant, it's the same situation here. Massive reduction to the debris field of the *Ocean Mist*.'

The Gorgon operator then reported. 'Same as the *Ocean Odyssey* Lieutenant. A life raft is still attached to the deck but it has sustained considerable damage.' The meteorological report followed. 'Lieutenant, we have a water temperature of -1 degree Celsius and air temperature of -15 degrees Celsius; wind speed is 35 kilometres per hour with waves to 8 metres.'

The radar operator cut in. 'Captain, we have a radar contact 6 kilometres south.'

The captain's response was instant. 'Okay gentlemen, hang on. We're going in low with all cameras on to get as much information as we can. Radar, keep an eye on the weather please.'

The radar operator barked out a response. 'Yes Sir.'

It took the Orion just over a minute to cover the distance to the radar contact. On approach, they dropped to an altitude of 300 metres and approached the target from the north. The water in the target zone was broken and confused. There were objects in the water that appeared to be of varying lengths – from several metres to in excess of 20 metres. At the speed the aircraft was going, it was difficult to determine what they were. Several observers on the Orion all attempted to speak at once. The sergeant brought them to order. 'One at a time gentlemen – you'll all get your chance.'

One by one, the observers related the same confused message. What they were looking at was not making very much logical sense and the report from the Gorgon operator made the least sense of all the reports. The lieutenant ordered two more sweeps across the new target zone – one from the south and one from the west – to ensure that they collected the maximum amount of information possible about the objects. After the final sweep was complete, they set a new course to intersect a predicted target zone, 165 kilometres northeast of the first target zone. This zone was based on computer projections on where a released life raft might have been blown to from the location of the *Ocean Odyssey* debris zone.

The observers continued to monitor the carpet of swells below as they made their way to the new zone. The Orion had risen to an altitude of 4000 metres, to maximise the efficiency of the heat seeking cameras and other detection equipment on board. While in transit, the lieutenant contacted Timothy Wiley, Race Headquarters, the RCC and the Air Force to report on their findings and to advise he was continuing the search of the drift target zones for any possible life rafts.

By this time, the rescue charter had been airborne for two hours. Timothy slumped by the window upon receiving the news from Lieutenant Stewart, staring at the ocean below. His mind was in turmoil. The only hope that Penelope was alive now came down to the improbable possibility that she somehow launched the other life raft and managed to escape the wreckage. Unable to stare into the dark ocean any longer, he closed his eyes and drifted into a fitful sleep.

The Orion took another hour to complete the grid calculated to be the location of any raft that could have been blown out of the *Ocean Odyssey* debris drift field. The Orion now set a course back to the *Ocean Odyssey* debris field, 2 kilometres south of the previously taken course. This course ensured that they also searched a 4 kilometre corridor between the debris fields.

On reaching the *Ocean Odyssey* debris field, the Orion set course for the projected location of the *Ocean Mist*'s debris field. The Orion took another hour to complete searching the new *Ocean Mist* grid. No contact was made with a possible life raft and the Orion backtracked to the debris field without detecting a life raft.

The lieutenant made a summary report that was relayed to the rescue charter, Race Control, the RCC and the Air Force. In his report he advised that both the deck of the *Ocean Odyssey* and *Ocean Mist* still had an attached life raft and that a sailor could not have survived by using the deck-mounted life raft. The Orion continued its search to cover the possibility that a sailor may have escaped in the below-deck life raft.

After a comprehensive search of the new target zone, calculated from currents and winds in the area over the last thirty-six hours, the Orion had detected no life rafts or survivors. The crew of the Orion therefore concluded that based on the available information and meteorological conditions at the sites, none of the three sailors survived the disastrous event. The crew transmitted their condolences to friends and relatives.

The lieutenant, in a separate communiqué to the Air Force, reported the unusual radar contacts – a detail left out of the public report. He was advised to transmit all the available information to the Antarctic Division in Hobart for assessment. He advised Timothy of the radar contacts and they both agreed that they should review the information on Timothy's return to Perth.

At 10.30 am Perth time, the rescue charter arrived in the search grid. Timothy had decided to retrace the Orion's search grid for the *Ocean Odyssey* and to increase its size by 50 per cent. The hours dragged on as the rescue charter flew up and down the grid, systematically eliminating more and more of the target search zone.

At noon, the rescue charter had completed the wider grid and was preparing to make its last run back to the debris field when their radar operator detected a contact, 12 kilometres south of their position.

'Radar contact due south,' he shouted into his microphone. 'Sorry Sir, that was a bit loud.'

'That's okay comms, coming about.' The pilot banked and flew directly towards the contact.

As they approached the contact the aircraft dropped to 1000 metres, cameras were engaged and everyone on board was glued to their windows, trying to catch a glimpse of the radar contact. They flew over the contact area, banked and returned at 200 metres, just above the stall speed of the aircraft.

'We appear to be approaching some form of disruption in the water,' said the pilot. 'It's very low in the water and very hard to make out … we'll be relying on the radar and photographs to work out just what we have here.'

The pilot made two more slow flyovers, collecting as much information as possible about the mysterious disruption in the water.

'That's it for this time,' he announced. 'Nav, can I have a new course for Perth please?'

He banked and climbed to cruising altitude. The data was transmitted to the RCC and the Orion, which was still in transit to Perth.

Timothy and Jack poured over the photographs of the disturbance in the ocean. Timothy turned to Jack. 'This area here – what do you think that is?'

Jack shook his head. 'Absolutely no idea; I'm out of my depth on this.'

Timothy continued. 'It appears to be deforming the wave – never seen anything like this before. What deforms a wave?'

Timothy and Jack continued to pour over the photographs for the next two hours. They sat back in their chairs and faced one another. Jack shook his head, caught Timothy's eye and raised his eyebrows, his hands outstretched with palms up.

'This is the first time that I can honestly say I have no idea. I can't make any sense out of the photographs! Radar has a contact; we can see some deformation in the water from the contacts but we can't make out what it is. I'm completely baffled.'

Timothy took one more look at the screen. 'I think we need to get these photographs to the Hobart Antarctic people straight away and get them involved in this. This is their backyard – let's hope they can make some sense of it. I think that I'm going to try and get some sleep … I'm sure the Air Force will have another long debrief for us when we get back to Perth.'

Timothy was struggling with his emotions. He got out of his chair, went back to his seat, grabbed a blanket, strapped himself in and closed his eyes. He wanted to avoid dealing with his loss and immense grief. Sleep came and immediately took him back to the days before the race started in London.

CHAPTER 21

Timothy woke to a familiar heavy hand on the shoulder. Jack was standing over him.

'Time to wake up; we're on final approach into Perth.'

'Thanks,' mumbled Timothy.

He looked out of the window at the gleaming blue ocean. It was so different compared with the Southern Ocean, with its huge, forbidding grey swells. Below, the ocean was bright and inviting. They were soon taxiing to the hangars where an Air Force limousine was once again waiting.

At the Air Force base, they were ushered into the briefing centre where they were met by Flight Lieutenant James Stewart and Flight Sergeant Harris. The lieutenant introduced them to two Antarctic Division scientists who had flown up from Hobart for the debriefing. 'This is Dr Frank Mellows and Dr Virginia Perry. They flew to Perth at the request of the Australian Government and the RCC, who are both eager to understand the cause of the catastrophe.'

Dr Mellows was approximately fifty years old with greying light brown hair. He was tall with a solid frame. His frameless glasses gave him a distinguished look of an academic. Dr Perry was a blonde, just under six feet tall, one hundred and thirty pounds but curvaceous.

The lieutenant convened the meeting, introduced Dr Mellows

and Dr Perry and handed over to Flight Sergeant Harris, who took the group through an analysis of the day's photographs before calling the doctors to the floor.

'Doctors Mellows and Perry will now take us through a detailed description of what is contained in the photographs and in the digital observations.'

Dr Perry took the lead. As she stood, she brushed her slightly dishevelled blonde hair behind her ears. However, she was unfazed and focused. It was the first time she had dealt with an unexplained event in her career – it had her total attention.

She turned back from the screen. 'We can see from the first photograph that there are several abnormalities from what we've come to expect in this area. Something appears to be distorting the waves but we have no clear visual image. If we look to the lower image, we can see a three-dimensional representation of objects that are varying in size from 15 to 20 metres and approximately half a metre deep. They have irregular edges and there is some indication that they may be tapered like a knife-edge. The physical data contained in the three-dimensional digital images indicates that these objects have a temperature between -2 and -6 degrees Celsius and a density of 0.949 to 0.9256. The objects are barely buoyant. What we can say clearly about these objects is that their physical properties are not those of sea ice. The only material that comes anywhere near having these characteristics is freshwater ice.

'I'll now hand over to Dr Mellows who may be able to address the phenomenon we are looking at.'

Dr Mellows looked back at the images, then turned to address the teams in front of him. 'Ladies and gentlemen, the images and physical data we see here is problematic to say the least. The question we have to ask is: what is freshwater ice in such an immense scale doing several thousand kilometres from the polar cap?'

He turned back to face the images, then back to his audience – he appeared to be grappling with huge conflicts in his mind.

'With such incredibly problematic physical characteristics … and temperatures that are lower than the surrounding water temperatures … and densities slightly elevated to normal sea ice …'

He turned back to the images and requested a map be put up on the screen.

'We can see from this map that the location of this ice appears to be 1200 to 1600 kilometres from the polar ice field.'

Dr Perry took her cue. 'We have been receiving messages from the French station at the Kerguelen Islands for the last twenty-four hours. They confirmed that they have been receiving mysterious fleeting radar contacts, occasionally representing objects or several objects, with a combined length of several hundred metres. These objects have been disappearing within four to twelve hours of contact.'

Dr Perry paused, looking at her audience, then continued.

'The disappearance of the objects is problematic in the overall resolution of this matter but until we can ascertain the source of the ice and have a better understanding of its formation, this problem will remain unsolved.

'The French research station has no vessel or helicopter capable of going out to inspect these radar contacts. As a result, without any conclusive information, no official report has been issued. The information we have now, as a result of these photographs and digital survey information, provides us with sufficient information to be able to issue a warning to all vessels travelling below the 48th parallel.' Dr Perry referred to her notes. 'I have been advised the RCC has already issued that warning.

'These objects appear to weigh in excess of 5 tonnes and the larger ones could exceed 5000 tonnes. Any of these objects making contact with a vessel has the potential to inflict serious, even catastrophic damage. The nature of the objects means that they would have a very small profile in the ocean, potentially meaning that they may be undetected by smaller craft with limited radar capabilities.'

Dr Perry gestured for other slides to be put up on the screens.

'We believe that the damage caused to the vessels in question is consistent with an encounter with a field of this objects. In the cases of vessels one and three …' She stopped briefly and looked around the room. 'Sorry, our identifiers. I mean the *Ocean Odyssey* and *Ocean Mist* … we suspect a single catastrophic impact of an object, exceeding 25 tonnes on our first and very rough estimates, coming down a wave and intersecting a vessel as it rode up or down the wave. In the case of vessel two … excuse me, the *Shanghai Sunrise* … we suspect a single object intersecting the vessel at a different angle to the first two vessels, or multiple objects, have hit the vessel consecutively, breaking it into pieces. With approach velocities in excess of 30 knots highly probable, the result is a horrific and devastating impact. Both scenarios presented are hypothetical, yet highly probable, based on the physical information presented in the photographs, in particular the weight and dimensions of these objects.

'Neither Dr Mellows nor I are capable of giving you reasonable information on the formation of these objects or how they came to be in the ocean so far from Antarctic ice cap. We are currently negotiating with the Australian, French and American governments for funding to send a vessel to the Southern Ocean to visit the Kerguelen Islands, to attempt to unravel this catastrophic set of events and explain the presence of these objects in the ocean.'

As Dr Perry surveyed her audience, Timothy slowly got to his feet and addressed her. 'Dr Perry, how much funding is required to send a vessel into the Southern Ocean to give us some indication of what caused this event?'

Dr Perry moved towards Timothy. The excitement on her face was obvious to everybody. 'A sum in the order of ten million Australian dollars could provide us with a wave-piercing catamaran out of Hobart. This vessel has the speed and manoeuvrability to avoid these objects and the radar and sensors to detect them, as well as helicopter pads and payload for the equipment required for the analysis and research.'

Timothy looked sternly at Dr Mellows and Dr Perry, then at Flight Lieutenant Stewart. 'Lieutenant, it is clear to me that we have a cause for this event. I'm prepared to fund the expedition as a private investigation – to intersect the debris field and collect relevant data. A secondary task of the expedition would be to visit the French base on the Kerguelen Islands. There may be an opportunity to intersect some of those radar contacts that they recorded. I suggest that Doctors Mellows and Perry meet with me separately to discuss a proposition and to get the wheels in motion to make things happen as soon as possible.'

A radio operator stood and indicated that he had a message to give to the assembled teams. He relayed a message from the RCC asking if the rescue should be called off based on available information. That would remove the involvement of the RCC and the Australian Air Force.

A second radio operator stood to relay a message. 'Race Control indicates that they are relying on the RCC and the Air Force to call the shots in relation to whether the search is over.'

Flight Lieutenant Stewart took the floor, looked around the room and addressed the teams. 'Ladies and gentlemen, this afternoon it has become obvious that we have not detected any signs of life from the search. Also, we have carefully determined that insufficient material was taken from the vessels for a sailor to sustain life in the climatic conditions in the target zones. Therefore, we can only conclude that all three sailors are lost.' The lieutenant looked down, then back to the assembled teams. 'God rest their souls. Having determined that the search has concluded, you can all now stand down.'

With the Air Force dismissed, the lieutenant motioned toward Dr Mellows, Dr Perry and Timothy. 'Please feel free to use our facilities and communication equipment to continue a search investigation for as long as required. Flight Sergeant Harris is at your service and the base has the authority to make any facilities available that you require. A car will be available to take you back to the airport or your hotels.'

'Thank you, Flight Lieutenant Stewart,' Timothy said as he shook the lieutenant's hand. 'Please thank your team for their efforts in this search; their professional conduct has been exceptional.'

With that, Timothy motioned Dr Mellows, Dr Perry and Flight Sergeant Harris to a table where they sat and discussed the next steps in sending a vessel back into the Southern Ocean, to unravel the tragedy facing them.

Two hours later, Timothy and the scientists departed the Air Force base. Timothy was heading to his hotel in Perth, and the scientists to the airport to catch the midnight flight back to Melbourne, and then another flight to Hobart.

CHAPTER 22

It was 10 pm at Race Headquarters in Perth. Dave Michaelson had called a meeting of all the team managers and communications managers. A few minutes earlier, he had received an update from the RCC. The team members entered the room, each one with searching gazes directed at Dave, James and Caroline. They were all met with solemn, expressionless faces. Dave motioned them to be seated.

'Ladies and gentlemen, we have an update report from the rescue target zones in the Southern Ocean. The specialised equipment on the Orion was able to determine that the safety rafts were still attached to the decks of both the *Ocean Odyssey* and *Ocean Mist*. Since we have now exceeded the survival time of a sailor surviving in the current conditions, the Race Coordination Centre has determined the three sailors to be lost at sea, presumed dead.'

There was a hushed silence in the room. This morning's hopes had been slim, but they had just been delivered the worst news possible – Penelope, Tony and Sam had been lost at sea.

Dave cleared his throat gently to get their attention. 'Timothy Wiley, the owner of the *Ocean Odyssey* team, is putting together an expedition with the involvement of the Australian Antarctic Division to determine the cause of this incident. The *Shanghai Sunrise* and *Ocean Mist* teams may want to consider joining the expedition. That's something you'll need to work out with Mr Wiley. I'll now request that the team managers and communications coordinators join Caroline and myself in our communication centre, to prepare communications for the press and condolence messages for the families of the sailors lost at sea. In these solemn times, we do pass on our condolences to all the team members. We're all part of a tight knit community and any loss is enormous. In the past forty-eight hours, we have lost our three top solo racers and that's a loss that we will feel in every major race for many years to come.

'We have had detailed discussions with the race sponsors, and it has been decided to terminate the race as of midnight, Southern Ocean time. Positions at that time will be used to determine the race winners. Due to these catastrophic events, sponsors believe that they will have the support of all the teams in this decision. That's all for this meeting, ladies and gentlemen. Our thoughts go with you.'

The team members filed out of the room quietly – the managers and communications coordinators followed. Dave made his way to the communication centre, closely followed by Caroline Murray. The team leaders and communication coordinators headed back to their offices, having to prepare their own communications for the team owners, and relatives of the deceased sailors.

VJ Gupter was finishing up a board meeting as his mobile phone rang. 'VJ here,' he drawled.

'VJ, it's Sanjay. I also have Michael with me. We just had an announcement from the Race Control Centre. They just received a message from the RCC. I'm sorry to say, VJ, but the news is not good. The Race Coordination Centre has declared all three sailors and vessels lost in the Southern Ocean. The race organisers have passed on their condolences to the teams and the relatives of the sailors lost.'

'This is too early!' replied VJ. 'It's not enough searching! How can they abandon the search after only thirty or forty hours?'

Sanjay hesitated and passed the phone to Michael.

'VJ, the last aircraft left the search zone approximately thirty-four hours after contact was lost with the vessels. The survival raft can only sustain life under the terrible conditions out there for thirty hours without fresh supplies. By tomorrow morning, it will have been in excess of fifty hours. It's a hard call, but it's one the RCC has made. Hold on, Sanjay has something to add.'

Michael passed the phone back to Sanjay.

'VJ, Timothy Wiley is chartering a high-speed catamaran out of Hobart to go to the search zone with scientists and attempt to determine the cause of the incident. You may want to consider supporting that venture to avoid any possible media fall out. It's something that you may want to review with your media advisers.'

'Good point – they never leave us alone,' mumbled VJ. 'Well, you two may want to wrap up the team there and head back to Mumbai. There's no point in staying in Perth. If there's nothing else, Sanjay, we'll leave it at that and I'll see you and the team back in Mumbai as soon as possible.'

'One last thing VJ. Do you want me to coordinate with your PR people to manage things with Sam's family and relatives?'

'Yes, please do that, and have them keep me informed, thank you.'

With that VJ hung up the phone and looked around his office. The last forty hours had been tense; the whole race drama had created a media nightmare for his business. His clients were very uncomfortable as a large media contingent was constantly around their offices, making business very difficult – they preferred their privacy. He felt that he needed to distance himself as far as possible from the limelight to make his customers feel more comfortable. He would have to have his PR team find them a high profile actor or actress to distract the media. He hoped that would keep the pressure off him until the race drama was all over.

Janice Yew left the communication centre and headed straight to her office. She immediately called Lee Chang.

'Lee here. What's the news?'

'Couldn't be worse, Lee. The RCC has just declared the three sailors lost. Based on the climatic conditions in the search zone, even if our sailor had managed to get into life raft, he would have been dead a couple of hours ago, due to hypothermia. The rafts need replenishing every thirty hours for a sailor to survive under the conditions being experienced down there at the moment.'

'That's a devastating outcome. Tony was a great sailor and a fantastic asset to the business. Can you handle the family for me please, and also coordinate with our media people to manage this properly? Please also advise the business risk department to notify the insurers of the event. Janice, we have a major business deal meeting here at 5.00 am tomorrow morning. Can you deal with all that and be in contact with me at about 3.00 pm tomorrow with an update?'

'Okay Lee. I'll email you a brief and talk to you then.'

'One other thing, Janice. The government needs you to be on top of this development. This is one of the reasons you were placed on that project. They have particular interest in anything that is happening in the Southern Ocean.'

CHAPTER 22

'Yes, I am aware of that. Timothy Wiley is putting an expedition together to go back and find a cause of the incident. I will make sure that I am on that expedition to represent your interests.'

'Excellent, I will rely on you to be on the expedition then.'

'All the best with your meeting, Lee.'

'Thanks Janice; good night.'

The next three days were a living hell for Dave, James and Caroline. They were taken to task by the media over every minute detail of the planning of the race, rescue preparedness, and knowledge of any climatic events in the Southern Ocean. They were getting enormous support from sponsors but the media was unrelenting in their quest to keep the story alive. Despite their intense questioning the media had no answers and there had been no hints of what might have caused such an unprecedented tragedy. They were, however, turning the story into a profitable media circus. Media-chartered aircraft were over the debris fields daily. Across the globe, banner headlines carried new theories as to what caused the sinking of the three boats.

With all the media attention, the Antarctic scientific community, oceanographers, weather forecasters, the RCC and the politicians involved, were finding themselves being pushed into the limelight and questioned relentlessly about all aspects of the tragedy. The media probing had been mentioned on the floor of Parliament in Australia, New Zealand, India and the United Kingdom. The US Congress and the governments of Argentina, China and South Africa also expressed interest and concern in the events in the Southern Ocean. The eyes of the world had been brought to gaze on the race and its coordinators and sponsors – and the ocean.

Timothy Wiley's expedition, while rapidly growing momentum, was suffering constant interference from governments, scientific groups and the media. Each interest group now wanted to be on board the vessel that was setting out to unravel the mystery. Timothy was standing his ground, only taking on board a small scientific team comprising the Australian Antarctic division, a single representative from each of the other two impacted teams and the Australian Air Force and Navy. Janice had insisted on representing the *Shanghai Sunrise* and Timothy had seen no reason to deny her that position. Competing media interests had attempted to find a similar high-speed long-range vessel but they had been unsuccessful. It appeared as if Timothy's team would have the Southern Ocean to themselves, to carry out their investigations away from the probing eyes of the competing media.

Two days after calling Lee, Janice got an unexpected call from him.

'Janice, Timothy Wiley has had the media blacked out from all coverage of the search and rescue for the missing boats. This is a serious development. I have been asked officially to provide our government with a direct feed of information from the search area. Are you able to assist?' asked Lee.

Janice had been waiting for this type of opportunity. Her income from the team was good, but would not last for long. This was her chance to make real money. 'Lee, I have been in contact with Timothy; he will accept me on the team. Can you provide all the equipment I will need?'

Lee didn't hesitate. 'Just send the list Janice,' he said.

'Then there will be danger money for work above and beyond normal duties,' replied Janice.

Lee had been expecting a business proposal; Janice was not naïve. She had a solid background in intelligence services, so the task was not beyond her. 'The equipment is no problem. The services fee – how much are we talking about here?'

'To cover the risk of getting caught and losing my current career, I would need five million US up front.'

Lee sighed. It sounded like a lot but she was right. Her career in professional circles would be over and there would be the possibility of jail time, if things went wrong. 'That's a bit steep, don't you think?'

Janice knew this response was coming and was prepared with a list of further requirements. 'More than fair, Lee. I will need guaranteed legal costs, just in case, and jail time at one hundred thousand per year if I go away, covered in escrow of one million dollars.'

Damn! thought Lee. *She heard me thinking ... She has it all covered!* 'Okay Janice, you drive a hard bargain. When can I have the equipment list?'

'You will have an email within three hours. Can I get details of what information the government is looking for?'

'The government is concerned that there could be some sort of influence on the environment or weather patterns associated with this incident. They are very concerned about protecting our massive solar and alternative energy associated businesses. It is very important that no-one gets data coming out of the Southern Ocean that could jeopardise that business. Do you understand?'

'Very clear. Just get me the equipment before the boat leaves.'

'Okay, Janice, take care.'

'Thanks Lee; talk to you when I get back.'

Janice felt that she had become secondary to the information. She wondered if the relationship had always been that way. But she was excited about the deal she had just made. She had covered all the bases and she had the experience to deliver the goods. She prepared her list of required equipment, checked and double-checked it again to be sure. She then drafted a plan, ran through it and double-checked her equipment list again. Once she was satisfied she sent her email to Lee.

CHAPTER 23

In London, the Prime Minister, Secretary of State for Energy and Climate Change, Secretary of State for Defence and Chancellor of the Exchequer met in private to discuss the emerging events in the Southern Ocean. The Prime Minister commenced the meeting after they were all seated.

'Gentlemen, this meeting is to focus on risks to the government's policies and the British economy as a result of intelligence reports from the Southern Ocean over the prior several months, exacerbated by the tragic loss of three vessels and their sailors in the ocean race. Very unfortunate matter.'

He nodded to the Energy and Climate Secretary, who continued.

'There had been extremely unusual thermal events occurring in the area, accompanied by unexplained radar images that have raised the possibility of an unexplained local thermal event. Risk assessment advisers have reported to the government that should anything destabilise trust in the government's climate change policy, a series of events would unfold that could bring the government down, cause global economic instability and eventually cause a massive financial and political meltdown.'

The Chancellor interjected at this point. 'The British government's policy on climate change was primarily based on the Stern Report, which had recommended expenditures of one to two per cent of GDP as being required to bring about the changes necessary to contain global warming. The British government had embraced the report in policy, worked towards a carbon price and committed the nation to a climate change policy and alternative sustainable energy lifestyle.'

With the European economic crisis raging, the British government and all the governments in the European Union member states were under extreme political pressure. Any hint of policy issues surrounding one of the pillars of the current economic policy would be catastrophic for the government of the day. The Prime Minister and his ministers had felt they had no choice but to manage the situation with extreme prejudice. After all, it was for the good of the nation and the people of the United Kingdom. At stake was the global warming agenda and the economy. They felt that such an issue gave them license to do whatever was necessary to control the developing situation as a matter of national and global security.

The Defence Secretary waded into the discussion. 'MI6 has been gathering intelligence on the events and has provided briefing papers on the Southern Ocean situation. In the briefing papers, MI6 has proposed implementing a program that would cover half the southern hemisphere. The Royal Navy will be called on to assist MI6 in providing vessels to observe and manage the unfolding situation. In their assessments, MI6 has deemed it necessary to involve the Australian government in containing the issue. They briefed the Australian security agencies ASIS at length on the assistance that would be required from the Australian government in containing the matter.

'The Prime Minister's office called on the Australian government to provide assistance in the matter. The request was classified as a matter of national security and briefing papers were provided for Australia's Prime Minister, Defence

Minister and Treasurer. The government in Australia was looking happy to oblige. Within hours of receiving the request of the British government, the Australian Defence Minister had been requested to provide ongoing intelligence reporting in relation to events occurring in the Southern Ocean and to provide strategic support and operations, to control events as they unfolded. The orders in the Prime Minister's Office included the direction, *"The events are to be managed with extreme prejudice if necessary."*

'Australian intelligence services based in Perth were put on high alert. Within hours, their command centre had tapped into all communications relating to the search, Race Headquarters and Timothy Wiley's team. At the Australian Secret Intelligence Service command centre in Perth, the local director has initiated a mission to support the request from MI6 and the UK government. In addition to that, the UK government has sent MI6 operatives to Perth. The Defence Minister and Prime Minister's office of Australia had ordered that the operation was a matter of national security with international political implications.

'By monitoring Timothy's phone calls, ASIS has established the need to infiltrate Incat, a ferry and defence manufacturer in Hobart, to ensure that the captain and crew of the ship that Timothy hired, is under its control. A team has been dispatched to Hobart with the authority to take control of the vessel being hired by Timothy. The Official Secrets Act has been invoked and a permanent liaison stationed in the Incat office, to ensure that the company and its officials do not divulge any information to compromise the mission. With their tactical teams in place, the security services is playing a watch and wait game as Timothy's plan begins to unfold.'

The Defence Secretary concluded with, 'Gentlemen, I believe we have the situation firmly under control.'

The Prime Minister looked to the gathered ministers for approval. 'If everyone agrees, gentlemen, then let's get back to work.'

CHAPTER 24

Hobart

12 July 2015

Five days had passed since the declaration that the sailors had all been lost. Timothy had stayed totally focused on the expedition to the Southern Ocean. Bureaucratic interference, the media, scientific groups and politicians were constantly trying to contact him for more information. There appeared to be a distinct uneasiness about the expedition and what it could uncover.

Timothy had relocated the *Ocean Odyssey* management team onto the *Spirit of the Southern Ocean*, as he had named the charter for the expedition. Miles Henderson and Gary Smith were good operators and Timothy decided that they would be an asset to the expedition team. He had supplemented the team with Caroline Murray, Janice Yew and Sanjay Singh, figuring a heavy contingent of communications coordinators would ease the burden on him with regards to the press and the other teams.

Both VJ Gupter and Lee Chang had requested representation and offered to contribute to the costs of the expedition. Timothy agreed to representation but declined financial aid to avoid losing control of the expedition.

Timothy called Miles and Gary to his office on the *Spirit of the Southern Ocean* in Hobart.

'Gary, Miles, grab a seat. Drink?'

They both nodded.

'Gary, Jim Beam straight up? Miles, uh, vodka and tomato juice on ice?' Timothy poured the drinks and continued. 'We haven't had a chance to discuss why Penelope was off course when she disappeared.'

That was the question Miles had been dreading for days. He took a good long drink before he captured Timothy's gaze and commenced. 'As you know, coming out of Cape Town, the other two boats headed south. They picked up speed as a result of the Roaring Forties and beyond. We gave the other teams almost three days before we made a decision on a course change. At that point, the other boats were going to be in Perth at least two days ahead of Penelope.'

Timothy sensed tension in Gary and Miles and was curious to find the cause. He turned to Gary. 'What will I find on the recordings about the decision making process?'

Gary found himself between a rock and a hard place but there was no point beating around the bush on this one. He knew no matter what he said, Timothy would listen to the recordings, if he hadn't already. 'Well, you will find a lot of conflict about what to do. On one hand, there was great concern about losing the lead and possibly the race if we didn't change course. There was a huge amount invested in the race and no-one wanted to see that wasted.'

Timothy was showing signs of severe agitation. His face has reddened as he gulped his drink. 'Go on, Gary.'

'Well, when the other two boats cleared the plateau, gaining speed and closing the gap, Penelope totally lost it. She insisted on a course change, threatened Miles with dismissal or worse.

She insisted that she had to win the race at all costs.' Gary was ashen, with tears rolling down his cheeks. 'In the end it was very ugly. She wanted to keep that lead and nothing was going to stop her getting that course change.'

Nobody said anything for several minutes as they stared into their drinks, absorbed in their own thoughts.

Timothy was trying to reconcile the reasoning for Penelope's bad judgement. The pressure he was putting her under to give up racing ... had that put her into a mindset where she wanted to win the race and use that to move onto another team? She had always been so competitive. Whatever her decision-making process was, it was against what he had *insisted* on, not just wanted. He owned the boat; the funding of the venture was his risk. He had offered her the option of withdrawing from the race to be with him; he knew she was stubborn but he had never seen or suspected this in her. Miles and Gary would have been terrified of her threats. That they didn't call him was a serious issue, but could he have controlled Penelope under those circumstances? Trying to explain the commercial agreement with the race committee would have caused the same outcome.

Poor bastards, thought Timothy. *They've probably been dreading this discussion for days.*

Finally, Timothy looked at Miles and Gary. 'Another drink, gentlemen?'

Both nodded again without a word. Timothy poured the drinks – doubles this time – then proposed a toast.

'Here's to a hard-headed woman. There's not a man in this room who could have stopped Penelope changing course.'

After a few more minutes of silence, Timothy shook both their hands and motioned them away from the bar to a table. Timothy was relieved that the tension was broken between the three of them. It wasn't obvious before, but none of them could have prevented the disaster. Penelope was too stubborn, even for him.

'Well guys, let's call the rest of this meeting a risk management meeting. I have some concern about the attention we're getting on this expedition from various self-interest groups. I'm curious about the politicians and their advisors – and all these economists, particularly those with close government ties. There are climate scientists, oceanographers and meteorologists as well. Given the little that we know, based on the photographs and scientific data we took from the wreck sites, this level of attention is extraordinary. I'd like both of you to start digging, very deep, as to why these groups are so interested in three missing sailors and their boats.'

Timothy took a long sip of his drink and continued.

'I need both of you to keep this investigation absolutely confidential. The last thing that we want to do, is to make these groups aware that we suspect something. I can just sense a high level of interference with our mission. You have a reasonable budget to get expert opinions, analysis and intelligence to assist in determining what is going on. Under no circumstances should these activities be divulged to the other team members on board.'

Timothy finished his drink and poured another round.

'The other matter we need to attend to while still close to Australia, is whether or not we have a memorial service for Penelope now or after the expedition. Any ideas?'

Gary fidgeted in his chair. 'Timothy I really think ...' He paused. 'We feel that's your call. You were close with Penelope so that's one you have to decide on.'

'Then that's not a hard call. Miles, put together a statement with Gary that expresses my and the team's regret at the loss and pass on our condolences to her family and relatives. Make sure I do that personally. Ensure that her relatives will be comfortable with a memorial after our return, when we should have more definitive information about the loss of the vessels and sailors.' Timothy turned to Miles. 'How does that sound?'

'Sounds fine. We'll draft it up and get you to sign off on the statements before they go out. Also, we'll do a significant cover story for our media outlets and have some footage to go to air around the same time on the media channels.'

'Okay, let's get down to business,' replied Timothy. 'Travelling time to Fremantle, being the closest port to Perth, will be approximately four days. We'll arrive in Fremantle around the 16th of July. We pick up the rest of the team members there and refuel. Sailing time to intersect the debris field will be approximately forty-eight hours. The crew has estimated that the debris could have moved up to 750 kilometres from its previous location, based on the prevailing winds and currents in the area. Just to make sure that we don't go around in circles for a long time, the rescue charter aircraft will go out ahead of us to find the debris and locate the objects that we saw in the photographs. The plan is to inspect all the debris and retrieve whatever we can. Once we have done that for all three vessels, we will then go in search of what may have caused this incident. Hopefully by the time we have completed retrieval of the debris, Rescue Charter will have located the mystery objects.' Timothy gestured to Miles and Gary. 'Any questions, gentlemen?'

Miles puts down his drink. 'I'm not exactly sure what Caroline, Janice and Sanjay will be doing while we're out there.'

Timothy smiled and looked down. 'Yes, I expected that question. It's all political – a bit of face-saving for the good of everyone involved. This way, we get to keep the politicians and the media off the boat, and also give a representative of the other two boats and the organisers a chance to pay their respects at sea. It also gives us a person on board to field answers in relation to their own vessels.' He paused. 'Just on that topic, Janice approached me to be on this expedition. She seemed a bit eager. I feel a bit uneasy about her. Let's keep an eye on her for now … I'm just not sure.'

Miles nodded. 'She can be pretty pushy, and her knowledge of logistics and military equipment doesn't seem to fit her profile. Happy to keep an eye on her.'

The captain of the ship walked into the room. He was formally dressed in his white uniform, tall, clean-shaven, muscular with inquisitive brown eyes.

'We'll be underway in five minutes, Timothy.'

'That's fantastic, Captain Delaney. Thank you.' Timothy looked at Miles and Gary. 'Let's go up on deck and see how this baby performs.'

This was the first time that Timothy had seen Captain Delaney at a distance; he took in the walk and the mannerisms of the captain as he walked away, noting that he appeared to have the sharpness of a naval trained officer.

Up on deck the scene was breathtaking. The wave-piercing Incat three-hulled catamaran was a technological marvel. She had the ability to cruise at 30 knots all day and had a range of over four thousand nautical miles. Its flight deck housed two helicopters and below deck, there was room for up to seventy cars. Part of the space below deck was occupied by cranes and other lifting equipment, to enable salvage from the three debris fields. The catamaran had a length of 70 metres and was similar to vessels in service with the Australian and American navies, which were deployed in Aceh after the tidal wave and for rescues after Cyclone Katrina in the USA.

Within minutes, the catamaran was cruising at 20 knots and Hobart fell away in the distance. The Derwent River was calm and glassy on this cold July day.

CHAPTER 25

Over the next five days, Miles and Gary spent all their time collecting vast amounts of data that they thought could have been relevant to why politicians, economists and scientists were taking so much interest in the outcome of an expedition to the Southern Ocean.

'Where do you want to start?' said Gary when they sat down to summarise their research.

Miles looked at Gary. 'Seems to be a pretty clear picture coming out of all of this. Governments across Europe and Asia, as well as Canada and some American states, have made decisions to move towards various forms of emissions trading and carbon taxes. That's resulted in a lot of political agendas and economic decisions around clean energy. Government inaction on climate change has seen elections lost; action has seen elections won. The emerging political strength is driving a multi-trillion dollar industry in alternative energy sources, efficiencies and business re-engineering. And just a bit of trivia, Gary – have a look at this one.'

'On the science and technology front, the Australian CSIRO had a series of several thousand buoys deployed in the Southern and Indian Oceans to monitor temperature, fresh and saltwater content. There had been no unusual occurrences reported in relation to those buoys. After what we just experienced down there, that is really unusual. The Antarctic Division people were telling us that the temperatures seen down there were 4 to 5 degrees below normal. I haven't seen a single report on that anywhere!'

Gary stood and approached the large screen. 'This is even more fascinating – the polar ice fields were subject to change in the Arctic. It was predicted that the ocean could be ice-free during summer within the following year of two. In the Antarctic, loss of land ice appeared to be accelerating. However, there was an unusual balance between the Antarctic and the Arctic at any point in time. In the Arctic summer months, the loss of sea ice was balanced by extra growth of sea ice in the Antarctic. The unusual phenomenon is well known in the scientific community, but not within the general public.'

Miles poured two drinks while Gary adjusted the electronic whiteboard. 'I think the common thread here is the way the politicians and economists have used global warming to bring about social, economic and political change,' said Miles. 'They appear to be potentially uneasy about the Southern Ocean for some reason. There's something else at play here and maybe not CO2 global warming.' Miles passed a drink to Gary and highlighted a section on the board. 'The French Antarctic base at the Kerguelen Islands had reported unusual radar contacts during the search. The radar contacts had not been confirmed and it was not known if they were the same objects as detected by the Orion in the debris fields. Their helicopter had been grounded and they had no other way of confirming what these objects were. That strike you as odd? Shouldn't they have called in a jet? This is starting to look really odd, Gary.'

'Miles, you're getting pretty dramatic. I mean, look at all the information we've been through in the last five days. Every man and his dog out there has his own real theory about what's going on in his own patch. Just take the ozone guys. They're saying that it's colder in winter and hotter in summer. I can relate to that. I don't know how it fits in with global warming though.'

Miles nodded his head pensively. 'You know, you've got something there. We've got all these scientists, each one is an expert in their own area, and they can prove that ozone or CO2 or whatever can have an impact on what's going on. Then we have the thirty year cycle guys who are saying this is part of the bigger picture ... that in effect, Mother Nature looks after her own. Did the pollies take a big gamble? Wow ... what a story if that's true! There will be a hell of a lot of Humpty Dumptys, having a great fall.' Miles looked excited. 'This could be fifty times the size of the *News of the World* phone bugging scandal.'

'Miles, do you want to do a summary for Timothy? It would be a great opportunity for the business to start running features on all these weather change theories – see if we can flush out a rat!'

'I like that. Yes, we could punctuate that with news from the Southern Ocean every now and then. If we're going to make that work, we should have a camera crew on board. I'm sure Timothy will support that. I'll have one waiting when we dock!'

'While you're doing that, I'll go and get Timothy so we can take him through our research and what we've come up with.'

Shortly Gary arrived back into the room with Timothy. Miles poured them all fresh drinks, sat down and began to explain the complex scientific, economic and political nature of what they had before them. Timothy was fascinated by the sheer enormity of what they were potentially dealing with. Historically, things like this had happened before, but never on a global scale. This would be enormous.

'Okay Gary, Miles, you've got a budget. I suggest a camera crew and a photographer meet us at Fremantle.'

Gary winked at Miles.

'This is definitely a lockdown now. I'll talk to the captain – we'll put tight security around our offices for you guys to work in. Let's get onto it. Well done guys. Let's go up to the bar and have a few more drinks and dinner after you line up the cameraman and the photographer.'

Gary, Miles and Timothy talked well into the night. There was a resurgence of energy in Timothy. He had been depressed since Penelope's disappearance and this was big enough to draw him out of the pain and give him something to live for.

The *Spirit of the Southern Ocean* docked in Fremantle early the next morning. It was a six hour turnaround. Caroline, Janice, Sanjay, a cameraman and a photographer came on board. The ship was refuelled and they departed.

The media throng in Fremantle was enormous, but no-one was giving statements other than Timothy talking to his own media representatives by phone. Timothy had taken several angry telephone calls from a number of politicians, economists and scientists, all of whom insisted that they should be on the expedition. Gary had started noting down the names of all the people making contact. Each one would be investigated fully for links to any interest groups as they worked through the emerging web.

Caroline finally caught up with Timothy in his office. She embraced him with a kiss on the cheek. 'I'm sorry for your loss, Timothy.'

Without a pause Timothy responded. 'Thanks Caroline, welcome aboard. I guess you want to update the agreement?'

Caroline tensed. 'Would it be insensitive to mention it now?'

Timothy sat down at his desk facing her. 'It's okay, please sit down.' He hadn't had a chance to think about the agreement since the search concluded. It was time to close all the loopholes now. 'Caroline, I'm blocking all other media companies from this venture. I have exclusive rights to the media coverage of the search and all events that occur out there.' Timothy noticed the change in her expression. 'You look concerned, Caroline.'

'You did just say exclusive rights. How am I supposed to take that?'

'Sorry, Caroline, my mistake. We still need the assistance of the race committee, but in a reduced capacity. I'm proposing that the share for the committee drop to five per cent.'

Caroline was visibly angry; she steadied herself. 'No less than ten per cent, otherwise you will get no cooperation, and that's final.'

Timothy sat back in his chair. Caroline had brought the first offer to him and it had boosted his coffers by a considerable amount before the disaster. He decided it would be worth keeping her on side for now. 'That's a lot for a little support, Caroline!'

Caroline didn't hesitate. She didn't want to lose the income for the committee or herself. 'Timothy, if we stand by you, this will be huge. Without us, it could drop off the media front page.'

Timothy didn't believe that for a moment but he would need the committee at some stage. 'Seven and a half per cent, final offer. I suggest you take it.'

Caroline sensed that things would be difficult if she persisted. 'Seven and a half it is. You push a hard bargain. In the meantime, is there anything I can assist with?'

Timothy felt inclined to include her more in their plans, but decided against it. 'No thanks Caroline, we're doing okay.'

Caroline rose from her chair. 'Okay, I'll leave you to it. A draft of the change to the agreement will be with you by the end of the day.'

'Thanks Caroline.'

Timothy watched Caroline as she gracefully slipped through the door and disappeared down the corridor. *Why hadn't Penelope been more like that?*

CHAPTER 26

16 July 2015

One day out of Fremantle, the outside temperature had dropped to 2 degrees Celsius; the ocean waves had increased to 6 metres and a westerly wind had reached 60 kilometres an hour. The charter aircraft had been out all day and was now on its return trip to Perth. It had not found a debris field; however, the Hobart Antarctic Division had provided new estimates as to where the fields could be. Their estimates were 50 to 100 kilometres outside the original search field. The Orion would be back in the morning to search the new area.

At dawn on the second day, the *Spirit of the Southern Ocean* had travelled just over 1300 kilometres and was still twelve hours from the original target zone. The charter aircraft left Perth at 2.00 am and was due to fly over them within a half hour. There was a sense of anticipation on the boat as the aircraft was picked up on the ship's radar. It passed directly overhead, waggled its wings in acknowledgement and disappeared into the western sky.

Ninety minutes later, the pilot called in his report. 'Charter to *Spirit of the Southern Ocean*.'

'*Spirit of the Southern Ocean* receiving.'

'We are reporting location of the debris zones – location report to follow.'

The pilot reported that each debris field was now an area of some two and a half kilometres square. Captain Delaney made a small adjustment to their course and reported that they should be in the target zone within ten hours. Unfortunately, the timing would only give them one or two hours of light before nightfall in the debris zone.

As the day progressed, the wind speed increased to 80 kilometres per hour; the waves were increasing to between 8 and 11 metres and the temperatures had fallen to -5 degrees Celsius. It was bitterly cold on deck; at times, there were snow flurries and the sky was dark and forbidding. The drift of the debris had been south-easterly, with the closest field lying just below 50 degrees south, out of the Roaring Forties and into the Furious Fifties. Captain Delaney advised that the weather would only get worse over the next few hours.

As they approached the first debris field, the temperature had dropped to -8 degrees Celsius. The wind had fallen slightly to 65 kilometres an hour and the waves were running at 6 to 8 metres. Captain Delaney came online with a stern warning – the wind chill factor of 65 kilometre per hour winds made the temperature on deck a numbing -47 degrees Celsius. The captain advised that only his trained crew would be allowed on deck, to partake in the salvage operations. The conditions were too treacherous for untrained personnel to be on deck.

The first debris field that they had located appeared to be that of the *Ocean Odyssey*. The deck had broken in two, in line with the mainmast. The crew battled the swells to secure the two sections of the deck and haul them on board. At times the swells smashed across the work deck like angry hands attempting to grab the equipment and operators. The task was dangerous and time consuming. The smaller debris was collected under lights by 10.00 pm.

The sections of the *Ocean Odyssey* were taken below deck into the massive storage area. The area had been cordoned off with partitions and was floodlit to allow reconstruction and inspections to begin. Timothy, Miles, Gary and the ship's crew were the only people allowed into the area. The crew had mounted the remains of the deck on a scaffold, allowing for inspection above and below deck. The two sections were brought together to form a continuous deck. The masts were missing, either torn away by the initial impact or worked free in the days of continuous wind and wave action. The breaking of the deck in two indicated the mainmast could still have been intact when the deck went into the water.

Timothy, Miles and Gary approached the scaffold. Timothy immediately headed up to the deck while Miles and Gary held back, then walked around the scaffold, mesmerised by the shattered hull and the carbon fibre hanging from the deck in short threads. Timothy walked down to the bow; he could see where fittings had been torn out of the deck. The bow had a few sections of rail intact – mid-ship the life raft was intact and securely restrained on the deck as it was when Penelope had sailed out of London. The winches and wheel had been torn out of the deck.

Timothy looked at Gary and Miles. 'Not much up here to tell us anything I'm afraid. The life raft is here and not much else.'

Gary pointed at the stern. 'You'd better have a look at this, Timothy. Part of the stern is still intact.'

Timothy moved to the ladder on the scaffold. 'On my way,' he said in a determined tone.

He joined Gary and Miles at the stern, where they were inspecting the torn section. About a metre from the stern, the torn section increased in depth to about eight hundred millimetres. It appeared as though the entire stern had been ripped out of the hull. They were joined by the salvage team, headed by Peter Dreyfus. Peter gestured at the stern.

'We've sent detailed photographs of that through to Hobart University. Hopefully their scientists will be able to give us some idea of what happened here.'

Timothy looked concerned. 'Are they under commercial confidentiality?'

Peter smiled. 'If they want to keep their grants, they're under confidentiality. But I'll remind them straight away.' He took out his phone and walked away from the scaffold.

Timothy moved under the scaffold, where most of the fittings were missing. He looked around him. It was an eerie feeling walking in the space that should have been the cabin of the *Ocean Odyssey*. He noticed the door arch to the galley and hesitated as his mind flashed back to the last time he was there. He struggled with the thought and then noticed that the hammock had been torn from its mountings. The pain became too intense and he struggled on his feet. He staggered sideways into the scaffold.

Miles rushed to his aid. 'Steady there, Timothy. You okay?'

Timothy looked dazed. He mumbled but could not speak. He had grazed his head against the scaffold and had a small stream of blood pouring down from the wound.

Miles noticed that Peter had finished his phone call and was approaching the scaffold. He called out, 'We need a hand here Peter and possibly a stretcher.'

Peter called for first aid, and soon after, Timothy was on a stretcher being attended to by the ship's doctor. Timothy was in a daze; his head was spinning. He was not able to speak to the doctor as he was examined; he was taken to the ship's first aid room and made comfortable. After a few minutes and a glass of water, Timothy was able to start answering the doctor's questions.

'Timothy, how are you feeling now?'

'Feeling better by the minute, thanks.'

'Where are you?'

Timothy answered without hesitation. 'On board the *Spirit of the Southern Ocean*, in the Southern Ocean, collecting wreckage and looking for answers.'

'So what happened?'

'One moment I was looking at the underside of the deck, the next I was in here. That's all I remember.'

The doctor was able to determine that Timothy had not been eating well since the *Ocean Odyssey* disappeared; he had been extremely stressed, depressed and also not sleeping well.

'Sounds like a good meal, some sedatives and a good night's sleep is in order. Your blood pressure is a bit low but that's to be expected.'

Timothy was relieved to hear the doctor's prognosis. 'Thanks, Doc.'

Timothy accepted the doctor's offer of dinner together. Afterwards he had a restful night's sleep, assisted by some prescribed sedatives.

Captain Delaney had released two beacons to drift in the remnants of the *Ocean Odyssey* debris, to ensure that they could find it again if required. The captain then set an automatic course for the *Shanghai Sunrise* debris field at low speed, to keep the ship stable in the high seas. The strong winds continued to blow through the night and dawn was very bleak. The deck of the ship was encrusted in ice and snow and the maintenance crew was called out to remove as much of it as they could to make the deck safe to work on. The captain had manoeuvred the vessel to be at the *Shanghai Sunrise* debris field at dawn. The crew worked diligently throughout the day and had recovered the debris field by 3.00 pm.

As one team was engaged on deck and collecting the debris, another team below deck had been laying out the puzzle and piecing together the jigsaw from the first photographs taken within twenty-four hours of the loss of the *Shanghai Sunrise*. Having collected all the debris, the below-deck team had completed assembling the jigsaw. Using their overhead crane, photographs were taken of the assembly of the two vessels. The photographs were issued to the university engineering and forensic departments. Peter Dreyfus called a meeting with Timothy, Gary and Miles to review the photographs; Dr Perry and Dr Mellows joined them. A composite image of the debris field after the destructive event was on one screen and the reassembled jigsaw puzzle below deck on the other. Just after they were seated, two additional screens were turned on. One was a teleconference with the Engineering Department of the Hobart University and the other was the Forensic Department.

Timothy, Gary and Miles headed back to their offices, reviewed the findings of the day's activities, and carefully prepared a report for Gary to take back to Peter, to be sent to the RCC. The three of them felt as though they were part of the media pack again – and this time, leading it. They had the strategies to have the story to themselves – a sensational world-first story, with potentially massive political ramifications. The three of them toiled over the communiqué. It was important to inform, but not to give away critical information that may alert the rest of the media of the bigger story to be had. Miles led the preparation.

'Okay guys, the facts we have to work with, is our printable hypothesis. The story has to captivate the audience. "Unidentified objects slice through ketches at waterline". It might be worthwhile trying to attach an emotional line about Timothy and his fragile emotional state, to add a bit more interest?'

Timothy nodded with a wry smile. 'That's the way I think we want it. So in summary, the *Ocean Odyssey* and the *Shanghai Sunrise* were destroyed by an object yet unidentified and the scientists are still working on the physical evidence that they have. At the moment, all that's been said is that either an iceberg or a wayward shipping container are the most likely culprits. They're hoping to properly identify the object that caused the destruction after viewing the last debris fields. The Hobart Antarctic Division and the university's Engineering and Forensics Departments have requested a statement be issued advising that ships should not enter below the 40th parallel until the cause of the loss of these three vessels has been finally determined.'

Timothy looked at Gary and Miles. 'When both of you have fleshed this out and tidied it up, we might show Caroline, Janice and Sanjay the debris and review the statement with Peter. I suggest Peter get a copy of it beforehand. Miles, you walk him through it, please.'

Miles acknowledged the request with a nod.

The statement was completed before 8.00 pm, at about the time that dinner was being served on the vessel. Timothy suggested that Peter get his copy before dinner. In the meantime, Captain Delaney had manoeuvred the vessel to within a kilometre of the *Ocean Mist*'s debris field. He arranged for marker beacons to be dropped and set an automatic slow course to keep the vessel stable during the night. They would be in position to commence recovery of the debris at dawn. It had been a long day for the captain and crew. The captain was looking forward to dinner with his guests and to see the report of the day's findings.

At the dinner table, Captain Delaney was seated with Timothy to his right, and Dr Perry to his left. Timothy was seated next to Caroline, who was beside Miles. Miles had Janice Yew on his left, then Gary and Sanjay Singh. The captain was masterful in keeping the conversation light throughout dinner, and it was not until after dessert that he raised the matter of the shattered remains below deck. 'Well. Timothy, I believe after today's work we have a preliminary report to issue.'

'That's correct, Captain. If you like, I'm happy to give a summary here, and then I'd like to invite you all below deck to inspect the reconstruction of the vessels – or rather what's left of them.'

Captain Delaney looked around the table. 'Sounds like a good plan to me – how do the rest of you feel?'

There was a unanimous nodding of heads around the table. Timothy delivered the technical report of the destruction of the three vessels. As Timothy summed up, Janice looked quite annoyed.

'Timothy, why weren't we invited to the investigation? Otherwise, I don't understand why we are here.'

'Janice, you're here as a representative of the *Shanghai Sunrise* team. The review was conducted by the technical experts. You were invited on this expedition to provide support in relationship to any questions pertaining to the *Shanghai Sunrise* vessel. Also, it allows you to transmit findings to your team rather than reading about it in the press. Last but not least, we will have an opportunity to pay our last respects at the calculated impact points of each vessel.'

Janice stood up and looked up and down the table. She had never liked the way Timothy took over when he entered a room. He and Penelope were always the centre of attention at all the race functions. It didn't end there either. The media always favoured the *Ocean Odyssey* team; they were always front-page news at every port of call. She hated the fact that she couldn't break their charisma and she craved that attention. She'd had enough of Timothy!

'Caroline, Sanjay, are you comfortable with this outrageous behaviour? Timothy thinks he is dictating why we are here and what we are doing.'

Caroline cleared her throat. 'From the race organisers' perspective, this is Timothy's private charter. He has graciously invited you and Sanjay to assist in relation to your vessels. The current situation allows our teams and colleagues to be advised prior to information being published in the media. I'm grateful for the generosity that Timothy has shown to the other teams and the organisers at a time when he is dealing with a very large personal loss. I believe you owe him an apology. I'm certain that I'm saying that with the full support of the race committee.'

Janice glared at Sanjay. 'What's your opinion?'

Sanjay gritted his teeth; he had never been a fan of Janice. She was too hard, too outspoken and always gunning for a fight. The team members were always very cautious around her because of her short temper and track record of winning, no matter the cost. Today he was going to have to take sides. There appeared to be no downside in siding against Janice as there was no race to win; there was no business deals to be done – it appeared to be just Janice being Janice.

'The *Ocean Mist* team appreciates Timothy's offer in having us here; Timothy is in charge. We accept his explanation of our purpose. We support Caroline's request for your apology to Timothy.'

Janice was seething. First Caroline, now Sanjay. Didn't they care? Why weren't they fighting to take a greater part in the outcome of the expedition? If they didn't stand up now, the expedition would belong to Timothy; and in the eyes of the world, what would the rest of them have done? A great big nothing!

They would be present at a commemoration at sea – big deal. No headlines or publicity, no gain at all. It wasn't her purpose – she had to add value for Lee Chang and force more involvement in the analysis.

How could she retrieve the situation? A dummy spit? An apology? It could give Timothy time to trip up and would give her a chance to stay close and maybe see the mistake. It appeared to be the best option. Humble pie: the nastiest dessert she had ever come across. This would be like two fingers down the throat.

'I'm so, so sorry Timothy,' Janice said. She got out of her seat and headed towards Timothy's chair, arms outstretched. Timothy stood graciously and accepted a hug and a kiss. 'I'm so sorry that I have been so insensitive ... I'm sure it is just the frustration and horror of it all and being cooped up. Not contributing is very, very frustrating for a person like me, who sees being out there and getting things done, solving problems, as a measure of success.' She turned towards Timothy with her finest expression of remorse and even managed a small tear.

Timothy noticed the tear. *That's a bit heavy*, he thought, *even for Janice. She never struck me as somebody who would bother to care about somebody's feelings – let alone mine.* 'Thank you for the apology Janice,' Timothy said aloud. 'It's graciously accepted.'

Janice gave Timothy one more hug and then headed back to her seat.

Timothy looked around the table. 'If we're all done here, I suggest you go back to your rooms, rug up, and we'll all meet on the C deck in fifteen minutes for the wreckage inspection.'

Shortly after they were all assembled on the C deck, Timothy motioned them towards the scaffold that held the remains of the

Ocean Odyssey. 'I suggest you all go up on the deck one or two at a time and observe the destruction for yourselves.'

On the deck, they were confronted by holes where the rails and fittings had been torn out of the deck. The deck was split in two across the line of the mainmast. The life raft was still intact, strapped to the deck. As they wandered under the deck in an area that would have been the cabin, they could see the same type of destruction there. There were no EPIRBs and other safety equipment to be seen.

One by one, they all went up the ladder, wandered around the deck and came back down in silence. They milled around in what would have been the cabin space, taken aback by the frayed edges of the deck and the destruction around them. As the last of them had completed inspecting the deck, and what was left of the cabin, Timothy addressed them.

'As you can see, this deck structure was torn from the keel and flipped over the stern. We believe the keel and the rest of the cabin sank to the bottom of the ocean. Are there any questions on the *Ocean Odyssey*?'

Caroline peered from behind Sanjay. 'Timothy, I'm not up to speed on all the safety equipment that the boats were carrying but shouldn't the EPIRBs have all started transmitting when they hit the water?'

'Not these ones. It's quite common for solo sailors to have their boats take on significant amounts of water. Having automatically triggered EPIRBs creates a lot of false calls under those circumstances. As a result, the race committee saw no problem in having these EPIRBs manually triggered. All of the sailors agreed this was the best course of action. It is highly unlikely that this kind of event was even considered by the race committee or the sailors.'

Caroline moved closer to Timothy. 'Do you think I should

put it to the race committee to reconsider that decision, keeping in mind the inconvenience and high cost of false alarms and weighing it up against this tragedy?'

Timothy turned to look at the remains of the *Ocean Odyssey*. *This is good distracting stuff,* he thought to himself. *Could not have scripted it better myself. Gets away from the detail and grief, keeps looking towards tomorrow.*

Then he noted Janice's impatient fidgeting. *Now she is a worry,* he thought. *I wonder what her game is.*

'Caroline,' he said, 'I think that's a very good point that the race committee will need to take under consideration. They will need to weigh up, after careful risk analysis, whether automatic EPIRBs would have made a difference in this case – and then they will need to assess other scenarios before making a decision. But it's certainly a consideration I would strongly support.'

With the pause in the conversation, Janice just couldn't resist; the old journalist in her came forward again. 'Timothy, is there an explanation for this straight line that runs almost to the back of the boat and into this huge chunk hanging off the back?'

'It's actually very simple. Imagine sails in full flight, pushing the vessel forward – in effect, trying to lift the deck off the vessel. If something slices through just below the deck, the sails are effectively going to help tear that deck away from the bow towards the back of the boat. You get to a point where the deck is just ripped off and flipped over. And that's exactly what appears to have happened here. Are there any more questions on that, Janice?'

'No thank you, Timothy,' replied Janice. 'I think that is perfectly clear.'

'In that case, let's move on.' Timothy led the group to the reconstruction of the *Shanghai Sunrise*. 'Again, one person on deck at a time please.'

CHAPTER 26

The team broke up – one onto the deck and the other under the scaffold to survey what would have been the cabin of the *Shanghai Sunrise*. There was not much difference between the cabin of the *Shanghai Sunrise* and the *Ocean Odyssey*. There was just not much there. On deck, it would have been a treacherous affair as they would have been required to walk on a surface that appeared to be made up of random jagged tiles that once were the deck of the *Shanghai Sunrise*. The crew had erected a metal walkway suspended above the deck to allow safe access. The vessel had been torn to pieces.

After the inspection the team congregated around Timothy. He anticipated that Janice would come to the fore again, posing the first and most difficult questions. Timothy was starting to detect that she had journalistic training. He did not recall ever having seen her résumé or her name on any journalistic articles. And yet she sensed a story and she had started digging. Timothy didn't like it at all; he really needed to know more about her.

Janice had been over the vessel from stem to stern, twice, but she couldn't comprehend how anything – whether it was an iceberg or a shipping container – could cause such different devastation on such very similar vessels, unless Timothy was hiding something from everybody. She knew that Timothy was very, very bright. He must have sensed something about her – the probing, the enquiring, the relentless pursuit. He must have suspected she had been a journalist by now. This was not good. How could she be less obvious? There was only one way, she concluded – to get one of the others to pose the difficult questions. But she found difficulties answering her own question. How could she do that when Sanjay was against her, and there was no way Caroline would front for her? It was so difficult – there was no way other than doing it herself.

'Timothy, the destruction of the *Shanghai Sunrise* is so

dramatically different from the *Ocean Odyssey* – how can you explain that? The *Shanghai Sunrise* has been torn apart, chopped into pieces. It looks like the difference between slicing the top off an egg and throwing an egg against a brick wall. You're telling us that the difference between the cause being an iceberg and a shipping container is that different. With me, you have a major credibility problem Timothy. Was it an iceberg or was it a shipping container? Or was it something else?'

Timothy reeled from the impact. This, to him, was a very good investigative journalist in full flight. Why didn't he see it coming? Why did Gary and Miles fail to notice or check her background? Or was it too much to ask? They were primed on sailing and organisational skills but this was way beyond that. There was going to be some extensive risk mitigation going on well into the night. Who was Janice? Who had she been? Where did she learn her skills?

He remained poised and calm. 'Fantastic observation, Janice. If you need a job as an investigative journalist, let's sit down and have a drink tonight; I think we have a job for you. A clear point we are making, in going back to the public, is that this is a preliminary report. The University of Hobart Forensics and Engineering Departments made a preliminary assessment based on photographs only. The final assessment will be made after they investigate the physical remains. Yes, there are questions to be answered. We only have the debris of two vessels to date and I'm sure the third vessel will present additional questions to those that we have here now.' Timothy stepped closer to Janice and spoke quietly. 'You're very good Janice; let's have that drink tonight.'

Janice was tense – the element of surprise was gone. Apart from getting Lee his information, she had been hoping to get a scoop out to the media. She had no choice on that one now; capitulating and joining Timothy's team appeared to be the only winning exit. But what was in it for her? As a team member, it was salary only. She wanted more than that – but she didn't have much time to think. All she could do was stall, accept the drink, tell him nothing, say she needed to sleep on it and think about it for the rest of the evening. She paused for what seemed like a long time.

'Sounds great, Timothy. Let's do that.'

Timothy looked back at the assembled group. 'That's it then, if there are no more questions. I suggest we head back to the bar and have a nightcap.'

Timothy then ushered the assembled group back to the lift and into the bar. He pulled Gary aside and instructed him to urgently collect intelligence on Janice. He then approached Janice at the bar and waved to the barman.

'A drink for the lady and I'll have a Scotch straight up please.' He flashed a winning smile. 'Now, Janice, tell me all about yourself!'

Janice stiffened. 'What can I say? I'm not sure what you're looking for.'

Timothy observed the tension in Janice's body; her pupils narrowed to pinpoints. She flexed her hands and then focused on his face.

'Well, it's simple. Down below decks, you were acting like a highly paid first-class journalist, and a damned good one at that! I'm curious about where your training has come from.'

Janice felt totally exposed now. She realised she had taken on a self-made media billionaire and she was being read like a book. This was not the way she liked to feel. It felt worse than a police interrogation and she knew that the outcome could be devastating. Her value to Lee's company could be dramatically depreciated if she didn't get the interview right. She struggled with her options. The only obvious answer was to delay the questions as long as possible to give herself time to work out the best way ahead.

After a long pause, Janice couldn't look Timothy in the eyes. 'I'd like to discuss that tomorrow – it's been a long day. What we saw below decks is very distressing. I need to get the images of that together in my head before I make any comments on what you're asking.'

Janice regretted making the comment before she had finished. She had just told Timothy that she was analysing angles before going forward. It was the last thing she intended to do. She had betrayed herself, and her body language was screaming the wrong messages to Timothy.

In the background Gary had been running his research on Janice. It was not good. She had been trained in counter-espionage with the CIA, she was an accredited journalist and had worked for the *New York Times* and several other major newspapers. She was a force to be reckoned with in global journalism. Gary transmitted this to Timothy on his mobile phone.

Timothy casually checked his phone, and sent an acknowledgement to Gary. He now needed to seriously evaluate the situation. Janice was a major threat to the expedition going forward. She had the journalistic skill and contacts to unravel their restriction of information to the public and that could unravel the world first scoop that they thought they were sitting on. How could he prevent Janice from destroying the biggest media event in the world since the Murdoch phone hacking scandal? It would be difficult but there had to be a solution. They had too much to lose.

'Yes, it has been a big day,' he said. 'I should have been a little bit more thoughtful. Would you like to have lunch tomorrow?'

Janice stiffened up again. *What game was Timothy playing now?* 'That sounds marvellous – let's do that,' she said, forcing a smile.

CHAPTER 27

Timothy didn't head straight back into his room after finishing his drink with Janice. He made a detour after she was out of sight and headed for his office, where Gary was waiting.

'Well, wonders never cease!' said Gary. 'Janice is a lot more than she makes out to be. I'm still trying to get a line on it but it looks as though she might also be an active member of the CIA.'

'That's all we need, a CIA agent and a top journalist. I don't think it could get any worse than that! But it does beg the question, what is a CIA agent doing on Lee Chang's team? Lee's into real estate – why would the CIA want anything to do with him? So what else can you tell me?'

'Janice appears to have strong ties with MI6. She's been photographed socially with a few of their top players. She's been seen in the company of at least two possible MI6 operatives, and one other CIA agent. In digging through the files from China, Janice is seen in the company of Lee and several very senior Chinese politicians. Very busy girl, our Janice.'

Timothy phoned for Miles and brought Miles up to speed when he arrived on Gary's investigation on Janice. 'With what we are playing with here, I think we need to do a serious risk assessment and come up with a strategy going forward. It's now 11.30 pm – I suggest we all get a good night's sleep and meet down here tomorrow morning to work on this problem.'

Gary and Miles nodded their agreement. They locked down the office, turned on the video surveillance and headed to their respective rooms.

Timothy was woken by banging on his door at 2.00 am. He opened the door to find Captain Delaney with one of his sailors, who was armed with a handgun.

'Sorry to trouble you. The alarm went off in the offices; we're just on our way back from checking them.'

'Did an intruder get in?' replied Timothy, fighting back a yawn.

'It was a very sophisticated attempt. The alarm only went off when our energy-use sensor detected that somebody had turned on a computer. Not only was this person able to get past all our alarms but they also got past our surveillance cameras. You're probably going to ask why we didn't catch them. Well, that's because of this ...'

The captain held out his hand, and on it was a small object, about the size of a small coin.

'We suspect it's some sort of motion detector alarm. My colleague here tripped it as he came out of the bridge. This little nasty was attached to the skirting just outside the bridge. If this is what we think it is, the intruder would have had at least a minute's warning to get out of the offices.'

Timothy's mind was in a scramble. This was a pretty aggressive act. He had better get Gary and Miles to check that nothing had been stolen. This was someone with sophisticated equipment and experience; who on board could assist them in securing their offices against this type of intrusion?

'Captain,' said Timothy, 'can you post a guard on the offices for the rest of the night? First thing in the morning, we need to do a bug sweep of some kind. Do you have any of that sort of gear on board?'

'No, unfortunately we're not that sophisticated but I'm sure the boys on the bridge can come up with something to do the job from what we have on board, by morning.'

'Thanks Captain. It would pay to keep an eye on the guard for his own safety. Good night, gentlemen.'

Timothy closed the door and slid back into bed. He had a fitful night's sleep, waking often, tormented by the break-in. What in the hell was going on? He jotted down a few notes, including one to follow up on how Janice came on board – was there any security check? There was a lot to learn from this incident and a lot of questions to be answered.

He was woken by his alarm at 6.30 am; he showered and met Miles and Gary for breakfast. Both of them were shocked about the break-in and even more shocked about the sophistication of the intruder. A few minutes later Captain Delaney joined them.

'Gary, Miles, I'm sure that Timothy's brought you up to speed on last night's break-in. The good news is that overnight our technical staff has been able to devise a bug detector. They're pretty certain that we now have the ability to detect any bugs that may be in your offices.'

'How long to do a complete sweep of the offices?'

'They started twenty minutes ago. I would expect them to take two to three hours to complete the job.'

'So if we go to our offices at 10 pm, then we should be okay?'

'Let's aim for that. I'll let the boys know. Now I won't keep you from your breakfast any longer.'

The captain departed and Timothy turned to Gary and Miles. 'That's a bit of good news. In the meantime, I'd say nothing is secure. I'll make sure they sweep our cabins after they finish the offices. I wouldn't be surprised if they were bugged as well. One thing I just remembered ... I'm having lunch with Janice. I don't think I should cancel that – any thoughts guys?'

Miles looked a little startled. 'Did you ask or did she?'

Timothy smiled at the question. 'She wasn't forthcoming when I bailed her up over drinks about her rather obvious journalistic training. So I invited her to lunch, to get on with the conversation. How much do I disclose about the break-in?'

Miles pounced on the question. 'She is a trained operative but it wouldn't hurt to try to rattle her. Make sure you're watching her eyes when you tell her. If she continues to look straight ahead, she's either brilliant or she doesn't know. She might just let her guard slip again.'

'Lunch it is then,' said Timothy. 'And just to be paranoid ... Gary, can you check under the table to see if there are any bugs?'

Gary disappeared under the table and came out about half a minute later. 'Nothing under there but we may want to only have discussions like this in secure rooms in future.'

Timothy and Miles nodded in agreement. The next few hours passed slowly and finally, the captain came down and joined them at the table with one of his officers.

'Well, gentlemen, you now have a bug-free set of offices to go back to. We found three bugs in each room. Not a happy finding but it does show that somebody has been pretty meticulous about ensuring that they get first-hand knowledge of everything going on in there.'

'Thanks Captain; is it okay to go back to our offices now?'

'Yes, we're all done down there.'

Timothy, Gary and Miles then headed back to the offices.

CHAPTER 28

The offices now had a permanent guard at the entry to the corridor. Additional security had been added to the air vents, limiting entry to the guarded corridor only. When Gary and Miles met with Timothy again in his office, there were no pleasantries.

'Miles, Gary, the situation has changed dramatically from last night. Our risk assessment needs to look at our security here, as well as trying to establish a reason for our offices being broken into and bugged. So let's lay out what we are looking at. Firstly we have Janice's association with the CIA, MI6 and the Chinese. Secondly, her background in journalism. And thirdly, the break-in. Miles, have you established a hypothetical?'

'I certainly have,' replied Miles. 'For reasons yet unknown, Janice could be working with all three agencies. She was on the spot and able to become part of our team heading into the Southern Ocean. Janice could also be a free agent. Remember her attack on Timothy about how everything was being conducted? She was aggressive about being left out. She wants part of the media action and with her training, she has both the resources and the ability to get all the information she needs.'

Timothy nodded and then continued. 'Another less probable scenario is that it's not Janice at all. That would leave Dr Perry, Dr Mellows or Sanjay Singh, and the entire crew, as possible suspects. We'll need to keep our minds open until we get some definite proof. We do need to remember the political, media and scientific harassment that we had prior to leaving on this expedition. It was intense but we do have extensive records of all the people involved. Let's get all that up on the board and see if we can make some sense of it.'

Gary had a bemused look on his face. 'Leaving anybody out, boss?'

Timothy stopped, looked a little mystified. 'Have I?'

'Is Caroline a suspect?'

Timothy quickly felt awkward. 'Now that's a very good observation. She would have to be on the suspect list ... a slip on my part.'

Gary's smile gave away his thoughts.

For the next hour and a half the three poured over the electronic whiteboard and computers, trying to piece together all the connections. It was not proving to be easy. The significant common denominator was that the politicians were predominantly involved in finance or economics, associated with climate change like carbon credits or carbon taxes. The scientists, on the other hand, were from a very wide cross-section – climate change sceptics, CO_2 experts, ozone hole experts, government-funded bodies like the CSIRO of Australia, and others. There was also a significant group of economists.

They then tried to cross-reference in the varying theories, supporting and repudiating global warming that they had previously researched. Gradually a series of theories started coming together. They added another layer to the complex web – who were the beneficiaries and who were the losers of carbon politics?

The winners: Government treasuries, lobbyists, economists and scientific bodies supporting popular theories, research institutions, manufacturers of renewable energy devices and their installation and maintenance. The prize? Trillions of dollars globally, the resurgence of employment – a powerful tool to turn around the global economic crisis if controlled well.

The losers: The alternative lobby, economists, scientific bodies, opposition political parties, and the whole non-renewable energy industry – including coal, oil and gas. This involved powerful politicians, lobbyists, scientists, economists and businesses, with trillions of dollars at stake.

The analysis now came back to Janice. Was she working alone to get a media scoop, or as a free agent to sell her information to the highest bidder? Or was she an operative working for one or more governments?

Miles turned to Gary and Timothy. 'I think we need to do a lot more research to find connections between Janice and any of these major stakeholders. For the time being, we need to treat Janice as a major risk and carefully monitor her until we find the connection. I'm going to suggest that we ask the captain to monitor all her phone calls. He may or may not agree to that – I'll leave that to one of you.'

Timothy nodded his agreement. 'It's just gone midday; I had better meet Janice for lunch. I'll leave you both to it and I'll see you between two and three. I expect soon after that, they will have completed the salvage of the *Ocean Mist*. We may be able to get an update on that as well.'

Timothy headed towards the dining room to meet Janice. When he arrived he found her already seated. Timothy joined her by the window. 'Did you get a good night's sleep, Janice?'

'It was a bit fitful, actually,' she replied. 'As I said last night, there was a lot to take in, with the report and physically touching the remains of the boats. And how did you sleep?'

'I slept very well, thanks. Would you like a drink?'

'A glass of red would be nice, thank you.'

Timothy went to the bar and ordered a red wine for Janice and a Scotch for himself. As he got back to the table, a waiter joined them and took their lunch order. Timothy watched Janice closely; she appeared to be calm and poised. However, she was fingering the stem of her glass, possibly a slight nervousness. This appeared to be a good time to mention the break-in.

'One rather curious thing did happen last night, actually.'

Timothy noticed that Janice's facial expression had hardened. Her fingers had stopped moving on the glass stem. She had moved her focus away from him, as if not wanting to hear what he was going to say next.

'Our offices were broken into in the middle of the night. Apparently it was an extremely professional break in.'

Janice looked extremely uncomfortable now and she sat back in her chair, avoiding Timothy's gaze. 'That's terrible. Was anything taken?' she said without looking at Timothy's face.

'Apparently not. A lot of trouble to go to and not take anything. It raised the suspicion of the captain, who was rather thorough. He was able to find and remove three bugs in each of the offices.'

Janice had gone distinctly pale and she appeared to shudder. She looked at Timothy, slightly bewildered. 'You'll have to excuse me, Timothy. I'm suddenly feeling very seasick.'

With that Janice got to her feet with Timothy at her elbow to steady her. Her head was in a spin.

'It's okay, I can get to my room alone. Thank you.'

Timothy stepped back as Janice walked out of the room and down the corridor. She was feeling numb – this couldn't be possible. How could these amateurs have unravelled her work? She disabled the cameras and the alarm system. She was alerted by her motion sensor that someone was coming. Could that be it? Was there a tertiary alarm that she wasn't aware of? The

CHAPTER 28

truth, she felt, was she had let her guard down. This was not good. She didn't have a plan B and she needed time to think. The seasickness ploy at least gave her time to come up with another plan. She reached her room and went inside, threw her bag into a chair and went straight to the fridge.

'Damn this!' she said aloud. 'No food in the fridge and one stuffed alibi if I order a sandwich from the kitchen.'

She slammed the fridge door, walked across the room and settled into a sofa. Firstly, she would check any additional security arrangements and find out if there was a tertiary alarm; secondly, she would check the air vents to see if she could get into the room. Last but not least, she would try to get onto Timothy's team. The latter probably seamed the least likely, after her performance to date. She settled back for a long afternoon fleshing out the strategies.

Timothy, in the meantime, had headed back to the offices after apologising for Janice's departure and finishing his lunch. He explained Janice's behaviour to Miles and Gary. They were totally stunned by her reaction. How could they have caught out a talented operative? The big question remaining was how dangerous she was now. Timothy looked at their work from earlier in the day and commented.

'Miles, Gary, I'm not getting a good feeling about this. The stakes are too high. All this commercial stuff is worth trillions of dollars! If Janice is working for somebody, then it could be anyone from hundreds of significant companies that stand to make millions out of the alternatives. Or even worse, we could be up against a country like China, where most of those alternatives would probably be manufactured. The question now is, do we shut her down, or do we leave her free to wander?'

Gary seemed a little flustered. 'What do you mean by ... shut her down, Timothy? Is that a "shoot and throw over the side" shutdown? Or something else?'

Timothy gave little laugh. 'How I would love to, Gary ... if only life could be that simple. I mean restricted to quarters or locked up. I'm not sure how we would make either of those work but I'm sure we can work something out. Either one would mean having the captain involved and on side. So I think it's time to get the captain involved.'

Timothy headed up to the bridge and approached Captain Delaney. 'How is the salvage going today?'

'The *Ocean Mist* is spread over a much larger area. We would like it finished today, but it'll probably be lunchtime tomorrow before we have all the pieces on board and assembled. I'm surprised to see you up on the bridge. Is there anything I can help you with?'

'There is, actually,' said Timothy. 'Can I speak to you in private, please?'

'How about my office?'

'Has it been swept for bugs, Captain?'

'No, actually. Michael, can you do a bug sweep of my office please?'

Michael nodded to the captain and headed off to his office. In the meantime, the captain and Timothy surveyed the turbulent scene in front of them. Salvage was occurring in a 45 kilometre per hour westerly, with waves to 10 metres and long 100-metre swells. For any other vessel it would be impossible, but the wave-piercing hulls of the catamaran provided just enough stability for the salvage to occur. Michael returned thirty minutes later and placed three more bugs on the desk in front of them.

Captain Delaney looked at Michael and then looked around the bridge. 'I think you should sweep the bridge and comms, Michael.'

CHAPTER 28

Timothy and the captain were shocked when Michael found a bug under the desk they were standing at, two more on the bridge, and four in the radio room.

Captain Delaney looked sternly at Timothy. 'My office, now.'

They hurried over and the captain closed the door behind them.

'Timothy, what's going on? What do you need to talk to me about?'

Timothy debriefed the captain on his investigation of Janice and her recent odd behaviour – leading up to her 'seasickness' just as he was beginning to press her on the bugs. 'I suspect she might be desperate enough to play her hand tonight and attempt to break into our offices and replace the bugs. Also to possibly put at least one in the radio room. We're not certain of her motivation, but we have a lot of theories. So for now I'm requesting that you work with us to apprehend her and when she is under lock and key, we can try to work out what she is up to.'

'Well, that is one hell of a conspiracy theory. This is your charter and I must say that I am very disturbed by the number of bugs we have found. It's like they're growing out of the woodwork. I will work with my security people and lay the traps.'

'Thanks Captain, we should get on with it. It's getting late in the day.'

'Leave it to me.'

Timothy and the captain departed the office; the captain headed to the bridge to brief Michael and the security team. Timothy headed back to meet Gary and Miles in their offices. When he returned, he briefed Gary and Miles about the bugs found on the bridge and in the radio room and about the captain taking on the responsibility of providing security and apprehending Janice, or whoever was responsible for the security issues. He also advised them that the recovery of the *Ocean Mist* would not be completed until lunchtime the following day.

The three of them spent the rest of the afternoon analysing, re-analysing and verifying the intricate details of the links between all the apparent players in the global warming debate, the political manoeuvrings, and the massive economic factors driving the process. By late afternoon, they were getting a little jaded – to make light of the stress, they threw a few James Bond style scenarios into the mix. It would make interesting reading but a nightmare to live through.

'Okay, here's a *what-if* scenario,' Gary said. 'If we're about to embarrass climate change proponents at the highest possible levels, who is the biggest loser? How could they protect their investments? Projecting this scenario … say ten to fifteen million jobs … new production investments valued at two to three trillion and annual sales of ten to fifteen trillion plus.'

Timothy raised his eyebrows. 'What is that based on?'

Gary smiled, picked up a sheet of paper and continued. 'The investment in solar, wind, fuel cells, electric cars, trucks, scooters, trains and tidal power – first in research, then production dollars, followed by government infrastructure. Then there's the trade in carbon credits. The investments are massive. Some governments have most of their policies hinged on their approach to climate. Changing the baseline on what is happening in the environment will have a catastrophic impact on most of those staking on the current theory and solution.'

Gary looked at Timothy and Miles seriously and shook his head.

'If this is what it's all about, then this is our boat ride into oblivion. I mean, for God's sake, this has to be serious. Who plants twenty-two bugs, twenty-three including the motion sensor, for a news story? Somebody wants to know everything, absolutely everything that we're finding out here. They're leaving nothing to chance – they had our offices covered, the captain's office covered, the bridge covered, the radio room covered, and we're still looking.

'I'm getting very scared Timothy, I'm scared for my life. These sort of people don't stop at bugs! We're sitting ducks out here with no armaments, civilian radar only and no air coverage. There is nothing stopping a hostile party, especially a sovereign one, from using lethal force against us. A stealth submarine could send us to the bottom without a trace. A drone could launch missiles from just beyond our radar reach and we wouldn't even see it coming. That's before we start on the possibility of explosive device being brought on board in Fremantle. We hadn't considered the sort of risk back then – we had no real security checks.'

Timothy patted Gary on the shoulder. 'That's a pretty disturbing set of scenarios … I know how much you love your espionage thrillers.'

Gary managed a chuckle at that and took a deep breath. 'It's unlikely that the senior crew are involved. They would have had no need to bug the bridge or the radio room, so we can probably exclude the captain from a suspect list.'

'You're right,' Timothy continued. 'And if we leveraged those scenarios and project the bulk of all the new technology combating global warming through to where it is being manufactured, then we have the uncomfortable link between Janice and Chinese bureaucrats, and various heads of power and security agencies. It all helps support your hypothesis, as scary as it is.'

Miles was staring at his colleagues, looking distinctly uncomfortable. 'What would it take – one or two torpedoes to put us to the bottom? Kaboom! Lost without a trace, gone the way of the sailing boats. With all that stealth crap, we would never see it coming.'

Timothy felt it was now time to pull the process back into proper risk analysis. They had done the hypotheticals, they had considered all the vectors and the risk analysis now really came down to whether Janice was working alone or with someone else on the boat. 'Guys, they're scenarios. We're the media – now let's find the facts. Miles, I need you to go up to the bridge to analyse all the CCTV footage on the boat to see if Janice had been spending time with any particular passenger. While you're there, ask whether or not radio communications on and off the vessel were being monitored and recorded – and if they could be in the future if they're not. Gary, you and I will need to keep looking at this data, to see if we can find any obvious links that will help us understand more about what's going on.'

CHAPTER 29

By late evening, Captain Delaney and his security team had finished laying their traps. To be able to catch the intruder, they needed to be able to lure whoever it was into Timothy's office area. There were two possible doors that they could leave open. They needed to remove the new security grills from the air ducts and to alarm the security system's control panel. By the time dinner was finished, the security team had finished laying their trap.

Back in her room, Janice was still busy trying to work out how to gain access to Timothy's offices. She had a small batch of the latest high-tech bugs. These bugs were extremely expensive but she needed to use them as her last resort. First, she needed to gain access to the offices and hopefully the radio room. She only had four of the bugs, so they needed to be in the most effective places possible.

At 1.30 am Janice headed out into the corridor. She approached Timothy's offices from the corridor behind them, hoping to find air ducting leading to the offices. Janice proceeded slowly and carefully, checking around each bend of the corridor with a small endoscopic camera that allowed her to poke the camera around the corner, using the black skirting to camouflage the endoscope.

The corridor behind the offices did indeed contain a large air duct that would allow her to gain access to the offices through the roof space. Janice cautiously proceeded to the bridge, to see how many people were there. She was planning to go to the bridge after she had planted the office bugs under the guise of requiring more medication for seasickness. This would give her an opportunity to leave a bug in the radio room. She found that there were only two officers on the bridge that evening and nobody in the radio room. She would be able to find a way to give herself a few seconds in the radio room to plant a bug. Next, she needed to check on the level of security at Timothy's offices.

She cautiously proceeded and, using her camera, she was able to observe a solitary guard, sitting in a chair facing down the corridor towards her. The guard had no reading material or other distractions. He was facing away from the offices, which were constructed of solid partitioning without windows. This would enable her to enter the rooms unobserved from the air ducts. Janice made her way to the staircase leading down to the next level. This was the level that housed the electrical switch room for the security and other systems. The corridor was not being guarded; Janice cautiously checked as she went along to see if additional security had been added. It took twenty minutes to sweep the room. She had found no additional security and proceeded to the panel containing the alarm system controls.

Unbeknownst to Janice, the tubular frame of the door now contained a passive wireless alarm. A simple mercury tremble switch had issued a single pulse as Janice opened the door.

On the bridge, the duty officer picked up the phone. 'Security, this is the bridge. We think we have an intruder in the electrical switch room. The door trembler on the security panel has just been activated briefly.'

The security team had been on stand-by all night; they were

crowded around the duty officer waiting for their orders from the bridge. They finally came.

'Send four armed men to the switch room. Two other units of two men, fully armed, are to be stationed at either end of the corridor. The captain has authorised lethal force if required. Take care.'

The teams were assembled in a few seconds and filed out into the ship's corridors, on the alert for intruders.

Janice had waited a couple of minutes after disabling the alarm. Her sensors picked up no movement approaching in her direction. She had just completed bridging out the alarm system to Timothy's offices when the door burst open. Four heavily armed and uniformed security personnel filled the doorway.

'Freeze!' the lead shouted at Janice. 'Raise your hands slowly; lock your fingers behind your head!'

Janice complied. There was no point in trying to fight her way out of this – they had her outgunned and there was no feasible escape.

'Turn and face the panels! Press up against the panels!' shouted the lead.

Janice felt the cold steel of a barrel pressing into the base of her skull, the steel of a handcuff clicking into place on her right wrist.

The lead shouted again. 'Now, very slowly lower your hands and put them behind your back. Do not stop leaning against the panels!'

Janice felt the tension in the room and moved her arms very slowly down her sides and behind her back. A handcuff clicked in place on her left wrist and the gun barrel was moved from the base of her skull.

'Now stand up very slowly, step back, then lean forward and balance your forehead against the panel. You are going to be searched. Keep your weight on your forehead. Resist, and you will be shot.'

Janice was afraid. The warning, *resist and you will be shot*, had punctuated the serious position she was in. She sensed military efficiency and training all around her. It appeared as though the crew were not merchant seamen after all. That would mean she was not the only person with a mission other than recovering the debris of the three race boats.

The search was extremely invasive; only a strip search would have been more effective. The search revealed a small 38-calibre pistol, one double-edged fighting knife, one small notebook computer with multiple electronic leads and four very small bugs in a zip-lock bag. Condemning evidence.

The lead barked a command. 'Inform the bridge. We have the intruder. We're heading to the brig now.' He turned to Janice. 'Step up against the panel, turn around very slowly and take four steps forward.'

Janice complied with the command, very slowly and cautiously. She was now in the centre of the room. Two security men fell in behind her and the other two led her out of the electrical switch room. Janice rapidly surveyed the situation. She had two armed men in front and behind her, and another two at each end of the corridor. Even if she could take out the four men around her, the other four would certainly take her out. For the time being, all she could do is watch and wait. There would be nowhere to hide on this boat and the outside temperature was probably -25 degrees Celsius, so there was no point in escaping yet.

Janice's whole escapade had lasted less than forty minutes. She now found herself behind bars in the brig. The handcuffs were removed and the cell was locked. A guard was left sitting in a chair at a desk 4 metres from her cell. Janice surveyed the grim cell. It had a bunk, a table shelf, and an exposed toilet next to a hand basin and shower recess. The floor was finished in a grey rubberised material. The walls and ceiling were smooth and the front was metal bar panels. The right-hand panel automatically moved forward before moving to the left to allow entry and exit. The only visible controls for the door panel appeared to be a solid steel welded box lock. Again, escape from this room would be very difficult but not impossible. She decided to get some sleep. It had been three days since she had had a decent night's sleep.

The next morning, Timothy, Miles and Gary were just finishing breakfast when Captain Delaney joined them. He took a chair at their table.

'Around 1.45 am last night, we apprehended Janice in the electrical switch room. She had just finished bypassing the alarm system to your offices and was carrying a sophisticated small computer and attachments to give her access to the switch room via our electronic keypads. She was also carrying a 38-calibre pistol, a double-edged fighting knife and four state-of-the-art superbugs. Those little babies are worth more than fifty grand each at the moment.'

'A gun and knife? This appears to go way beyond a little eavesdropping.'

'That's right, and I think it's about time you and I had a long discussion about what's going on here. Would you mind coming to see me on the bridge sometime this morning please?'

Timothy was surprised – this was an interesting development. The captain had been quite obliging without question, up until now. 'Absolutely, Captain.'

With that, the captain left them to finish their breakfast. As soon as he was out of earshot, Timothy turned to Gary and Miles.

'New research task this morning. Gary. I seem to recall when we took on this charter that there was a reshuffle of the crew just before we left. We have the names of a few key players, but go through the databases and find out if any of them are Navy or intelligence-based. I would focus mainly on Australian, New Zealand or South African origin because of the accent.'

The morning disappeared rapidly, as they researched Captain Delaney and the crew. It was about 11.30 am when Gary called a meeting in Timothy's office.

'You're spot-on Timothy, everybody that we have names for comes up on the databases as being Australian Navy or ASIS.'

Timothy looked annoyed. Why hadn't he been advised that this had become a military operation? He was going to have to get the captain onside quickly to ensure that they not only had success in their objective of a world scoop, but also ensured the safety of himself and his team.

Timothy headed up to the bridge, meeting Captain Delaney there. 'Captain,' he said firmly, 'based on what you've told us about the bugs, it's probably best that we speak in my office. I believe it's the only secure place on the vessel at this time.'

The captain agreed and followed Timothy to his office. 'Take a seat please,' said Timothy when they arrived.

The captain rested back in his chair.

'Captain, we spent the morning doing extensive research on you and your crew, or at least those of them that we know the names of. We now know that it is highly probable that all of you are Navy, and/or ASIS operatives. All this efficiency in security and just getting it done has exposed you. What is the mission?'

The captain looked startled. 'Of course, I'm not going to confirm or deny any of that. But what's the point you are trying to make?'

'Basically, our research has shown us that Janice is firstly an operative, was once a highly proficient international journalist, and has had recent contacts with high-level officials in the UK, the US and China. We can only assume that her mission here is to gain information on the loss of these three vessels. It's conceivable that what we will find out here may cause significant turbulence in the world of global warming, politics, big business investment and overall credibility. As a result, I need your assurance that you can provide us with security and protection. At this point, Captain, my team is feeling highly vulnerable.'

Captain Delaney looked sternly at Timothy. 'Our mission is classified so I can't confirm or deny anything. But I can assure you that we will provide you with all the protection you need to complete this charter. To date, you and your team have been reasonably open with your evolving understanding of the situation. I believe we share a common objective and as long as we continue to discuss strategies, I can't see us having any issues. After the briefing on the *Ocean Mist*, we will start the interrogation of Janice. You're welcome to come along to see how the proceedings go.'

Timothy graciously accepted the offer. 'Just tell me where to be, Captain.'

'Meet me on the bridge after the briefing when you're ready, and we'll go down together.'

Timothy went back to Miles and Gary and filled them in on the agreement he had made with the captain. After lunch the team inspected the *Ocean Mist*'s debris. The inspection occurred in total silence. The debris was almost identical to the *Ocean Odyssey*'s, with one exception being that the deck had not been split in two. The teams dispersed and the captain motioned Timothy, Miles and Gary to join them in debriefing. The captain addressed the assembled group.

'Two hours ago, we set course to intersect the target location agreed upon by the Orion and the controllers on the Kerguelen Islands. They have identified several targets in the area of the original loss of contact with the three sailboats. Our sailing time to those locations puts us there just after dark. Due to the unknown dangers, we are planning to stand off the final location by two to three hours, and only proceed into the target zone one hour after dawn.'

Afterwards, Timothy waited on the bridge as requested, but the captain asked him to leave – promising the interrogation of Janice would happen and Timothy would not miss out.

The next morning Timothy was on deck at dawn.

'Good to see you bright and early, Timothy,' said the captain without looking at him. Captain Delaney looked out the windows and waved his hand. 'About 50 kilometres from us out there, we might find the objects that sank the sailboats. We're just about to launch a helicopter to go to intercept the target zone.'

The radio barked a message. 'Two minutes to helicopter launch.'

As the helicopter launched off the deck, Timothy and the captain waited for a report, which did not take long.

'Helicopter to base.'

'Base receiving.'

'Captain, we can report that we have intercepted objects in the ocean.'

Captain Delaney interrupted. 'Pilot, please make your report when you return to the vessel.'

'Captain, we're going to do three flyovers to get photographs, thermals and other data on the objects. Do you want us to transmit the data to the ship?'

CHAPTER 29

The captain was about to speak when Timothy took him by the arm.

'Captain, at the moment the only secure place on the boat we know of is my offices. I suggest all the reporting is done there.'

The captain agreed and instructed the pilot to make his detailed report on arrival back in the vessel. Fifteen minutes later the captain, Timothy and the flight crew met in Timothy's office.

The helicopter pilot presented his report. 'Captain, we can report that we have intercepted objects in the ocean with a length of 20 to 60 metres and width of 10 to 40 metres, with a mass of 40 to 150 tonnes. The objects are moving in waves of up to 15 metres with swells of up to 50 metres. These objects are pitching around like sailboards – at times a large one may stand 40 metres above the waves, providing an enormous radar contact. At other times, smaller ones provide no signal at all. A small vessel encountering these objects in the waves would be torn to pieces in seconds. God help them – they wouldn't have had a hope. Their radar wouldn't have seen these objects.'

Timothy, Gary and Miles were mesmerised by the photographs. The objects would have been absolutely destructive if one of the ketches had encountered them in the ocean. Survival would have almost been impossible. Timothy turned to Captain Delaney. 'Captain, I'd like myself and my cameraman to be on the next flyover of these objects.'

'No problem – the next flight leaves in five minutes.'

Timothy started barking commands like a military man. 'Miles, make sure my cameraman is ready to go in five minutes.'

Miles responded instantly, clicking his heals with a beaming smile and a mock salute. 'Yes Sir!'

Six minutes later the helicopter was airborne with Timothy and the cameraman on board. Several minutes after take-off, they were over the target zone. Beneath them, the ocean had changed character with huge ice sheets pitching and riding the swell like surfboards. The cameraman was hanging out the door, getting the photographs. This was sensational stuff, with 80 to 100 tonne sheets of ice riding the swells 2000 kilometres from nowhere.

When Timothy's expedition got back to the boat, the captain already had the next expedition planned. The next task was to retrieve samples of the ice sheets. To do this, the team would fire rocket-propelled grenades close to the edges of the ice sheets. Retrieval nets would be used to scoop the ice from the ocean. Fifty minutes later the helicopter was inbound with one and a half tonnes of sample ice.

Dr Perry and Dr Mellows were there to whisk the samples away to refrigeration. Their teams were ready to commence analysis and details of the samples would be available within the following hour. The helicopter team retrieved another 8 tonnes of samples over the next four hours. The samples were chosen randomly from various objects in the ocean, in an attempt to get a good sample distribution of the objects they were dealing with.

A briefing on the objects was called in Timothy's office at midday. Dr Mellows and Dr Perry were to conduct the briefing. Timothy, Miles and Gary found Timothy's office a little crowded when the doctors and the captain packed into the confined space. The captain was unapologetic for the crowding.

'Dr Mellow, Dr Perry, can you present your report please?'

Dr Perry eased her way to the front of the room, surveyed the faces and commenced with a slight smile. 'We must say, our analysis is breathtaking. Beyond a doubt, around 1500 kilometres from the Antarctic ice shelf, we are encountering sheet ice that, for all intents and purposes, is 100 per cent freshwater. This is just staggering. We are over 1500 kilometres from any source of fresh water, more than a thousand kilometres from any sea ice that we know of, and we just have no explanation for this.'

CHAPTER 29

The whole room sat in silence until Captain Delaney spoke. 'Dr Perry, what other analysis …' He paused. 'What can you do to give us some idea of what's going on here?'

'Captain, we need to try to come up with a theory as to how this could occur. We've already started on that process and we have part of a plausible answer. A lot more research needs be done before we can take this much further. We are, however, doing more detailed studies of the ice samples to see if we can determine where they came from. We should have some indication on that by the morning. Apart from that, there is nothing else we can report on at the moment other than getting back to our teams and continuing to work on the ice samples.'

The captain waved the doctors out of the room, sat and faced Timothy. 'That leaves us with a very hard call, Timothy. What are we going to report back to the world at large? We certainly don't want to get Dr Perry and co offside when we rely so much on their research. I suggest that after you write your stories, we meet with the doctors to get some agreement on the communiqué within the hour.'

'We'll get straight onto it Captain, thank you.'

Over the next hour, Miles, Gary and Timothy worked hard on the communiqué. It came down to a very chilling photograph of a huge ice sheet breaching off a fifteen metre swell. Just after they completed the statement, the captain, Dr Perry and Dr Mellows came back into Timothy's office.

Timothy addressed them. 'We've asked you back here to discuss a media release that we feel we need to make in relation to the discovery of these ice fields. Here is a copy of the statement that we intend to issue. We want to work through it with you, to ensure that we have agreement on the content.'

The statement read: *1500 km from anywhere, ice takes three lives and destroys three racing boats. These eighty tonne monsters* shattered the three sailing boats that they encountered in the Southern Ocean. Scientists are currently assessing samples, attempting to explain how they happen to be in the ocean and how they were formed.

'There will be photographs of this breaching monster to accompany the headlines and statements, Timothy continued. 'Please, spend a few minutes on the statements, then let's discuss how you feel about them.'

Dr Perry read the statement twice. It was something she would prefer to have published in a scientific journal, rather than in the public press. But these were the conditions she was working under. The statement left room for other scientific input, didn't give too much away on what was going on, and would perhaps make funding a lot easier for the additional research required. She basically couldn't be more pleased with the statement. She looked to Dr Mellows, who nodded his head in agreement.

'Timothy, you're funding this trip. We do, however, appreciate you not disclosing important scientific aspects of this finding. But please release enough information to get everybody interested. We're happy to sign off on a media release. Now we do need to return to the lab to continue our work.'

Timothy nodded, and the doctors headed back to the lab. 'Well, that was smooth,' he said after they had left the room. 'Let's get stuck into it and finish the scoop.'

Over the next three hours, they put together a full-page tabloid spread and multimedia extracts, beginning with pictures of the massive ice sheet, then the sailors preparing for the race and finally, photographs of the smashed vessels below deck. The headline read, 'Horrific death of three brave sailors in the Southern Ocean'. Timothy felt he would own the headlines for the next four weeks. He decided to keep the arrangement with Caroline private to protect confidentiality of the agreement. The loss of

Penelope was becoming confused by the buzz of the massive media win before him and the proximity of Caroline. He sensed his confused emotions and decided that he would have to keep an eye on that.

Miles transmitted the newsflash around the world and gave Caroline and Sanjay a copy each. He and Gary were very excited about the scoop. He could only see this story building. He was feeling secure now with the knowledge that the crew was Navy. At least that was better than being protected by merchant seamen after what they had experienced with Janice.

Later in the afternoon Captain Delaney came down to talk to Timothy about the delayed interrogation of Janice. The captain had received additional information and was about to interrogate her. Feedback from the CIA told them that she was now a rogue agent, working outside her brief. The CIA wanted to take custody of her as soon as they arrived back in Australia. The next two to three days would be the only chance that they would get to find out what Janice was doing on the boat. The captain invited Timothy to observe the interrogation.

They both proceeded down to the brig. Timothy was seated behind a one-way mirror in the observation room. The captain entered the room where Janice was sitting. She looked slightly dishevelled and had her hands handcuffed.

'Janice – if that is your name – we're going to establish over the next day or so what you've actually been doing on this vessel and who you report to. So let's start at the beginning. First of all, we know that you're a CIA operative. Secondly, the CIA has listed you as a rogue agent and wants to take custody of you as soon as we get back to Australia. The other option I have as captain of this vessel, is to offload you at the Kerguelen Islands. They would then ship you wherever, when the next supply vessel arrives in six months' time. You're looking down the barrel of at least half a year in unpleasant custody before you get back to civilisation.'

Janice was quietly listening to the captain. Six months on the Kerguelen Islands would be absolute hell; she was going to have to negotiate a better alternative than that.

The captain continued. 'The first thing we need to know is who you are working for.'

Janice looked the captain squarely in the eye. 'I'm the team manager of the *Shanghai Sunrise* team, for Lee Chang.'

'So are you telling us that Lee Chang has directed you to bug this vessel and collect intelligence information in relation to what sank these vessels?'

'That's not the question you asked me, Captain.'

'Then who are you doing the surveillance for? If not Lee Chang?'

'I'm not permitted to tell you that.'

'Is that not able to? Or not prepared to?'

Janice started working through the possible answers. She was not sure how far Captain Delaney would go. She was now more than certain that he was Navy which meant that this was a military operation, and she was in a very difficult situation. 'That's something I need to think my options through on, Captain. I'm not prepared to say anything now.'

Captain Delaney had anticipated this kind of stalling tactic. He stood up, collected his notes and moved to the door. 'You're not going to find my colleagues as pleasant as I was,' he said as he left the room.

He was replaced by a hard-faced sailor with no distinguishable rank insignia. The sailor recommenced interrogation from the top, using the same line that the captain had used. Janice sensed that this was going to be a very long interrogation, unless she did a deal.

The captain joined Timothy in the observation room. 'Timothy, this could run for a couple of days. I don't think you need to hang around for this. I'll bring you in if there are any breakthroughs.'

'Thanks Captain, I was just about to go to sleep.' Timothy laughed. 'Just call if you need me. Oh, there was one other thing I needed to clarify. How should we run the memorial?'

'Due to the serious nature of the ice sheets, we're planning to manoeuvre the vessel within 50 kilometres of our targets, then send out the helicopter with representatives on board. What are your thoughts on that?'

'I agree totally with that, Captain.'

'I'll announce the plan at dinner then.'

CHAPTER 30

Timothy entered the dining room just before Caroline. She grabbed him by the arm. 'Can I sit next to you?' she asked with a mischievous flutter of her eyelids.

Timothy was in an equally a good mood. 'Now let me see,' he said. 'Hmm, the most gorgeous woman on board wants to sit next to me. To say yes or to say no, that is such a hard question … the answer's yes, of course.'

'Thank you Timothy,' Caroline said with a little purr and nudged up closer to him. She liked the mood Timothy was in. Caroline had been cooped up in her cabin for over five days and she was bored out of her mind. Yet, she had written reports back to the race committee and extended the deal with Timothy. She had inspected all the wreckage, and the following day she would pay respects at sea for the committee. After that, there was nothing to do. With the possibility of another ten to fourteen days at sea, it was time to try to make things interesting.

'Would you like cocktails first?' inquired Caroline.

'I couldn't resist,' Timothy replied, enjoying the warmth of Caroline next to him. He sensed seductive danger but he threw caution to the wind; his life had been hell throughout this disaster. It was time to forget, and try to revive his life. Penelope had died tragically while defying him. That would have made a difficult relationship and he hadn't seen that in her before – a total disregard for him and the investment he had in her and the race.

At the bar, Timothy turned to Caroline. 'What will it be?'

Caroline looked deep into his eyes; she held his gaze while she replied. 'Gin and tonic, please.'

Timothy got the bartender's attention with a polite wave of his hand. 'One gin and tonic please, and a Black Russian, no ice. Thanks.'

Caroline and Timothy spent two hours at the cocktail bar, by which time they only had eyes for each other. Timothy had blotted out the pain, consequences and reality with five Black Russians, whereas Caroline has been a little more cautious, having two Champagne cocktails after her gin and tonic.

Caroline observed the room and nudged Timothy with a delightful laugh. 'Timothy, everybody's leaving, I think we're embarrassing them.'

Timothy gazed into her eyes; they were twinkly like diamonds. 'Sorry Caroline, but I think dinner is almost over. They're being polite.'

He guided her from the bar and they settled at a table not far from the windows. It was a howling blizzard outside, but inside it was a comfortable 23 degrees, and Caroline's eyes kept glowing. Caroline moved her chair around a little so that her shoulder touched Timothy's.

'Mmm, that's better,' she said.

'Delightful,' replied Timothy, gently slipping his arm around her waist.

Their dinner proceeded well into the night; the conversation was mischievous and taunting. Caroline was enchanted by Timothy, his wit, his humour and his attention. From time to time, he lightly brushed her hand or shoulder, or pressed against her thigh. She was becoming dizzy with his taunting approach. She wanted to scream at him, 'Take me!'

Timothy sensed that he had Caroline wound like a violin string. He watched the tone change in her eyes as a touch caused an explosion of excitement. Leaving her without a touch of flattery for five minutes caused an ignition in her eyes; the colour deepened and they looked as though they would consume him – demanding attention, demanding more contact.

Finally, approaching midnight, they left arm in arm. Outside the door Timothy turned to Caroline. 'My room … what do you think?'

Caroline wrapped herself into his body and gently nudged him against the wall. The heat of her body was intoxicating. 'I'm all yours,' she replied.

Two minutes later they were in Timothy's suite. Neither of them had time for pleasantries, intrigue or foreplay – they had just survived four hours of foreplay. Minutes after entering Timothy's suite they were locked, naked, under the blankets on Timothy's king-size bed.

Timothy's mind was blank, his pain numbed by alcohol but his body and soul recharged and activated by Caroline's hot passion and delicious body. Tonight was just about sex. Their bodies reacted to one another's, and there was a fever in the air. They lived off one another's passion until three o'clock in the morning and then fell asleep in each other's arms.

When Timothy woke, Caroline was sitting beside the bed wrapped in a fluffy white bathrobe. She was looking at him with gooey eyes. 'You're so wonderful,' she said.

She threw off the bathrobe, dived under the sheets and wrapped herself around Timothy. They did not emerge until ten o'clock in the morning.

CHAPTER 30

The first memorial flyover was due at 11.00 am. They had breakfast together and headed towards the helicopter deck. Caroline, Timothy, Miles, Gary and the camera crew boarded the helicopter. The flight time to the target site was fifteen minutes. Timothy, Miles, Gary and Caroline dropped wreaths into the ocean. The moment was solemn, grey and cold; the wind chill had the temperature of -60 degrees Celsius, and the waves were 10 to 15 metres. The water temperature was hovering near -2 degrees. The conditions were almost identical to when the *Ocean Odyssey* had disappeared at the site.

As they hovered over the area, an ice sheet rose vertically out of the ocean 40 metres in front of them. The pilot had to bank to avoid hitting the ice. Caroline screamed as everybody in the cabin scrambled to grab hold of anything to brace themselves as the helicopter banked.

The cameras were rolling and it was history in the making.

'Flight Lieutenant, get us back to the ship immediately,' demanded Timothy. 'Get Dr Mellows and Dr Perry on the next flight. We'll cancel the memorial. It's important we understand what's going on here. This appears to be a major part of the answer.'

Timothy had been caught up in the moment; it was unbelievable. As they commemorated a disaster, the cause of the disaster recreated itself in front of them, as if trying to snatch them from the air. He'd failed to notice the terror on the faces of Caroline, Miles, Gary and the crew. He had totally ignored Caroline's scream. As he saw their faces, his adrenaline rush began to subside. He found it necessary to breathe deeply and hold onto a seat to maintain his balance.

'Sorry team – I got lost in the excitement of the moment. Is everybody okay?'

Caroline shook her head. 'I think I've bruised my arm, not broken but it is a bit sore.'

Miles moved forward and took a look at Caroline's arm. 'That's a nasty bruise. Nothing broken, thank goodness.'

Timothy moved back and sat beside Caroline. He gently pressed against her side and whispered to her, 'Sorry about that. I got overexcited about my work.'

Caroline looked at his face. She hadn't seen him like that before; he was very animated, focused and couldn't wait to get the scientists back to analyse what was going on. She loved that intensity in him.

The lieutenant immediately came about and requested that Dr Mellows and Dr Perry were available for departure on their return; ETA twelve minutes. As soon as the helicopter touched down, Dr Mellows and Dr Perry scrambled aboard; Gary and Miles were left standing on the deck.

Timothy briefed Dr Perry and Dr Mellows on what they had just seen and showed them the video footage on the way to the target site. The doctors were startled by the videos. The images were of an ice sheet emerging vertically from the ocean, so it was highly improbable that the ice formed on the ocean surface. Nature was answering her own questions. How could sheet ice form beneath the ocean surface and rise vertically? They spent thirty minutes over the site to see one more ice sheet rise to the surface. It breached to a height of 35 metres then eased back into the waves, almost invisible to the naked eye. The doctors were in a dither. Here was the proof that they had found something absolutely amazing, and it appeared to defy science itself.

Dr Perry was so entranced by the ice sheet that she almost stepped out of the helicopter; one of the crew grabbed her just in time. 'Hang on Doctor, you can't step out here.'

Dr Perry gasped as she was manhandled back into the helicopter. 'My goodness, that was silly of me …' She exclaimed as she retook her seat, her complexion pale as she realised how close she came to falling into the ocean.

CHAPTER 30

Timothy looked around the cabin; there was a restraining barrier on the wall. 'Let's have that barrier up please, I don't want to lose any more of the team to the Southern Ocean.'

When they arrived back on the vessel, Timothy requested that the dedications be completed that afternoon. Timothy, Garry, Miles and the captain went into lockdown. A news release was put together and signed off by Drs Perry and Mellows and the captain. The news release headline read: 'Science, please explain: disaster source identified.'

After agreement on board, the news release with footage was released to the world at large.

Timothy was expecting mayhem, and he didn't have long to wait. The previous day's news release had left everybody with the impression that small icebergs had caused the incident. Today's news release left no doubt that this was something totally new.

By 2 pm, high level complaints were pouring in. They included the governments of the United Kingdom, Germany, France, the Netherlands, Spain, Portugal, Denmark, Sweden, Iceland, China, Russia and India. All these governments were demanding that the Australian government intervene and advise when information was going to be released to the public about such sensitive matters.

Unbeknown to Timothy or anybody else on board, the captain had advised the Australian Prime Minister of the latest communiqué before it had been released. Since coming to power in 2013, the Prime Minister had been looking for solid scientific evidence to challenge the carbon tax and climate change approach of his predecessors. He could use this data to confound and silence his opposition critics on the important issues surrounding climate, coal and coal seam gas. This media release was his white knight. He wanted alternative strategies, without denying that carbon emissions were contributing to climate change. Until science explained what was going on, he had as much breathing space as he needed, and he was not going to stop this communiqué going to the public.

His actions were justified to the British government as 'keeping the public informed without divulging the scientific cause'.

Sanjay Singh took the last memorial flight out over the Southern Ocean that afternoon. Doctors Mellows and Perry accompanied him out of compassion and scientific curiosity. Timothy's photographer joined them to cover any new photographic possibilities that could arise on the trip.

The photographer was not to be disappointed. Halfway back from the memorial, the radar operator advised them of more contacts in the ocean. The crew manoeuvred the helicopter over the new sheets, hovering 50 metres in the air. The passengers were all horrified to see a large sheet of ice breaching and coming within 10 metres of the helicopter. The pilot immediately took the helicopter higher and reported the incident back to Captain Delaney. This second near miss graphically demonstrated the extreme danger of these objects rising in the ocean.

The last sheet to rise was in the order of 80 to 120 tonnes and almost transparent in the ocean. The helicopter hovered for another five minutes as the photographer took shots of the ice sheets. Dr Mellows and Dr Perry took as many physical readings as they could.

On arrival back at the ship, Dr Mellows, Dr Perry, the pilot and the photographer had a debriefing with the captain, Miles, Gary and Timothy.

'Timothy,' said Dr Perry, 'from what we observed, the ice sheets were rising almost vertically from the ocean. The velocity with which they exited the water tended to indicate that they were rising from a considerable depth. To breach a 110 tonne object 40 metres into the air requires a massive amount of momentum. The buoyancy of freshwater ice in saltwater is relatively high but the breach height indicates that the ice came from a considerable depth.

'We estimate that approximately five to ten sheets are appearing in each of the impact zones on a daily basis. This means that depending on prevailing winds and ambient temperatures, up to thirty sheets could have been in the target zones at any point in time. Sailing in this part of the ocean was like sailing into a minefield.'

After the debriefing, Timothy joined Gary and Miles back in their offices.

'Right gentlemen, let's go for another scoop. The headline will be, "Breaching ice sheet near collision with helicopter in the Southern Ocean". We have heaps of graphic footage, zoom right in and make 10 metres look like 10 millimetres. Let's build the story. We'll use some of the words from our previous articles to pad this out and give it life. What do you think, Miles?'

'Timothy, I think it's amazing. It doesn't get any bigger than this. I've started writing an article about you and how you came out here to find out what happened to your boat and Penelope. The collision of global warming, politics, and the world economy may mean that that article has to become a novel, hopefully a bestseller. This whole story has a life of its own. Timothy, I hope you have the energy and the money to keep going.'

'That's a big ask, Miles. Where to next? This now appears to involve the UN, the IMF and I would say the ratings agencies as well. The latter, I would say, is the most important. So much of the economy of many of the major countries in the world is underwritten by the carbon reduction economy. If we add the value of solar, wind, tidal, electrical transport of all types, fuel cells ... that's R&D at all levels, production plants, suppliers, sellers, installers and maintainers. You have an industry that is so enormous that a change in global policy would cripple countries and bring governments down. The outcome could be a global recession. It's reminiscent of Y2K but on a scale a thousand times bigger. If you can work on that communiqué before dinner, I'm off to see the captain about ... Janice's interrogation.'

Timothy appeared on the bridge and approached Captain Delaney. 'Good evening, Captain. How is the interrogation going?'

'Ah, Timothy, I was just about to give you a call. Let's pop down to the brig.'

They both went down to the brig and into the observation room. The scene had changed dramatically. Janice looked dishevelled and rattled; her eyes were red and her complexion very pale. Her speech was broken and strained.

'So, Janice, who are you collecting this information for?' said the interrogator.

'I ... I ... I'm collecting it for myself.' She rocked backward and forward in her chair, then commenced again. 'I'm collecting it for Lee Chang. No, no ... I work for Lee Chang.'

'But what would Lee Chang want with this information?'

'But ... but ... I work for Lee Chang. He can buy very expensive favours from the officials, this ... information can't hurt anybody. It's not espionage ... it's not trade secrets, I don't ... I don't ... even know what it is.'

'So how much are you getting for the information?'

'I don't know.'

Janice collapsed on the table. The interrogator picked up a bucket and dumped water on Janice's head and back. Janice snapped back upright, dripping water.

'So Janice, how much are you getting for information?'

'Umm, I … I …' she paused. 'Two million,' she said quietly before collapsing on the table again.

This time the interrogator got up and left the room. He entered the observation room. 'Do you need any more, Captain?'

The captain shook his head. 'I believe we have all we need, thanks. That will be all. Thank you, Corporal.'

The corporal left the room. The captain addressed Timothy. 'I believe that's the summary. Janice was selling the information to the Chinese via her boss. In return the Chinese government granted favours to Lee in his property deals. Explains the high tech gadgets and the overall sophistication of what she was doing. The Chinese will not be happy with this. The Australian government has a lot to lose in getting them offside. I believe our instructions will be to make Janice disappear. I'm not sure if handing her over to the Americans will do that. They're intent on their own political agenda, which isn't the same as the Australian government's.'

Timothy couldn't believe he was in the middle of this conversation. Political power-plays at the highest level and now discussing the disappearance of an individual. He had to draw the line. 'Captain, how you handle the prisoner and all that stuff is up to you. I'm here for the facts and the story. We're working well together and I'm sure our agendas will stay the same, based on what we know at the moment.'

Captain Delaney nodded. 'We seem to be in agreement then.'

Later that evening at dinner, Timothy was seated next to the captain, with Caroline on his left. Caroline was looking delightful, her low-cut dress screamed for attention. All evening Timothy's attention was on the captain. Caroline was seated next to Sanjay, whom she found boring. She slowly began to realise that this was Timothy's game. She then worked out how to play.

Under the table she ran a hand gently along Timothy's thigh, up his groin. She felt him tense. Caroline sighed inwardly. This was a victory. She continued to tease Timothy all evening. After dessert she suggested Sanjay join her for a drink at the bar. Sanjay couldn't resist the offer. Caroline sat at the bar facing Timothy, both of them trying to contain their growing frustration.

One by one the tables emptied. The captain and Timothy were seated at a table, Caroline and Sanjay seated at the bar. The captain called it a night and Timothy joined Sanjay and Caroline. They drank and shared stories until 12.30 am when Sanjay appeared to sense the chemistry and decided to leave. Timothy gave Sanjay three minutes to get back to his room, then he took Caroline by the arm and steered her out of the room. They headed straight for Timothy's suite and were barely through the door before embracing in a breathless kiss and sinking to the floor. Their excited breathing began to synchronise; their actions became focused, intense, and systematic as they left a trail of clothing across the floor.

It seemed like half an hour since they had come through the door. They made it to the bedroom – naked, breathless and at fever pitch. They stood and Caroline arched against Timothy; he lifted her and turned to the bed, easing her onto the bed and entering her effortlessly. Her ankles locked around his back. The next thirty minutes were ecstatic for both of them; they eventually collapsed in each other's arms and fell asleep.

Janice didn't eat her meal until late in the evening. She was feeling extremely depressed and irritable. The interrogation had totally disorientated her – she had lost complete track of time and felt it was now time for her escape. Even though she was highly trained, she failed to recognise her own impaired judgement.

CHAPTER 30

She rapidly ate her meal, waited five minutes then forced herself to convulse, writhing on the floor until the guard rushed in to assist her.

'You alright, Miss?'

As soon as he reached out to touch her, Janice planted a foot to the bridge of his nose, sending him reeling back into the bars without his pistol. She quickly retrieved the pistol from the ground and followed through with a powerful blow from the pistol butt to the guard's temple. The blow made a sickening sound as the guard's skull cracked beneath the blow. As he fell, his two-way radio dislodged from the clip on his shoulder, landing heavily on the floor with a loud crash.

Janice heard approaching footsteps and sprang from the lock-up. A guard entered the room, rapidly surveying left then right. Janice fired first, when she and the guard made eye contact – his eyes glazed over and without a sound, he sank to the floor.

There was nowhere to hide in the room. Janice dropped to the floor, facing the door. She was in a sitting position, legs out in front of her and the pistol aimed at where she anticipated the centre of the next guard's chest would be. The guard sprang into the room, his rifle aimed well above Janice's head. They both fired simultaneously; the guard only managed a single shot before he succumbed to the wound to his chest.

Janice felt a twinge in her left shoulder. She looked at it in disbelief – the ricochet from the guard's bullet had torn through the flesh just below her shoulder. She was bleeding profusely.

In her distraction, she didn't notice the hissing gas canister that was lobbed into the room until it was too late. Her first breath of the acrid gas forced a second breath, after which she lost consciousness.

Some hours later Janice woke to find herself back in her cell, her left arm bandaged around the shoulder and her right arm manacled to the bed.

Timothy was woken by banging on the door at 6.00 am. He grabbed a bathrobe and went to the door, where he found Captain Delaney in a very distressed state. Timothy took the captain into the suite's dining room. 'Are you okay?'

'No I'm not. Janice attempted a breakout. I have two dead sailors, one critically injured. Janice is injured as well.'

'I'm so sorry, Captain. Is there anything I can do?'

'We can't bring my men back. In our risk mitigation, we had planned for her to attempt a breakout as we neared the Kerguelen Islands or Perth, most probably Perth. We had not anticipated her cracking like this though.'

'We can manage the media for you, if you want to play it down or show as espionage and attempted escape. That should smooth it over with the CIA. There doesn't have to be any mention of the interrogation or her cracking.'

'Thanks Timothy. You wouldn't have any Scotch in here, would you?'

'No, but it's your ship. Let's go open the bar.'

With that Timothy led the captain out of his suite and back to the bar, where over the next two hours, they drank half a bottle of single malt. Timothy suggested that they rest until lunchtime, then sit down and review how they were going to proceed with releasing information about Janice's injury and the death of the two seamen on board. They both headed to their rooms.

Timothy quietly entered his suite. It was 8.00 am and Caroline was sitting at the table waiting for him. He walked up to her and gave her a kiss.

She pushed him back. 'Scotch at this hour of the morning?' She saw the look on his face. 'What's wrong? What happened?' She took Timothy by the hand and searched his eyes for a clue.

Timothy thought about what he should tell Caroline; at this stage, as little as possible was probably the best option, considering the captain hadn't decided on a line of action yet. 'Two seamen died last night; Janice was involved. I can't go into more details until after lunch and would appreciate it if you say nothing to anybody about this.'

Caroline looked distraught. 'But wasn't she seasick and confined to her cabin? I don't understand what happened.'

'I'm sorry, I really can't discuss it until after lunch, until I have a chance to talk to the captain again. Do you want to go up for breakfast or have it sent down?'

'Sent down please,' replied Caroline.

They had breakfast together in silence. The deaths had cast a shadow over everything. After breakfast, Timothy headed back to his office. He needed to brief Gary and Miles about the deaths and Janice's injuries. He called them into his office. After they were seated he gave them the full summary of Janice's confession to spying and espionage, her attempted breakout and the disastrous results.

Miles gently waved his hands in an expansive gesture. 'This just gets better by the moment.'

At this stage Timothy had to inform them that they would be waiting on discussions with the captain at lunchtime, before proceeding with the espionage and death stories. Miles and Gary complained bitterly, and Timothy conceded that they should continue their research around the espionage.

At lunch, Timothy found Captain Delaney seated with another sailor he hadn't seen before. The captain introduced the sailor as his intelligence officer, Malcolm. After ordering lunch, they discussed how they would present the events of the last twenty-four hours to the media. Malcolm suggested a straightforward approach: that Janice was caught in the process of bugging offices on board the ship. In the process of being apprehended, she put up a fight. In the ensuing firefight, two sailors were killed and one critically injured, and Janice was shot and killed. Investigations were continuing.

Timothy mentioned that he had hoped to get more out of Janice before they made port and was then handed official documents from the Australian, American and UK governments. The incident was being labelled as classified and any other information other than the 'official line' was being covered under the Official Secrets Act. Janice had now become a tool of espionage. Officially, she was dead – ASIS would take custody of her in Perth.

Timothy shook his head. 'That's a disappointing outcome, Captain. We could have outed the Chinese, MI6 and the CIA over this one. Why do the politicians want to wrap it up and keep it as a hand grenade to use later?'

'I'm sorry Timothy – this one was way out of my league. I can only do as ordered from the top down. Neither of us can go against the Official Secrets Act of three countries, certainly not without a long stretch in jail.'

'As usual, Captain, I'll get you to sign off on the news release before it goes out. If we're done here gentlemen, I'll excuse myself.'

The captain and Malcolm nodded their agreement.

Timothy left. As he walked, he realised the presence of the captain aggravated him for the first time. *Bloody bureaucrats!* he thought. He felt uneasy about being aggravated by the captain as he was relying on him for his safety and the safety of his team and he had been a loyal and good friend.

Timothy got back to his office and sat down again with Gary and Miles. Four hours passed while they worked on the latest communiqué. It was slowly beginning to come together in a cohesive statement. The situation felt surreal but Timothy pressed on. The captain signed off on the final draft without so much as a question. He had come to trust Timothy. The media release that was sent out from the vessel that night read:

Attempted espionage in the Southern Ocean: three dead, one critical
Breaking news

Today in the Southern Ocean, things turned dramatically deadly on the Spirit of the Southern Ocean when one of the passengers was killed attempting to bug sensitive facilities on the vessel. In the ensuing gun battle with the ship's sailors, the passenger and two crew are dead, with a further crew member critically injured. The captain has reported that the secure facility has not been breached. Details of the deceased and injured will be released when the next of kin have been informed.

The newsbreak was then padded out with another half a page reminding readers of the headlines of the story to date: the disappearance of three vessels, the discovery of a possible cause and now, attempted espionage. Timothy, Miles and Gary were very pleased with the final press release. It had the headlines to grab attention and enough detail to bring new readers up to date on the story. It was a good story. It was time to hit the bar and have a good dinner.

They arrived at the bar at six o'clock, and Sanjay and Caroline were at the bar with Captain Delaney, who looked tired and depressed. Today, he had lost two seamen and another one was critically injured – he was obviously taking it very personally. Timothy walked straight up to the captain, put his arm around his shoulder and enquired about the health of the injured sailor.

'Thanks Timothy. He's off the critical list. It was very close – we almost lost him. Damn, she is a good shot. She took down three of my best. It's unbelievable.'

'I'm sorry for your loss, Captain – next round is on me.'

They all sat around the bar sharing pleasantries and working hard to move the conversation away from the day's grim events. By seven o'clock the drinks began to work their magic; the conversation had strayed to life after the return to Perth and Hobart. Dinner was a well-lubricated affair and the mood gradually turned slightly intoxicated and jovial as the night drew on. It was a moment of relief in a very difficult day.

By eleven o'clock, only Caroline and Timothy were left alone at the bar. Here were two people so totally in the moment, like moths drawn to a flame – once alone, there was no today or tomorrow. They were living in a cocoon of sexuality, intrigue and spontaneity. They continued to look at the bar as if they were sitting alone. Timothy slowly moved his hand, reaching down to touch Caroline's. Their fingers intertwined. They both turned and their eyes met. They both stood very slowly, their gaze unbroken. They walked in unison towards the door; not a single word was uttered. Timothy led the way back to his suite, unlocked the door and Caroline entered first, heading straight for the bedroom. Timothy went to the bar, opened a bottle of Champagne and poured two glasses. He then proceeded to the bedroom, to find Caroline already in the bed, sheets pulled up to her chin.

CHAPTER 30

Timothy was a little bemused by Caroline's impatience, but he couldn't see her clothes anywhere so for all he knew she could be fully clothed under the bed sheets. He sat on the bed beside her, holding out the champagne to her.

Her eyes flashed wildly. *Damn!* she thought. *He's taking all the fun out of it.*

Caroline hesitated, then sat up in the bed, allowing the sheet to fall away. Her gorgeous breasts were full and smooth, her nipples reacting to the cool air in the room and her growing excitement. Timothy could barely contain himself. He passed Caroline the champagne and they both sipped from their glasses without shifting their gaze from each other's eyes. Timothy blinked first – he placed his glass on the bedside table, stood and removed his jacket, tie, shirt and trousers. He watched Caroline intently the whole time. Caroline put her glass on the table beside Timothy's and slid back under the sheets, not braking Timothy's gaze for a moment. Timothy walked around the other side of the bed, slipped between the sheets and turned off the light.

Timothy was immediately drawn to the intoxicating heat of Caroline's body; within seconds their bodies were intertwined. The sex was silent, fast and furious – twenty minutes later they both fell asleep still intertwined in each other's arms. The sadness of the day was long forgotten.

Overnight the British, Chinese and Indian governments had called an emergency meeting of the UN Security Council to consider the events unfolding in the Southern Ocean.

The meeting lasted over twelve hours with an agreement reached for the UN Security Council to take control of communications and any investigations into the cause of the recent disaster, including the current search charter. There had been serious concerns raised into the possible economic impact of un-vetted reports about climate change that could negatively influence the global economy and cause severe regional instability, political unrest and possible riots. Britain in particular had been very adamant that the UN Security Council be used to manage the situation on behalf of all member states.

Britain got the support of China and India; her ally, the USA, did not waiver either. The rest of the Security Council, seeing no reason to reject the motion, unanimously passed the resolution.

CHAPTER 31

The next morning Captain Delaney came up to the table that Caroline and Timothy were sitting at. He was looking formal and strained.

'I have some bad news Timothy. The UN Security Council has taken jurisdiction over what is going on here in the Southern Ocean as a matter of global security. I've been ordered to shut down communications to the media and submit all the information to the UN.'

Timothy was flabbergasted by the news. 'Are you telling me that I can't get any news out?'

'They are my orders. As much as I don't like them, I have to obey my orders.'

'Nothing personal Captain, but we will have to see what my lawyers say.'

The captain retreated, leaving Timothy very aggravated. Caroline grasped Timothy's arm. 'How can they do that?' She looked very upset.

'I'm not really sure,' replied Timothy. 'But this is too big a story not to allow the press freedom on it. The news has to get out!'

After breakfast Timothy headed back to his office where he discussed the captain's announcement with Gary and Miles. Gary was given the task of getting in contact with Timothy's lawyers to seek their advice. In the meantime, Timothy met with Dr Mellows and Dr Perry, who were continuing their research into the ice objects in the ship's freezer.

'Good morning Timothy,' said Dr Perry. 'I'm happy to see you in the lab. Grab a seat and I'll give you an update.

'The structure of the ice from the sheets is very unusual. It appears to resemble ice that would normally be found on the top of a flowing stream, with a few important exceptions. We will continue to analyse the ice and work on various theories with Hobart University and other research bodies until we are certain about the ice formation.

'On another matter, Timothy, can I get additional scientific experts brought in to the investigation?'

Timothy decided to do a trade-off. 'Firstly I'll need a special favour. I can agree to fund additional scientific input, and in return, I need the use of your communication links.'

'Are you having problems with the on-board communications?'

'You might say that.'

Dr Perry did not hesitate – the funding was all that she was after. At this stage, she was oblivious to the political battles going on around her. 'Not an issue; use it whenever you require it.'

They were due to commence their return voyage to Fremantle, but Captain Delaney had taken a request from the Kerguelen Islands to make a visit and share information about the findings. Due to the embargo placed on information by the UN, the captain politely refused the request citing the need to urgently return to Fremantle. Since the UN's announcement, the Navy had been in constant contact with the captain. He was under strict orders to prevent any formal communication from the vessel to the media. He was frustrated and tormented by the orders, as up until that moment, he had formed a very good working relationship with Timothy. He couldn't imagine the impact that the orders were going to have on that relationship.

In the meantime, Timothy called Caroline up to his office. She knocked and entered. 'Nice office.'

'Thanks, take a seat.'

Caroline sat down and watched every move that Timothy made. His office was meticulous and Spartan. A desk, keypad, mouse, screens and no papers on the desk, a small filing cabinet, a side cupboard and nothing else.

'I have an offer to put to you, however the matter is highly confidential. Are you comfortable with that?'

Caroline thought about the question briefly. 'Yes, I'm comfortable with confidentiality.'

'Caroline, I want you to join my team to broadcast to the world. We have been gagged by the UN and our government from broadcasting what is happening out here, so you could end up in jail if we're not lucky. Are you still comfortable with the proposal?'

Caroline's heart was beating so loudly that she could barely think.

'Take a few minutes to think if you need them Caroline.'

'Thanks.' *Jail*, thought Caroline, *was anything worth that?* The opportunity to work with Timothy was pretty compelling. 'Timothy, what if I end up in jail?'

'My company will get you out no matter what it takes,' replied Timothy with a smile.

'If I can get your assurance on that, then I'll take the role.'

'I'll have legal draw up a contract.'

Caroline was thrilled by the opportunity to work closely with Timothy. Her feelings for him were very intense and every moment away from him seemed like an eternity.

Timothy, Miles and Gary commenced work on a press release.

Their brainstorming created a sensational headline. For the following twenty-four hours they toiled over the content. The content included advice given by Timothy's lawyers that the captain's actions were illegal. Timothy had a contract for the use of the vessel and its facilities from the owner, including the hire and control of the vessel and its captain and sailors. In effect, they believed that this contract made Timothy the commander of the vessel and the captain's actions could be said to be an act of mutiny on the high sea. To complicate the issue even more, the legality of the Australian government having replaced a civilian crew with a naval one appeared to also have serious political and legal implications.

Timothy was uncomfortable and for the first time in his life felt that he could be slightly in over his head. However, the story was sensational – never before had there been an opportunity for a media individual to take on the UN. This was beyond exciting! Timothy felt focused. If he could get this right, he felt that he would be untouchable.

Finally the news release was ready, the headline to the world read: 'UN Security Council party to global conspiracy'.

Gary, Miles and Caroline were very uncomfortable with the headline. Based on the captain's orders and the UN Security Council's declaration, Timothy would undoubtedly be in the brig by the end of the day.

'You'll be locked up within the hour,' said Miles. 'What are your instructions for us after that?'

Timothy looked at the three of them sternly. 'You keep communicating no matter what.'

Caroline reluctantly took the press release down to the offices of Dr Perry and Dr Mellows, sending it to Timothy's media empire.

Forty minutes later, Timothy's office doors burst open and three armed sailors entered, followed by Captain Delaney. The captain read a terse statement. 'Timothy Wiley, you are under arrest for defying the UN Security Council ban on communication, in relation to the Southern Ocean incident. You will be held in the brig until we arrive in Perth, at which time you'll be transferred to the nearest naval military base and handed over to the UN for processing.'

Timothy motioned for calm and said nothing. He was handcuffed while his film crew continued to film – the full incident had been documented.

The captain ignored the film crew. The advantage taken by the Prime Minister in previous communications had made these oversights easier than he thought. It had become clear to him that the Prime Minister was using the situation, so he saw no apparent harm in continuing down that path. He just needed to avoid a deliberate breach of orders.

As soon as Timothy had been removed from the office, Caroline took command. 'We have our orders. Gary, Miles, let's get on with it. Miles, can you supervise the editing of the arrest please?'

Neither Gary nor Miles had challenged Caroline taking over the leadership of the team. Neither of them wanted the responsibility. They commenced assembly of the next press release while the film crew edited the footage of Timothy being arrested with Gary looking in from time to time.

Gary and Miles wove a web of conspiracy and intrigue; Caroline felt empowered but frightened by the experience. The headline read: 'UN arrests media baron to prevent conspiracy disclosure'. Who was the captain going to arrest for this one? Caroline again used the Hobart University facilities on board to transmit the press release. The repercussions were almost immediate – Caroline had barely returned to Timothy's office before the doors were again burst open by Captain Delaney and his security team.

'Who sent the news release?' demanded the captain.

Miles immediately raised his hand. 'I did, Captain. You have no authority to prevent the media from reporting on this. Our legal advice is that your actions are an act of piracy. Your actions in overriding Timothy's authority on board are an act of mutiny!'

The captain stood back in a daze. 'Mutiny?'

'That's the opinion of our lawyers, with Timothy commissioning the venture and you reporting to Timothy, who is on board. I'm not a lawyer, but you should check with your own lawyers!'

'I'll do that, Miles.'

Again the captain did not query how the message was transmitted. This time Caroline was suspicious, but put it down to the doubt that Miles had caused with his statement about legality and mutiny.

Miles was handcuffed and marched to the brig. Again the film crew had been filming the entire event. Caroline instructed the crew to edit the film while she prepared the news article with Gary.

Two hours later the latest release was ready: 'Southern Ocean charter mutiny sanctioned by UN'.

The article carried footage of the captain and his security team arresting Timothy and Miles on Security Council orders. The repercussions for the world community were significant. At this time it was not clear why the UN Security Council had taken this action. The article created uncertainty as to whether the UN could be involved in such an abuse of power. The public scrutiny would be intense.

Caroline negotiated the corridors carefully. Again she managed to publish the article via the Hobart University facilities on board. She and Gary were prepared this time as Captain Delaney and his security team burst through the doors. This time Gary took responsibility for the article being published; he was handcuffed and escorted to the brig. Again there was no search or questioning as to how the article had been transmitted. Caroline was left alone in the office while Gary was escorted to the brig.

Caroline had the editor's seat. The news release read: 'Demand freedom of the press for jailed Southern Ocean journalists and media baron!'

Caroline took three hours to complete the article, and then had it transmitted. This time only the captain entered Timothy's office.

'Caroline, I've placed the ship on lockdown. You should proceed back to your cabin immediately and not leave it unless escorted by one of the crew. The crew are authorised to shoot on sight if you fail to obey these orders.'

They were twenty-six hours' sailing time from Perth when the ship was locked down.

Across the world, there was mayhem. One and a half million people were in a rowdy protest outside the UN in New York. Similar protests were occurring in many major cities across the world. The public wanted to know what was going on in the Southern Ocean and why the UN Security Council was taking such an interest in three lost sailors and the cause of their deaths. There was global outrage about the censorship of the media by the UN Security Council on what appeared to be an environmental story. The complicity of major governments in the censorship was fuelling the global outrage. Protestors globally united in demanding that the UN immediately release Timothy and his employees.

A social media tsunami was in the making. Every politician in the countries supporting the arrests appeared to be a target for a relentless barrage of tweets, blogs and denial-of-service attacks as the public, political and social change machine turned against them. Global media came out in support of their colleagues; governments were under siege by the media and the people of their own countries. Rioting spread around the world, as trust in the political system began to crumble. The Security Council in New York was in crisis control; they worked through the night in an attempt to resolve the issue.

Governments, one by one, contacted the UN demanding that the Security Council release Timothy and his employees and allow media freedom around the Southern Ocean event. As the hours dragged by, reports began to flood in of damage, injury and deaths as the riots escalated.

Sixteen hours out of Perth, the captain received an urgent communiqué from the Australian Defence Minister. He was to immediately release the prisoners and remove the lockdown, allowing communication with the media and other external bodies.

CHAPTER 32

Upon his release, Timothy and his team immediately set about preparing a global broadcast to update the world about what had occurred in the Southern Ocean. The captain took Timothy aside.

'Timothy, the Secretary-General of the United Nations has requested that you issue a calming message as soon as possible to assist governments in quelling growing riots.'

'Captain, I'm not inclined to fulfil that request.'

The captain moved closer to Timothy. 'I suggest you go online and have a look at what's happening around the world before you make that decision. The riots are unprecedented.'

Timothy went to his desk and scrolled through various media outlets and began to appreciate the severity of the issue and why the UN had requested assistance. 'I can see the problem now. I will consider the request and will act on it as soon as possible.'

In the news release supporting the UN, Timothy appealed for calm and requested that everybody return to their homes and continue to watch the broadcast, as they believed it was the best way to support Timothy and his team in getting to the truth about the ice sheets. In the broadcast, Timothy introduced Miles, Gary, Caroline and Sanjay. Each one would take it in turns to stay online during the rest of the voyage.

Afterwards, Timothy took his team back to his office. 'Well

everybody, congratulations! That was phenomenal. We have the attention of the world ... We've taken on the UN and won. The next step is to get material ready for our non-stop broadcast for the next sixteen hours. I suggest we do two-hour shifts starting with Miles, Gary, Sanjay, Caroline then myself – and then we start again. I think the best format that we can have, is to introduce ourselves, explain why we're on board, then read through the various news releases in detail. Perhaps we'll add a comment or two, but we won't stray from the content. How does everybody feel about that?'

Everybody was smiling; they all nodded and there were high-fives all around. This was beyond their wildest expectations. They had a global audience to deliver to.

'Next step,' Timothy said, 'I think everybody should relax and do just a little prep work for their time on air. The video team will broadcast you with a ninety second delay just in case you have bloopers, so relax and enjoy the broadcasts.'

With that they all departed the office, leaving Miles with the first two-hour shift. Timothy and Caroline headed towards the bar, hand in hand, both of them beaming.

As they walked to the bar, Timothy quietly spoke to her. 'Your delivery of the final plea for support for a free media focused the global protest. Without a doubt, you have proven to be the hero of the media team. Think about it: you brought the UN to its knees by evoking global condemnation of the act of suppressing free media.'

Caroline squeezed his hand and looked straight ahead. She was in a bit of a daze after the whirlwind events of the last half hour.

Until now, Timothy had seen his relationship with Caroline as purely being one of business and a casual sexual relationship. In the last ten hours, their relationship had changed dramatically.

CHAPTER 32

He felt slightly breathless in her presence, as this stunningly gorgeous woman had stepped up to the plate in very difficult circumstances. That demanded his respect.

They arrived at the bar arm in arm; not a word had passed between them since they left the office. Words couldn't describe the electrifying sensation that passed between their clasped hands. Timothy eased Caroline onto a barstool, his arms gently rising up her sides. He cupped her face in his palms as she closed her eyes, her long lashes accentuating her stunning face. Caroline was breathing slowly, savouring every moment. She had worked very hard on her relationship with Timothy; she felt that she was in love with him and she wanted the moment to go on forever.

Timothy eased closer to Caroline's face – she was absolutely gorgeous. Their lips touched. The first touch was like igniting a fireworks display. She flung her arms around his neck and the kiss was long and passionate.

Caroline pushed Timothy away and sank her head into his chest. 'I think I'm falling in love with you, Timothy,' she murmured into his chest.

'I love you,' he said in reply with a twinge of remorse.

Caroline sat back looking into Timothy's eyes. 'I was so worried for you when they took you to the brig. All I could do was get the message out and pray that the world community would come to your rescue. You really are amazing. In a few days out here, you've captured the imagination of the world. The people now see you as a hero. They came to your rescue.'

She clasped her fingers behind Timothy's neck and drew his lips to her own, in a very long lingering kiss. This time Timothy pushed Caroline away and looked up and down the bar.

'No bartender. What would you like a drink?'

'Champagne would be lovely,' purred Caroline.

They lingered at the bar for half an hour before wandering

into the restaurant, where they found Captain Delaney sitting with Sanjay. The captain motioned them over.

'No hard feelings I hope?' he said.

'No hard feelings – orders are orders.'

Caroline and Timothy sat down at the table with the captain and Sanjay. For the next two hours, the conversation revolved around the orders from the UN and the possible repercussions they would have on the UN following the global riots.

The captain informed them that a UN Security Council meeting was being planned for the day after their arrival into Fremantle. The conversation then drifted onto trying to understand why the UN was still persisting down this course. None of them were able to come up with a credible reason for the meeting. While they were talking, an officer came down to the bridge and spoke to the captain privately.

Captain Delaney turned back to the group. 'Time for the news headlines; look at the television screen.'

Splashed across the large screen in the dining room was Caroline reading the last news report before the ship went into lockdown. Caroline was very excited to see herself on the large screen. 'Wow, where did that come from?' she exclaimed.

'Our film crew are the best,' Timothy replied. 'You wouldn't have even been aware that they were filming all the work that went into getting out the news over the last twenty-four hours. When you get your broadcast time, I'm sure they will introduce you to a lot of footage you can use.'

Caroline stared at the big screen, beaming. 'Timothy, your team is absolutely amazing. That's me up there but they've made it so intense, so spontaneous, so amazing, I can't stop watching!'

The captain rose to his feet. He was totally besotted by Caroline and had barely been able to take his eyes off her after she came into the room. 'Off the record, I'd like to propose a toast

CHAPTER 32

to Caroline for following through on getting this important story out to the world. Congratulations Caroline.'

By this stage Caroline was almost blushing. She had noticed the intensity of the attention she was getting from the captain as she entered the room and was starting to feel just a little bit uncomfortable. The captain's comments made her relax a little. 'Thank you, Captain. I appreciate the toast and I graciously accept it on behalf of the team. And off the record, Captain, the team includes you.'

The captain allowed himself to smile briefly.

'I'll second that!' said Timothy, raising his glass to the captain.

'What a day,' said Caroline, 'and to think we don't even know what it's all about yet!'

Caroline had opened the door for the next hour's conversation. They delved into all the theories that had been put on the table to date but still could not quite work out what was going on. It was late in the evening when Dr Perry and Dr Mellows entered the room. They were immediately bombarded with questions about why the UN Security Council should be so interested in what had been occurring in the Southern Ocean. The doctors spent the next few hours working through their theories but were unable to come up with a conclusive reason. They did, however, let slip that their presence had been requested at the UN Security Council meeting scheduled the day after the expedition was due back in Perth. Both the doctors were excited about the meeting; they conceded that presenting to the Security Council would elevate their work to global significance.

By midnight only Timothy and Caroline were left in the restaurant. Caroline was due to commence her broadcast at 2.00 am and Timothy at 4.00 am. They decided sleep was pointless and headed back to Timothy's suite.

Both Caroline and Timothy's broadcasts were very well

orchestrated. The film crew had the production experience – and with input from Miles and Gary, they were able to prepare scripts for both Caroline and Timothy prior to them arriving. Careful instructions to follow the cue cards and a ninety-second delay in transmission were all that was needed, to deliver a seamless and polished broadcast. Caroline stayed to watch Timothy and near the end of the transmission, she was startled by an arm on her shoulder. Miles had entered the room but Caroline had been too engrossed in Timothy's broadcast to notice.

'Congratulations Caroline, it looks like you have a career in presenting in the media. Your presentation last night has had sensational reviews around the globe.'

Caroline stood up and kissed Miles on the cheek. 'Thanks, Miles,' she said. 'I couldn't have done it without you and Gary or your amazing film crew.'

Miles put his arm around Caroline and kissed her on the cheek. 'Welcome aboard. I'm sure you know he's falling in love with you.'

Caroline looked at Miles, beaming. 'Thanks Miles, I've fallen in love with him too.'

'I'm happy for both of you,' said Miles sincerely. He'd been concerned about Timothy's mental state since the death of Penelope. Timothy had thrown himself into the search in the Southern Ocean without what appeared to be a moment of grief. Miles didn't feel that had been a very healthy decision – a man had to have feelings and a time to grieve. Now he saw Timothy pulling his life back together again. He felt that by the time they reached Fremantle in the morning, Timothy could be almost his old self again.

Timothy came bounding out of the studio. 'Well, you two, what're you up to? I saw kisses and smiles from in there. What's going on?'

Miles came to the rescue. 'Mutual admiration for our journalistic skills. You must have seen it by now – we're both brilliant ... and Caroline saved your butt.'

'Enough of that Miles – get yourself in there and keep the show going.'

'Yes boss!'

Miles headed into the studio with a smile and a wink at Caroline to commence his broadcast.

Timothy and Caroline headed off to bed. They were still six hours from Fremantle and they hadn't slept yet.

CHAPTER 33

After the interrogation and failed breakout, Janice was very depressed and despondent. She had now failed her mission. Her injury was only a scratch, which she was thankful for. Lee did not have his data feed from the Southern Ocean and she had her two million dollars – but there was no way she could collect on the jail money. That was something she had not thought through. If the link had been in place she could have made her plan work; she could have done the jail time and come out to three million plus interest.

This kind of failure usually had an agent put on a hit list to protect the backers. Her prospects of survival beyond a few weeks onshore were grim. She had to test the defences of the crew and then break out prior to arrival in Perth. She was a good swimmer, so a twenty-kilometre swim to shore was within her capabilities. A 'lost at sea' disappearance was her one hope of survival. Her first objective was to move the two million to an untraceable location.

Janice observed the guards for twenty hours before making her move. Overpowering a single unsuspecting guard was easy for her. Ten minutes on a computer and a redirect to her emergency transmitter backup had her money shifted and untraceable. Janice then locked herself back in her cell. The guard didn't see what hit him so he would presume he had fallen asleep and toppled onto the floor, or that it was a third party. Either way, Janice herself was blameless. Her plan was working well. The guard had not recovered by the time he was due to report and an armed group of three sailors came to investigate. Janice pretended to be asleep and the guard was revived by his colleagues. Then a heated conversation commenced.

'There's been some comms from below deck; did you fall asleep again?'

'Look at the lump, how could I get that? She must have done it!'

'She's locked up, stupid. Did anyone check the lock?'

There was silence followed by heavy footsteps as someone checked the cell door. A gruff voice reported.

'It's locked and secure.'

'She must have an accomplice on board.'

'Let's call the master-at-arms.'

There was a muffled series of conversations. After a brief delay, the master-at-arms arrived. The guard was further questioned, then attention turned to Janice. She was startled by a metal object being rattled along the cell bars.

'Hey prisoner, wake up! We need to talk to you.'

Janice turned over to find six men staring at her, three carrying assault rifles that were pointed at her. The guard she had ambushed looked angry and confused.

'What's the problem?' Janice enquired with a lazy yawn.

The master-at-arms stepped forward. 'Did you see what happened to the guard?'

Janice wanted to laugh but contained herself. 'He's right behind you ...' she replied, faking confusion.

The master-at-arms turned bright red; he was furious. 'Enough!' he screamed. 'We found him unconscious on the floor with a large bump on his head – did you see what happened?'

Janice felt little comfort from the bars between them but continued to taunt the master at arms. 'Did he fall asleep …' she paused. 'Again?'

The master-at-arms turned to the guard and exploded. 'What does she mean, "again"? Well, sailor? What does she mean by "again"?'

It was the sailor's turn to go bright red. 'I have no idea Sir, I've been hit from behind. I didn't see who hit me Sir!'

The master-at-arms turned back to Janice. 'Did you hear anything then, Miss?'

'Nothing until you woke me up,' Janice replied.

'Okay Miss. Stand back! Hands on the wall! Move your feet back! Now hold that position! Franks, Smyth, go in and search the room for anything that could have be used to pick the lock or hit Jameson.'

Janice heard the door being opened, then the room being disassembled behind her. She was confident that they wouldn't find an object that could be used to knock out the guard because she had used his own pistol. But the lock pick was an issue. It was in the flap of her boots between the tongue and the laces. It was secure but a spy would find it easily. Hopefully the sailors were not trained to that level.

One of the sailors queried the master-at-arms. 'Do we search her, Sir?'

'No sailor, not today. Now come out of there, both of you.'

The master-at-arms was very concerned that they had not found anything in the cell. That pointed to a second perpetrator on board. That would also explain who made the unauthorised transmission in the last half hour. Or, his sailor fell asleep. The master-at-arms checked the layout of the furniture and determined that it was almost impossible to sustain a bump on the back of the head that size from any of the furniture. He could had fallen asleep from a sitting position and fallen to the floor. The master-at-arms left instructions that a minimum of two guards be posted at any time in future and left with the balance of his team.

One of the sailors called out to Janice. 'Okay miss, you can relax now.'

Janice eased up against the wall, then slowly turned and went back to her bunk where she slid under the blanket and went to sleep.

The master-at-arms submitted his report to Captain Delaney. The report concluded that since the prisoner was in her cell, and all other personnel on the ship were accounted for, at the time the guard was assaulted and the communication transmission made, that there was an unaccounted for passenger on board or an accomplice. The captain, after reviewing the report, ordered a sweep of the ship for any unaccounted passengers.

After five hours, the sweep was completed without finding anyone or any transmitter. The unsuccessful search raised tensions on the ship. If there was no unaccounted for passenger, then one of them may be a traitor.

Two hours later after the search, Janice had become aware from the guards' conversations that the ship was nearing Fremantle and that it was a daytime return to port. That meant that she would need to escape as soon as possible and hide for as long as she could to avoid a long stay in the water during the day and risk detection.

She had been working on the guards to try to get them to relax which had started to work. Most of them were not battle hardened and saw her as a person, not a mortal enemy. From a lying position on her bunk, Janice rolled onto the floor and began convulsing. Both guards came through the door almost together. The lead guard dropped like a stone as Janice's booted foot made brutal contact with his throat. The second guard, eyes wide open, was about to shoot when he too succumbed to an upward moving boot to the nose. The second guard died instantly; the first was dispatched with a snap of the neck.

Janice moved fast, heading for the deck containing the remains of the ketches. There was enough wreckage there to provide a safe haven. Hopefully the dead guards would not be found for another couple of hours. She located her backup ID and credit cards, hidden for such an occasion. After two hours the alarm had not been raised and Janice moved cautiously to an upper deck where she had access to the water. It appeared that their course had taken them very close to Busselton. Approximately 5 kilometres from the coast, Janice slipped over the side undetected and began her short swim to shore.

The water was cold but Janice was trained for this type of swim. She had estimated it would be between two and three hours to the shore if the currents were neutral. After a few minutes, she realised that there was a considerable current taking her towards the coast. Janice was able to make the shore after only ninety minutes in the water. She managed to get to the tree line undetected. She was not absolutely certain of her location, but looking at the coastline she had estimated a location at least 200 kilometres south of Perth.

Janice moved quickly on the ground. To her north, there was a farmhouse that appeared to have a car parked outside it. It took Janice less than ten minutes to reach the farmhouse and survey the buildings. There was a sign on the back door.

Monday. Jack, Mum has been taken ill. Back in a couple of days. Don't need any work done until I get back.

Janice found the back door open. She entered and locked the door behind her. It was Tuesday; she could relax. A quick search of the farmhouse and she had a fresh change of clothes. The car keys were on the hook inside the back door. Janice took food from the fridge, water, and was in the car heading east an hour after arriving on shore.

She was now trying to plan her next steps. North to Perth would be like going into a lion's den. She knew as soon as the crew found the dead guards, the entire coast and road to Perth would be swarming with police looking for her. Albany was her target. She could dispose of the car near Albany so it wouldn't be found for a week or two and slip into the town. She had the wallets of the guards and her own backup ID. That would give her sufficient money to wire herself some cash, change her hair colour and a few other cosmetic changes that would give her an identity change, sufficient enough to move about the country without detection. Then she could plan on getting to Darwin where she could make an exit to Asia and then on to the US to disappear.

After four hours, the change of the guard at the cell was met with a grizzly scene. Both sailors had been dead for several hours. Timothy and his team were confined to quarters as an extensive search commenced. The ship was stopped 60 kilometres from Perth, the captain not wanting to enter port with a search in progress. The police and navy were advised of the possibility of a fugitive on the loose along the coast from their current location to Busselton and 7 kilometres out to sea. It took the crew forty-five minutes to determine that Janice was not on board.

CHAPTER 34

Timothy and Caroline went back to sleep after the search; they were awoken by the sound of air horns and sirens. The view from their window was amazing as hundreds of pleasure craft had come out to welcome them back to Fremantle. In the distance, no fewer than six naval vessels lay at anchor. The sky was buzzing with media helicopters angling for any view they could get.

'Come on, Sleeping Beauty, we have a helicopter to catch in forty minutes. You have an appointment in front of the cameras in a couple of hours.'

Caroline sat bolt upright. 'What do you mean, *in front of the cameras in two hours?*'

'Sorry, we forgot to tell you. Your reading of the news release was such a big hit globally, we thought you might like to be our spokesperson in Perth today.'

Caroline looked a little frantic. 'But my hair! I have no clothes to wear and my shoes just won't do!'

Timothy looked a little bit bemused. 'Hairdressers and the wardrobe departments of the studio are ready for you. You're a size six, your shoes are a size eight, you're five foot eight and a half inches and gorgeous, and they're ready. Now grab a shower and get yourself ready. We need to leave as soon as the helicopter arrives.'

CHAPTER 34

Prior to leaving, Timothy met with Captain Delaney, Dr Perry, Dr Mellows, Miles and Gary. He gave strict instructions that the ice samples were his property and would be released to no-one. He had arranged for refrigerated transport and armed guards to take the samples to a secure refrigerated laboratory facility where Dr Perry and Dr Mellows could continue their work. The transport would be driven on board, to allow the samples to be loaded out of the view of the public and waiting press.

Timothy's media team would tape the loading. Timothy also advised Dr Perry and Dr Mellows that their work was under contract to him and that they needed to advise the Security Council that any requests about their work needed to be directed to him. They were not free to divulge any information about their work to the Security Council or any other authority or the public.

Dr Perry and Dr Mellows were taken aback by the restriction but were contractually bound and had to comply with Timothy's wishes.

The helicopter arrived and Caroline and Timothy were whisked away to their associate studio at Channel Ten in Perth, where another of Timothy's crews were preparing for the two o'clock news conference. Upon arrival at the studios, Caroline was whisked away while Timothy made a beeline for the production department.

Upon entering the production department, Timothy was confronted by his lawyers and the production manager. The lawyers appeared to be very agitated and insisted on updating Timothy on the current situation. Even though the Security Council had released Timothy and his people, they were still insisting that the situation was a global security issue and they were attempting to take control of the samples and all the research. The courts had not allowed any restrictions on how Timothy was reporting developments or the use of any photographs that he may wish to broadcast.

The Security Council expected their appeal to be dealt with in the following two hours. Timothy requested that his lawyers block the council and prevent them from having their way. His belief was that what they had found in the Southern Ocean, was not a threat to global security and he was not sure why the council wanted to intervene. Timothy then settled down with Alex, the production manager, to go through the news report that Caroline would present.

'So, what do you think of the material?' he asked.

'Timothy, it's the most sensational material I've ever seen in my life!'

'Take me through it; we're on air in seventy-five minutes.'

They worked through every photograph and every section of action footage for the one-hour production, looking at the details and the careful balancing of words against images and live footage. Timothy was very pleased with the fine work his team had done in bringing the footage together in such a detailed report.

A hush came over the room when Caroline entered. Her teal silk dress with matching shoes accentuated her alabaster skin, dark hair and sky blue eyes. Her lipstick was red, providing a superb contrast for her stunning face. She immediately started working with the production team to familiarise herself with their process. There were fifteen minutes remaining until airtime.

Timothy was interrupted by a senior assistant. 'Excuse me Timothy, I have the Environment Secretary of State from the UK on the line. Do you want to take the call?'

Timothy nodded and reached for the phone. 'Timothy Wiley here.'

CHAPTER 34

'Timothy, Ben Bradshaw, Secretary of State for Environment, Food and Rural Affairs. The Prime Minister has asked me to phone you because we're getting reports here that you're not cooperating with the Security Council. What's the story?'

'Ben, it's quite simple. We have a story that has nothing to do with security and unless somebody shows me that it does – we are going to air it.'

'The Prime Minister is insisting that it doesn't. He still wants your assurance that you're not going to air with that material. Off the record, if you do, there could be grave ramifications for your business in the UK. Am I making myself clear, Timothy?'

Timothy felt threatened, but there was something very satisfying about this threat. He had struck a nerve and the UK government had twitched. Could they be driving this agenda? Timothy understood the repercussions, however he felt that he had to press on. 'Very clear, thanks Ben. Now I have to go. I have a broadcast to take to air.'

'Don't do it, Timothy. You'll regret it.'

'Goodbye Ben,' said Timothy and hung up the phone. He turned to the production manager. 'We struck a nerve, Alex. The English Prime Minister just had me threatened. So let's get on with it.'

The countdown moved to five minutes. Activity began to pick up around the studio; cameras began to roll and the technicians were poised. Five, four, three, two, one.

Caroline's face had taken over all the monitoring screens as she began with an introduction with a headline banner: 'Death and conspiracy in the Southern Ocean'.

Footage showed the three lost sailing boats in their former days of glory. She then took them to Race Headquarters in London where she introduced the three dead sailors with live footage edited from the race start briefing. The story quickly moved to the Southern Ocean on that fateful day, on July 6, when the unanswered radio calls were made and three sailboats went missing. The story wove in the media releases from 7 July and then moved to the discovery of the debris fields, and soon after, the confirmation of no survivors. Caroline now had tears in her eyes as she took the audience through live footage at Perth Race Headquarters, as the message of three lost sailors began to sink in. The story then moved to Hobart, where Timothy chartered the *Spirit of the Southern Ocean*, which then began the dash from Hobart to Fremantle, to pick up Caroline, Sanjay and Janice.

At around this time, the report came in that the global audience was approaching one billion viewers. Timothy and the producer were ecstatic. In the logistics room there was a very tense auction going on to sell the next forty minutes of advertising space. The auction was a risky strategy but it was paying off. Heartache and grief now filled the story as the *Spirit of the Southern Ocean* intersected the debris fields one by one, confirming as they went that none of the sailors could have survived and deliberating on how the sailing boats were torn to pieces.

Now, with the tension of the broadcast reaching fever pitch, Caroline took to the deck of the *Spirit of the Southern Ocean*, where temperatures were approaching -60 degrees Celsius and the wind was howling across the deck. They went in search of the fleeting radar contacts. The camera took them onto the helicopter that lifted off the deck and headed out across the grey swells towards the nearest radar contacts. As they hovered over a small group of ice sheets just metres above the swells, an ice sheet emerged from the depths and was projected vertically out of the water, coming within a couple of metres of the hovering helicopter. The tension on the set was explosive. Caroline was in control and directed viewers to the helicopter and back to the waiting ship.

CHAPTER 34

A sense of urgency built in the broadcast. They needed to collect ice samples as quickly as possible and get them back into the freezers on the *Spirit of the Southern Ocean*. Caroline built excitement as the sampling team approached the ice sheets. A rocket-propelled grenade was used to fragment an ice sheet and sent a massive plume of ice and water into the air. The crew of the helicopter secured a large fragment in a cradle, suspended beneath the helicopter. The fragment was taken back to the *Spirit of the Southern Ocean* and deposited into the freezer. Dr Perry and Dr Mellows were introduced as they commenced work on analysing the ice fragments.

Caroline now posed the question: How could these ice sheets exist 1500 kilometres from the nearest ice field? More importantly, how had they not been detected and posted as a marine hazard?

She reported no fewer than three satellites collecting data over this area of the ocean daily and that there was a base in the Kerguelen Islands, whose radar had been detecting these objects for some time. However, they had reported that they had not had the facilities to confirm the contacts and therefore had not reported them.

Another report came in on viewing numbers – at forty-five minutes into the broadcast the viewers were close to one and a half billion.

Caroline's story now took another twist, as she introduced Janice – portrayed as a foreign espionage agent. She explained that for reasons still unknown, Janice had been caught bugging Timothy Wiley's offices, the bridge and the radio room on the *Spirit of the Southern Ocean*. In the ensuing firefight, Janice had killed four sailors, seriously injuring another, and had been killed in the ensuing firefight. Images were shown of the room ridden with bullet holes, blood on the floor and the five bodies under shrouds in the morgue. The story then went to the seriously wounded sailor in a hospital bed, providing the backdrop to Caroline's faultless, dramatic delivery. Caroline now posed the question: Who was Janice working for and why was information about these ice sheets so valuable to someone, that they were prepared to kill?

Caroline had the story at fever pitch and she introduced the UN Security Council's ban on the transmission of information from the Southern Ocean, followed by Timothy, Miles and Gary's arrests and her own effective house arrest in her room. The images that Caroline now addressed were flashed from all around the world as people came out in support of Timothy and his team. They then descended into the riots that followed the UN Security Council's orders for suppression of media. The next images were of the amazing welcome back to Fremantle for the *Spirit of the Southern Ocean*.

In the background, Caroline exposed the frantic manoeuvrings in the Federal Court by the UN Security Council to take possession of the ice samples and all the research. Finally, in the most sensational part of the report, explosive news once again.

'Some ten minutes before this broadcast,' said Caroline, 'Timothy Wiley took a phone call from Great Britain's Secretary of State for the Environment. In that call the secretary threatened Timothy Wiley and his business with severe repercussions in the UK, if this broadcast went ahead.' With her eyes flashing and her emotions running high, Caroline appealed to the camera. 'To the Environment Secretary, and the Prime Minister, of the United Kingdom – and the UN Security Council – it's time to tell the public what you know.

'This is Caroline Murray for Wiley International, signing off with the question: Doesn't the public deserve to know what's really happening in the Southern Ocean?'

The camera panned out and Caroline heaved a sigh of relief.

CHAPTER 34

The production manager rushed onto the set to congratulate her and the production team began calling out and clapping. *Sensational, 60 Minutes material* ... Caroline was surrounded by an ecstatic team. She looked sensational and was beaming.

Where is Timothy? she thought. *Why isn't he here?*

She then spotted him in the control room, feet up on the console, sitting back in his chair with his hands behind his head, smiling at her. She instantly got goose bumps as Timothy's casual knowing smile made her feel as though they were almost one person. The whole time she was broadcasting, she had felt him behind her and with her – a reassuring force watching her back, but not interfering.

I've got to make this go on forever, she thought.

She was then brought back down to earth by the noise on the set. The outer crews were pouring onto the set and the applause was becoming deafening. She reached out to Alex, the production manager. 'Alex, can you get me out of here please? I'm exhausted.'

Alex let out a piercing whistle. 'Okay everybody,' he roared. 'Caroline would like to pass on a few words of thanks before she heads off to get some well-earned rest.'

Caroline took the cue, waved, smiled and headed toward the control room, with Alex a few steps behind her. They reached the control room where the blinds were closed. They entered to find Timothy seated alone facing them. He motioned to Alex to sit, then sprang to his feet and embraced Caroline.

'You were sensational! You took the ratings to up over two billion viewers by the end of the show. Beyond sensational!'

Caroline could no longer contain herself; her hands clamped around Timothy's neck and she planted a long, passionate kiss on his lips and only broke the kiss when Alex issued a quiet cough.

'Sorry Alex,' mumbled Caroline. She sheepishly sat in a chair and flashed a smile at Alex.

Timothy looked at both of them and looked at his watch. 'We should expect an outcome from the courts in the next hour. Also, our conclusion from the phone call with the Environment Secretary and mentioning Janice and the UN Security Council, would have set the cat among the pigeons. I think we can expect a lot of attention from all the wrong people. Both Caroline and I will have full-time bodyguards for the foreseeable future. Our hotel doesn't have a helipad on the roof, but we managed to get clearance to get a helicopter into the station and then land on the edge of the city on the Trinity College grounds. Alex, do you want to join us?'

'No thanks, I have a lot to do here.'

Timothy had arranged for Miles and Gary to meet them at the hotel, while they would wait for the outcome of the UN court action.

As they walked through the production area, Timothy stopped in front of a screen showing a local news broadcast. Apparently, the local and international media were outraged at the inability to get access to Timothy or Caroline. Sanjay had been unable to make comments due to the confidentiality agreement he had entered into before going on the expedition. The only way the global media could report this event was to buy feed material from Wiley International. Timothy smiled at the screen and nudged Caroline. 'Your commission is growing.'

Twenty minutes later, Timothy led Caroline into his suite where Miles and Gary were waiting. Miles planted a big kiss on Caroline's cheek. 'You were sensational, Caroline. Absolutely brilliant!'

Gary was a little awkward but also managed to plant a kiss on Caroline's cheek.

'How are the laboratory facilities?' asked Timothy. 'Are Dr Perry and Dr Mellows happy with the facilities?'

Miles responded. 'Facilities are very good – the added security is phenomenal. They even have rubber-tracked tanks. You would think that they were looking after the crown jewels.'

'That's standard business,' said Timothy. 'The bar is open and the food is a minute away.'

Timothy had a barman brought in and they relaxed as the food arrived. Miles turned on a large television and used the screen-in-screen facility to bring up the four local major channels. Caroline's face was on all four channels. Miles turned the sound down and left the images on the screen. For a moment, Caroline was mesmerised, then she contained herself and searched the room for Timothy. She felt she wanted to be close to him.

It was 5.00 pm when the lawyers arrived. Apparently the judge had stopped proceedings to view the telecast. He had given the Security Council a further twenty-four hours to produce a compelling reason for taking control of the samples and the research and failing that, he indicated that he would remove all restrictions on what Wiley International could or could not do with the samples and the research. Timothy was congratulated on his big win.

Timothy walked over to Miles and leaned down beside him. 'Miles, has the room been bug-swept?' he whispered.

'The room is clean but I can't vouch for the barman. We swept him on the way in,' replied Timothy quietly.

Timothy ushered him into the next room for a quick meeting. 'I need you to get on to Dr Perry and Dr Mellows and tell them they have eighteen hours to come up with something. I believe within twenty-four hours, the Security Council may take over everything. This will be the last chance for us and the doctors to have our names on this discovery. We will need at least three to four hours with their material to get another story out.'

'I'm on it boss.'

Miles picked up the phone while Timothy headed back into the other room.

The lawyers had gathered around Caroline like bees to honey. She appeared to be polite and putting up with them and Timothy decided to leave her with them for another ten or fifteen minutes.

In the meantime, he rang Alex and gave him the heads up to have the production team ready for the following day. He suggested that they could start work immediately on the lead-in story so that they only had to add the latest news to the final story.

Timothy was in planning mode. He approached Gary and suggested that he make sure that all the research material was ready to be handed over to the production crew if required. Gary said his goodbyes and headed off. Miles came into the room as Gary was leaving. Gary briefed him and they both left together. Miles waved goodbye to Caroline, who was starting to look a little impatient. Timothy noticed her impatience and stepped in beside Caroline to find the lawyers discussing the intricacies of attempting to deal with the UN.

'Now now, gentlemen, that's way over my head. I suggest you finish your drinks and go back to the office to work out how we're going to keep on top of this.'

After they left, Timothy quickly dismissed the barman as well.

'Alone at last!' moaned Caroline. 'Why did you leave me so long with those awful men, Timothy?'

'You need to be able to hold your own in any group. I had a pile of work to assign to the other guys – sorry, but that kept me away.'

Timothy sensed a change in Caroline's attitude. He couldn't quite put his finger on it. He also sensed a change in himself and as he remembered the previous night's declarations of love, it now began to feel true. A lump came up in his throat and the image of Penelope flashed back at him from the newscast. He didn't fight it – he had learnt, in times of stress, not to engage the thought and let it move on by itself. That was the best way to deal with it.

Caroline gently steered him towards the couch. Timothy gained his composure, swept Caroline off her feet and carried her to the bedroom. They fell asleep fully clothed within minutes, exhausted by the lack of sleep in the last twenty-four hours and the intense workload of the broadcast.

CHAPTER 35

Timothy and Caroline slept through the night undisturbed, waking at 6.15 am just as the first hints of dawn painted the eastern sky. It was going to be a busy day. There was a briefing with the lawyers at 7.00, another with Dr Mellows and Dr Perry at 7.30 and then at 8.00 am they were to meet for breakfast with Miles and Gary.

The lawyers painted a tense picture. The UN Security Council had swung into action at the request of the UK government, which was pushing the line that anything that could impact on low-lying island countries Kiribati, Micronesia, Vanuatu and the Marshall Islands should be managed by the Security Council. Even though the issue had been on the agenda for in excess of five years, the UK was able to push it through the Security Council in several hours. It was now emerging that the UK was involved in a massive amount of lobbying with all the member countries of the Security Council prior to the vote.

The lawyers were continuing to work frantically to deny the Security Council their wishes in court. This was still uncertain as the UN was now challenging the ability of the Australian Federal Court to deal with the matter and was pushing to refer the matter to the International Court of Appeal. The lawyers were advising that they could give Timothy and the doctors another twenty-four hours with the samples.

CHAPTER 35

In London, the House of Commons was debating action to be taken against Timothy's companies. They were hoping that the media would side with them as there had been a flood of complaints about the feed charges they were incurring.

A more immediate concern was that Lee Chang had arrived in Perth and in a press conference, demanding answers about what had happened to Janice and access to the ice samples. A Chinese Navy Houbei-Class trimaran had entered the Port of Fremantle as part of an impromptu visit, to strengthen naval relations between the two countries. The connection between Lee Chang and the Chinese vessel was unclear. NASA and the Chinese government had deployed geo-stationary satellites over the Southern Ocean and were streaming the data to the UN Security Council. This information was not available to Timothy and his team but he would have a private satellite over the region within six hours.

At 7.30, Timothy and Caroline had a phone conference with Dr Perry and Dr Mellows. Timothy was eager to get a progress report.

'Good morning, doctors. I hope the facilities are up to your needs?'

'They're brilliant, thank you,' replied Dr Perry.

'Sorry to be so blunt, but how close are we to a report?'

'We're positive about having a report to issue by 3.00 pm. We're reluctant to discuss progress and feel that we needed to get back to our work, if you don't mind?'

Timothy was a little stunned by Dr Perry's frankness. 'Like your focus and enthusiasm. We'll let you get on with it; I look forward to your report at 3.00 pm.'

'Thanks Timothy.'

Timothy looked at Caroline and smiled. 'Let's go get breakfast.'

Timothy and Caroline arrived ten minutes early to breakfast, enjoying a few minutes of not having to deal with a barrage of information and decision-making. They were just finishing a fresh juice when Miles and Gary entered the room. Miles made a beeline to Caroline, giving her a quick kiss on the cheek. 'Looking absolutely gorgeous,' he whispered in her ear.

Caroline gave him a quick peck on the cheek.

Miles seated himself at the table and Gary said his good mornings and sat next to Miles.

Timothy took charge as soon as they were seated. 'Miles, can you take us through the day's itinerary?'

'Well, we have a deadline of 3.00 pm for the doctors to present information for another broadcast. The Australian Federal Court was scheduled to hear the United Nations appeal at 5.00 pm. Caroline also needs to resign from Race Management to allow her to continue to broadcast. We have received a formal complaint from Race Management about her continuing involvement.'

Timothy took a call then at the breakfast table. He was momentarily surprised to be greeted by Lee Chang; his minders had successfully been keeping the Chinese magnate at bay, until now.

'Timothy, we have a lot to talk about, I'm going to cut right to the chase. I lost another person in the Southern Ocean – this time off your charter. I think you owe me big time.'

Timothy was taken back by the aggressive approach. From the interrogation, he knew that Lee had placed Janice on his charter to spy on them. Lee was clearly not aware that Janice had broken under interrogation – Timothy needed a little more time to understand where Lee was coming from. 'How do you come to that conclusion?'

'I placed Janice on your charter to assist with communication and identification of the wreckage of our boat. All this talk of espionage is nonsense. If that was Janice's doing, it had nothing to do with me or my business. You owe it to me to be frank and open about what you found in the Southern Ocean for all my assistance in providing Janice to support your work down there. Also, as a fellow competitor, I have a right to know how I lost my sailor and my boat.'

Timothy was now starting to get the picture. 'What sort of information are you after?'

'Firstly you can give me a private briefing on all the findings you have from the Southern Ocean and allow my team access to the ice samples to help us understand what occurred down there. As a business owner, you would understand how important it is to have the correct information for your insurance companies when putting in a substantial claim.'

Timothy had to concede it was a good argument – he would have substantial insurance claims to make for the loss of his ketch as well. However, he was not prepared to allow Lee or his people anywhere near the samples at this stage. 'That's very clear, thank you Lee; unfortunately, I won't be giving you access to the samples. Your needs are going to be better met by the final reports, which will have the technical backing of the universities and scientists involved. Allowing you access to the samples sounds more to me like a fishing expedition for information. I'm not sure what you're looking for in that but I'm certainly not going to concede to your request. You'll be sent a copy of the final report. Goodbye.' Timothy hung up without waiting for Lee's response.

Lee sat staring at the phone – this is not an acceptable outcome; Beijing would not be pleased. He pondered his options. He was aware that Beijing had sent a naval vessel to Fremantle and on board, there were technical experts, scientists and senior representatives of a shadowy group from within the Ministry of State Security. He quickly concluded that he had no option but to contact his superiors and provide all the information he had.

He was about to pick up his phone as it rang.

'Lee, it's me. Don't say my name aloud.'

Lee reeled under the impact of Janice's voice – he had believed the news reports that she was in fact dead. 'Where are you?'

'Now that's a question I can't answer. I just called to let you know that the news reports are incorrect. Beyond that, the mission failed because the military was in charge of the boat. It's not clear whether Timothy knew that or not but the mission failed. Please don't look for me or send anybody; for all intents and purposes you must believe the news report. I love you Lee … goodbye, have a good life.'

Lee sat in his seat stunned. That was valuable information; if the military had been involved in Timothy's expedition from the start, then his superiors may not be as hard on him. He began to sense a glimmer of hope.

He immediately called Beijing and informed them. To his surprise they conceded that if this was the case, then having one person trying to do the job would have been an exceptionally difficult task, even for a trained operative like Janice. They indicated that his role in the matter was now closed and other operatives in Perth would now take on the task.

Lee didn't feel secure but he certainly felt a little better than he had felt several hours previously. It was now time to pack and return to Beijing.

Caroline dialled Dave's number and he answered almost immediately. 'Caroline, good to hear from you. Where are you?'

'Dave, I'm in Perth. You would have seen the news broadcasts by now – Timothy has made me an offer I can't refuse. Dave, I'm sorry but I have to resign from your team.'

'I'm very sad about that, but under circumstances I can understand. I'm not sure if you're aware, but I am back in London and James is there in Perth – in your hotel, I believe.'

'If James is here than that's something I will have to deal with.'

'You're one tough lady Caroline but James is not going to take it well.'

'That's my problem.'

'Caroline, what do you know about the ice? Do we have a future in round-the-world racing?'

'Dave, there will always be a future there. A few ice cubes can't wreck that.'

'Thanks Caroline, all the best for the future.'

'Thanks Dave.'

With that conversation Caroline had formally entered a new world of passion, excitement and intrigue. Beside Timothy, ever moment was exhilarating; she was now legally free to be on Timothy's team officially. She now had to meet with James to make sure that their relationship did not interfere with her relationship with Timothy.

Caroline headed out into the hotel, accompanied by a security guard at Timothy's insistence. She went to the foyer and made a request at reception for James's room number. She proceeded up to James's room and rang the doorbell.

James opened the door and was stunned to see Caroline and a guard. He waved her into the room; the guard stayed outside. 'Caroline, I'm so happy to see you!'

'Sit down James – there's something we need to discuss.'

Caroline took control and looked sternly at James. 'James, since I left London things have changed. It's over. I can't explain it; things just happened. You have to let me go.'

James went into deep shock; he sat down hard in a chair, head in his hands. 'Did everything in London mean nothing to you?'

'At the time it did, but now it's the past. We have to move on.'

'So I just have to accept that?'

'You have no choice James. It's over.'

With that Caroline walked to the door and left James sitting with his mouth wide open. James was too shocked to move initially; he then raced after Caroline. By the time he got to the lift it was gone and Caroline with it. He was on the thirtieth floor and he made a dash for the stairs. Desperately, he negotiated each floor with two bounds, one to the middle landing and the second to the floor below. When he reached the foyer, Caroline was nowhere to be seen.

He rushed towards the doors but was confronted by two well-dressed men who flashed identification at him. James stopped in his tracks, attempting to step around them, but they moved with him.

'Get out of my way!' he hissed.

'She had a car waiting; she's long gone,' one of the agents replied.

'Shall we go back to your room? We need to talk,' said the other.

'I'm not talking to anybody,' insisted James. 'Now get out of my face or I'll call the police.' He pushed past them and headed towards the doors.

James had no idea that Caroline was in fact in the penthouse suite in the same hotel above him.

James found a porter at the taxi rank. He had a photo in his wallet but unfortunately the porter didn't remember Caroline having come out in the last ten minutes. The porter insisted that he would remember if Caroline had come out. James ran back into the hotel through the doors and the agents were still standing there.

'Okay you bastards, she never went out the doors.'

'Let's go back to your room and talk about it, James. That's the only way we're going to say anything to you.'

James was starting to feel very uneasy. *Alone in my room with these two? Not likely*, he thought. 'You buy me a drink at the bar, the *public* bar.'

'Let's do that then,' came the reply.

James and the two agents headed into the public bar where they sat and drank for the following two hours. It was early morning but James didn't really care.

'So James, do you know anything about the relationship between Caroline and Timothy?'

James felt indignation and anger at the question. 'I was in a relationship with Caroline in London and at that time, there was no relationship between Caroline and Timothy. He was in a relationship with Penelope. Why is MI6 interested in Caroline and Timothy?'

The agents became very evasive. 'It's a matter of security, James. We can't divulge anything.'

James was feeling very uneasy about the agents. How could a few icebergs in the Southern Ocean have anything to do with the United Kingdom's security? Even he wasn't stupid enough to believe that. 'So what do you really want from me?' said James.

The agents looked straight ahead in silence. 'Your country needs you; it's a matter of national security. We can't answer too many more questions.'

'What a lot of hocus-pocus!' said James. 'I'm not cooperating until you tell me exactly what's going on and what I'm getting into.'

'Another drink?' replied one of the agents.

'Why not?' said James. 'The day can't get any worse.'

The drinks arrived and the conversation continued to move between James and the agents, as James attempted to find out what was going on and what his actual involvement would be.

'Come on guys, you need to tell me what's going on. I'm not going to get involved unless you level with me.'

James got to his feet to make his point. His eyes rolled back into his head and he slumped into the arms of the two waiting agents.

When Caroline got back to Timothy's suite, he was engaged in a very animated conversation.

'Listen, you sanctimonious son of a bitch, your orders come from the Prime Minister; you are the Environmental Secretary! You keep threatening me and my media in the UK and you can say goodbye to your career.' Timothy hung up the phone, looking very agitated. 'There you are Caroline – you would have loved that! They're threatening to kick us out of England, seize all our assets and shut us down.'

'Timothy, you need to be careful. Please talk to your lawyers, please do that now.'

Timothy got straight onto his lawyers; the repercussions of losing their UK assets were enormous. He spent the next hour talking to the lawyers and a QC was brought in to advise him, and the lawyers in particular, on British law.

The QC addressed Timothy after a long discussion of the facts. 'Timothy, we can only assume that the Environment Secretary was bluffing you, in an attempt to get you to back down and to hand over control to the UN Security Council. But you should prepare himself for anything to be thrown against you due to the very unusual circumstances and the high stakes, possibly even lethal force. Your security should be put on high alert. Effectively the minister's comments have made the state your lethal enemy. It's very unusual, but if the wording you gave me is correct, there is no other way to interpret it.

'I have never encountered a similar matter before in my legal career. I advise you to call on all your political allies in the House of Commons and House of Lords to question the government closely on what was going on and what pressures were being brought to bear on you and your team by the government.'

There was an air of extreme tension after the conversation, underscored by the QC's comment of the state being Timothy's 'lethal enemy'.

Timothy finished the telephone conversation and looked absolutely exhausted. He looked at Caroline, bewildered. How could his country turn on him when all he wanted to do was report the news? What was going on in the minds of these madmen?

Caroline put her arm around his shoulder. 'Are you okay?' she asked.

'No I'm not,' he replied. 'It looks as though the Prime Minister is treating me as an enemy of the state and that could mean they will do almost anything to stop us. I'm not sure what that means yet but it's very serious.'

Timothy called a meeting with Miles and Gary. He advised them of the serious nature of the threats from the UK government. Miles took charge of security, bringing in a corporate security team – experts in matters of kidnapping, assassination and ransom. Miles had used the team before and could guarantee their efficiency. The team was made up of ex-agents and military personnel who were experts in their area. The agency had a team in Perth and they were deployed within the hour to bolster security.

At noon Timothy took a call from his lawyers. The lead counsel had placed the call. 'Timothy, Phillip Cochrane here.'

'Yes Phillip, what's the news?'

'Timothy, the UN Security Council has failed to have the matter transferred to the International Court of Appeal and the court has determined the jurisdiction lies with the Australian Federal Court. Unfortunately, the UN's now pulling out all stops to convince the Australian Federal Court that the UN has jurisdiction over the matter. They appear reasonably confident of winning the appeal. For now it buys you more time with the ice samples.'

'That's the only positive development then. When is the appeal being heard?'

'Tomorrow at 10 am in Sydney, in the Federal Court.'

'Keep me informed on progress, Phillip.'

'I certainly will; keep safe.' With that Phillip hung up the phone.

At that moment it appeared that Timothy had no friends or allies in the global arena; he was under pressure and felt that he needed to find a substantial ally.

He was about to put the phone down when it rang. The next incoming call was from the American Embassy in Canberra. Timothy had met the American ambassador before.

'Timothy, Ambassador Dick Cleary. I believe you've been marginalised by your own government and you're coming under serious pressure from the Chinese and other governments. I'm able to offer protection and support in view of the serious nature of the pressure being brought to bear.'

Timothy did a quick analysis of the statement. 'So Ambassador, what does your government want in return?'

CHAPTER 35

'Full cooperation. Nothing more, nothing less. An open book.'

Timothy liked the frankness of the ambassador's reply. 'Do it Ambassador, you have my full cooperation. We keep all the rights to public disclosure.'

'Your liaison will be there in thirty minutes. Your backup will consist of a navy trimaran carrying Viper and Black Hawk helicopters for tactical support. We believe our boat will be able to keep up with yours.'

'Thank you, we'll stay in communication through your liaison officer.' Timothy felt satisfied. Between his 'mercenaries' and the American support team, they should be able to take on almost anybody.

It was rapidly approaching 3.00 pm. A helicopter was waiting at Trinity College to transport Caroline and Timothy to the lab for an update with the doctors and research teams.

There was tension in the team – Timothy and Caroline were fitted out with flak jackets and helmets and there were six heavily armed security people accompanying them. They were assured that the helicopter would be shadowed by a fully armed Black Hawk helicopter, launching from an American vessel currently stationed off-shore.

At 2.45 pm, Caroline and Timothy were driven down Hay Street and onto Trinity Avenue, accompanied by their armed security personnel.

'This way please,' directed the security chief. As they reached the helicopter he cautioned them. 'Watch the step.'

They stepped out of the van and crouched over against the draft of the helicopter blades.

The first indication of a problem came when a guard screamed, 'Bogey on the roof!'

Timothy was knocked off his feet by a solid blow to his back.

There were two eruptions in the ground as bullets slammed into it.

'Tight formation,' screamed the security chief.

Immediately there were guards pressing against Timothy and Caroline. Caroline was crouched over Timothy who was on the deck struggling for air.

'Get them in the van now,' came the screamed order. Caroline was blanketed by security men who quickly moved her back to the van.

In the meantime, a firefight had erupted between the Black Hawk helicopter and apparent snipers on an adjacent WACA rooftop. The report came in that the snipers were down and the Black Hawk was going in to secure the site.

Surveillance cameras fitted overnight by the security team had captured the whole scene. One of the guards was down on the ground, lying motionless, and he was being attended to by a colleague. The colleague waved for assistance and two other guards rushed out to assist him.

In the meantime, Timothy and Caroline had been secured in the van. Timothy was treated for his injuries; the blow to the vest had left him with a fist-sized bruise from the impact of the guard protecting him.

Fifteen minutes later, a report came in that the area was now secure.

'All clear,' the security chief announced. 'Are you ready for another attempt to leave?'

Both Timothy and Caroline answered in unison. 'Let's go.'

They were escorted to the helicopter and managed to depart without further incident.

CHAPTER 35

Twenty minutes later, they were at the secure lab facility with Dr Perry and Dr Mellows. The incident at Trinity College was not mentioned.

The doctors were very excited and able to report in detail on the ice structure. Timothy interrupted. 'Can a copy of the report go to the studio, please? And let's get them on the line so we don't have to explain the report to them.'

'I'll do that straight away,' Dr Mellows replied.

A few minutes later, with the studio on the line, Dr Perry commenced her report. She looked very animated as she stood before them; her excitement was obvious.

'Ladies and gentlemen, the amazing fact is the ice sheet is made up of fresh glacier melt water; origin unknown. The formation was extremely unusual – it resembled ice that would normally form on flowing rivers or streams. The most confusing thing about the ice is that the only source of freshwater ice near where the incidents had occurred, was the Kerguelen Islands, which were 1500 kilometres away. The only other possibilities were Heard Island or Antarctica, both of which were in excess of 2000 kilometres away. An enormous amount of additional research is required back in the Southern Ocean to determine how and where the objects were formed.'

The cameras had been rolling for the duration of the report. 'What additional equipment would you require to go back to the Southern Ocean to continue their research?' Timothy asked the doctors. 'Could I have a list of equipment and what kind of team would be required, please?'

Dr Perry beamed. 'You will have the list within the hour.'

The Trinity College incident had made Timothy more determined to get to the bottom of this than before. Nothing would stop him now.

The next stop for Timothy and Caroline was the production

studio. As they got to the studio, Timothy took a call from the US military. He stepped into a separate room to take the call. Timothy listened intently to the report given to him by the warship commander.

'Timothy, three bodies were recovered from the rooftop opposite your hotel. Two of them were MI6 agents known to us and the third was a civilian who was still gagged and tied when recovered.'

'Do you have an identity on the civilian?' asked Timothy.

'James White. I think you might know him from the ketch race management team. He had been executed – shot in the back of the head. It looked like the MI6 guys used a handgun on him at point blank range.'

Timothy was silent for a long time. 'Captain, were the British aware that we had been given the support of the US?'

'No. The outcome of this engagement could have been very different if they had known.'

It was now obvious to Timothy that the MI6 agents had been caught off-guard by the helicopter support. 'You said you removed the bodies. How much trouble are you going to be in, if I report this today?'

'None at all; the bodies are all where they're supposed to be and the local police are in charge.'

'Brilliant, then we'll get back to reporting. We appreciate your continued support, Captain. We should be leaving here in approximately three hours and we will appreciate your backup.'

Timothy rested back in his chair for a moment. Caroline had broken up with James that morning. How could MI6 have been over the situation so quickly? It would be interesting to find out how James became involved and whether MI6 had actually led him to his death. Timothy didn't have time to think about it but felt he should follow up it in the future. His mind returned to the present – he had a lot of issues to juggle. How would Caroline react to the death of James? Would she be able to deliver the news?

There's only one way to find out, thought Timothy. *Let's go deliver the news.*

Timothy burst into the studio, immediately walked up to Caroline and put his arm around her shoulder. He motioned her to a chair. Her brilliant blue eyes were wide open.

'Caroline, we need to go over all of this. I need to know fairly quickly if you can deliver the news this afternoon.'

Timothy motioned Miles and Gary over.

'Okay, a quick update about what happened this morning with the assassination attempt. The US Navy has been able to determine that the assassins were two MI6 agents. They had a bound and gagged civilian with them as a fall guy. They'd planned to execute him to make it look as though they had come to our aid and gotten rid of the assassin. Their plans were upset by the helicopter and our security. We have all this on CCTV footage including the MI6 agents trying to unbind the civilian after they had executed him. While they were trying to do that, they were themselves killed by fire from the military helicopter. I'm sorry Caroline, but the civilian was James White. MI6 probably lured him out here to use as a fall guy in an assassination attempt, to make it look as though a jilted lover had killed me.'

Timothy watched Caroline carefully. She was shaking and breathing deeply, then slowly composed herself. 'Those bastards, let's get on with this and bring them down!'

Her eyes were teary she was on her feet. Caroline felt her head begin to spin; she steadied herself against the door. She was in a blind rage but she couldn't afford to lose control now. She turned to Timothy. 'Hold me while I walk please,' she said.

Timothy obliged with an arm around the shoulder; they walked into the studio. Inside the writers were assembled. Caroline went off to make up and wardrobe and the rest of the team settled down to thrash out the script.

CHAPTER 36

'Headline suggestions please!' called Timothy.
The suggestions came thick and fast. 'UK government orders assassination of Timothy Wiley'. 'UK government fabricates love triangle jealousy to kill Timothy Wiley'. 'UK government prepared to kill innocent national as decoy'. 'Are the UK government and the UN Security Council cooperating in assassination attempt?' 'Scientists baffled by Southern Ocean freshwater ice sheets'.

There was an enormous amount of material available for the news broadcast. The rooftop footage of the assassination attempt was gruesome but had been made available by Timothy's security team. The execution of James was graphic and chilling; not since the Rainbow Warrior incident in New Zealand had a European power been put in such a precarious position. Heads were bound to roll in London following the broadcast. By now the Prime Minister should be aware that his two MI6 agents were dead but the rest of the details were under wraps.

Timothy addressed the room. 'Ninety minutes team; let's get it together.'

For the next ninety minutes, the room buzzed like a well-oiled machine. At 4.45 pm Caroline was in the news chair and the countdown began. A quick check of the local news channels had Miles reporting that there had been no report from the police about the MI6 agents being killed.

'Timothy, can we report those shootings even though the police haven't issued a statement on that yet?'

'It's news, Miles – first in, best dressed. They can explain the delay after the news.'

The ten second countdown commenced. Caroline was looking feisty; the monitoring screens all filled with her face. The broadcast commenced with the accusation of complicity between the UK government and the UN Security Council to assassinate Timothy Wiley and gain control of events in the Southern Ocean. The release progressed to the rooftop shoot-out between the MI6 agents and the US Navy helicopter. The sickening scene of the agents shooting a bound and gagged James White was on the screen for thirty seconds, the caption calling for the resignation of the Prime Mister of the United Kingdom and the UN Secretary-General. The story built on the fact that James had previously been in a relationship with Caroline who was now involved with Timothy, and how the MI6 agents were hoping to make the incident look like a love triangle jealousy killing. At that point Caroline broke down momentarily, recovered and glared back into the camera.

'What kind of heartless bastards are you?' she sobbed. 'How is freshwater ice sheets destroying ketches, 1500 kilometres from the nearest source of freshwater, a matter of global security?'

Caroline took a moment, wiped the tears from her eyes and regained her composure to take the story back to Dr Perry and Dr Mellows.

The story progressed into the unique nature of the ice and the need for urgent additional research, to find out how it came to be where it was. The news broadcast included a statement from Timothy Wiley, vowing to find out how and why the ice was

CHAPTER 36

forming and creating such a hazard in the Southern Ocean. He stated that regardless of the blocking techniques and attempted assassinations, the *Spirit of the Southern Ocean* would set sail the following day to look for the cause of the ice sheets. The vessel would be fitted out overnight with additional research equipment to enable the scientists to do the necessary research to discover the source of the ice sheets.

The broadcast ended with a challenge from Caroline. 'To the British Government, you attempted to kill us today for exercising our right to freedom of speech. You failed as the world watched. The eyes of the world are on you now.'

The broadcast team erupted into applause for another sensational delivery by Caroline. The celebrations were getting into full swing when Timothy was motioned towards a ringing telephone. He took the call in a sound booth. It was the captain of the US naval vessel, indicating that he had been authorised to escort and protect the *Spirit of the Southern Ocean* on its voyage into the Southern Ocean. The captain indicated that he was in communication with the captain of the *Spirit of the Southern Ocean* and they would coordinate departure times to provide support and security. Timothy went back to the celebrating team and announced the American commitment of support. The announcement was met with wild excitement as the team sensed imminent victory.

As the team calmed down, Miles advised them that they were all required on board the *Spirit of the Southern Ocean* the following morning at 8, to ensure the broadcasts continued for the next two weeks. He advised them to go home and pack a lot of warm clothes as the temperature in the Southern Ocean could be as low as -50 degrees Celsius. Timothy took Miles, Gary and Caroline into a separate meeting.

'Miles, I'd like you and Gary to prepare an open communiqué

to send to the UN Security Council and the Secretary-General, offering them the opportunity to send ten scientists and their equipment on the venture into the Southern Ocean to investigate the source of the ice sheets.

'Acceptance of the offer is provisional on all pending legal action being terminated. In light of the events of today, it is highly unlikely that any legal action attempted by the UN or the UK will be successful. The scientists are welcome, but all communication rights will belong to Wiley International. That is our only condition. The offer is only valid until the *Spirit of the Southern Ocean* is out of helicopter reach of Perth.'

One hour later Timothy, Caroline, Miles and Gary were seated at Timothy's bar in his hotel room. The barman was back and there was food on table. They started with a glass of champagne.

Timothy proposed a toast. 'To Caroline's amazing delivery!'

Glasses clinked.

'Thank you, gentlemen,' said Caroline graciously. 'It would be impossible without your amazing teams.'

'Hear, hear!' said Timothy. 'To an amazing team effort.'

The discussion then turned to the preparations for their departure the following day at 10.00 am. Security had been beefed up enormously. The production team was required to arrive at 8.00 am and go through full security checks before being allowed on board. The scientific teams would be placed in quarantine for twenty-four hours to allow for security and equipment checks. No-one other than the contract security team or the ship's security team would be allowed to have any weapons on board. They would be shadowed at all times by a US Navy ship for additional security. Gary and Miles were happy to have the additional security for the venture.

The US ambassador interrupted the evening at around 8.00 pm. It appeared that the Chinese were unhappy about the impending departure. The Chinese had requested that the Security Council authorise them to prevent that departure. An emergency meeting of the Security Council was being convened.

They all looked at one another in disbelief. What common interest could be driving the Chinese and English governments? The conversation continued on this intriguing topic until 10.00 pm, when a phone message came in for the US ambassador, who was pleased to announce that the US had vetoed the attempted resolution preventing the *Spirit of the Southern Ocean* from leaving the following morning. The matter did not even get to a vote. There were cheers in the room and a round of champagne.

It had been approximately four hours since Caroline's broadcast to the world. In the background, there had been intense activity. The local police were working with the US Navy and the private security provider in investigating the deaths of the three men killed in the firefight. The security guard injured in the firefight was in a critical but stable condition in the local hospital. He had taken a bullet for Timothy by pushing him down when the alert was raised.

The UK government had been in damage control since the broadcast. The Defence and Environment Secretaries of State had been locked in discussions with the Prime Minister. There had been a steady stream of lawyers, ministers and politicians in and out of 10 Downing Street since the broadcast. Even though there was a growing media pack outside, there had been no media release in relation to the events in Australia earlier that day.

At 11.15, Timothy received a call from Miles. 'Turn on CNN. I'll talk to you later.'

'No, both of you come up now,' replied Timothy.

On CNN the UN Secretary-General was making an announcement. The UN was accepting an offer made by Timothy Wiley for UN sponsored scientists to accompany him on his expedition into the Southern Ocean to find the source of the ice. As a result, all legal action in relation to the ice samples had been terminated. Going forward, the UN would cooperate with Wiley International in discovering the source of the ice. The Secretary-General distanced himself from the action of a Security Council member in the United Kingdom, whose actions, he stated, 'Had not been sanctioned by the UN.'

The Secretary-General took the opportunity to commend the United States and China for positioning geo-stationary satellites over the Southern Ocean to provide support for what had now become a global expedition. The satellites would provide continuous real-time detection capabilities for finding the ice. The champagne flowed as Timothy, Gary, Caroline and Miles congratulated one another.

'We'll probably only realise in a week or two that this was one of the biggest moments in our lives!' said Timothy.

Their attention was once again drawn to the television screen. This time, it was the media pack at 10 Downing Street. The Prime Minister had just announced that he had asked for and received the resignations of the Defence and Environment Secretaries of State over the action they had taken against Wiley International in Australia. The Prime Minister went on to announce that based on legal advice, all action against Wiley International had been terminated. The Prime Minister terminated the news conference abruptly. He was on his way to face a very angry parliament. The reporters covering the announcement immediately began speculation about the ability of the Prime Minister to survive.

CHAPTER 36

'Absolutely astounding!' shouted Timothy, as he took Caroline on a quick dance around his suite. 'There's no stopping us now – we own this story!'

Miles began to smile. 'Since we began this venture, Timothy, the company has trebled in value. By the end of the expedition, it may treble again.'

'Miles, take a note I need to spend more time out of the office; that's how I add shareholder value,' joked Timothy. 'I would normally suggest we go out and paint the town red, but unfortunately our security level is still very high!'

Miles and Gary thanked Timothy and once again headed off to their rooms.

Caroline snuggled up to Timothy on the sofa. They sat quietly for a while before calling it a night, neither wanting to detract from the enormity of what they just witnessed on CNN.

CHAPTER 37

With the acceptance of the offer of scientific inclusion by the UN, support statements were given by various governments for the expedition.

Miles met Timothy and Caroline at breakfast where they discussed a series of emails.

'Congratulations, that's a formal apology from the Prime Minister of the United Kingdom. Apparently he had taken a battering in the House of Commons; there was even talk of a vote of no confidence. The Secretary-General of the UN has also sent his formal acceptance of your inclusion offer and a formal cessation of all legal activity.

'You may want to read this one privately – it's a bit sensitive.' Miles winked at Timothy then handed him a printout of the email.

Timothy stood up and walked to the window as he read the email.

The board of Wiley International had sent their congratulations and were suggesting that Caroline be offered a seat on the board to provide day-to-day journalistic insight. Timothy decided to keep that one until a little later. He had to stop his imagination as to what he could do with such an offer.

Timothy came back to the table and sat down beside Caroline; the email was secure in his jacket pocket. 'Back to the emails,' he announced.

CHAPTER 37

Miles read out the next email. 'The police had decided that Timothy and Caroline would not need to be interviewed about the deaths of the MI6 agents and James White. They seemed satisfied to accept the reports of the US Navy and the security team.'

'That's a relief,' exclaimed Caroline.

'Security at the docks had its hands full processing the large scientific contingent. At this stage, it looks as though departure will be at least two hours late.'

After breakfast, they headed back to their rooms to pack.

There was a huge media throng on the docks hoping to catch a glimpse of Timothy and Caroline and to engage them in discussion. To avoid the media and maintain security, Timothy, his team and the doctors were flown in by helicopter with a Viper escort. They arrived uneventfully on the deck of the *Spirit of the Southern Ocean* at 11.30 am and were greeted by Captain Delaney and his security team at the helideck.

'Welcome back Timothy, Caroline. Wonderful to see you again.'

The captain was momentarily captivated by the transformation in Caroline. When she left his ship, she was a little dishevelled, wore no makeup and looked very strained and tired. Now she was radiant, brimming with confidence and taking in her environment, flashing that gorgeous smile. Timothy was a lucky man.

He was brought back to the helipad abruptly as a seaman nudged him. 'You okay, Captain?'

The captain didn't respond and tried to hide his embarrassment with a quick update of the security arrangements. 'Timothy, your offices and expanded media centre has been swept for bugs. We now have the latest technology so we will continue to sweep the rooms daily. All points of entry into your offices have been secured and the bridge and communications room are also secured. Extra security has been posted to the offices to prevent unauthorised entry.'

'Thanks Captain; we will head straight there and get to work. I'll get Miles to come to the bridge with details of the expedition as soon as he settles in. By the way, good job on the security upgrade ... I hope we don't need it.'

With that, Timothy and his team headed to their offices.

The doctors had prepared a presentation on the overview of the issues being considered in solving the ice sheet origin. Dr Perry delivered the presentation late in the afternoon.

'I'll try to keep this fairly pedestrian so that it is not drowned in technical jargon. It looks as though the Southern Ocean weather is being distorted by several known effects, including the ozone hole. These effects are potentially influencing the growing ice sheet cover in winter in the southern hemisphere. Then we have the impact of high levels of fresh water flowing into the oceans in the northern and southern hemispheres from melting freshwater ice in the glaciers and ice shelves in summer. On the recent historical side, the weather influence in Australian and New Zealand during the preceding twelve months had been of massive cooling. On one hand, there was scientific evidence that the temperature of the world was increasing, while the winters are getting colder. The scientific community had no less than six other potential influences to investigate, as part of the search for the reason why the ice event had occurred.

'The scientists on board have a challenge in front of them. We have a source of freshwater ice from Antarctica and/or the Southern Ocean islands. What we are working on, is how we get ice 1500 kilometres away from the potential source.'

Dr Perry took questions and then headed back to the lab.

CHAPTER 37

It was 12.30 pm when the *Spirit of the Southern Ocean* sailed out of Fremantle, heading to a point 2500 kilometres south-west, where the sailboats had first encountered the ice sheets. The captain gave the passengers an arrival time of between sixty and seventy hours from departure.

The ocean where they were headed had swells of 140 metres and waves of 9 metres, a wind chill temperature of -60 degrees Celsius and winds up to 75 kilometres an hour. One advantage the scientific team had this time, was the overhead geo-stationary satellite hired by Timothy. Until actual readings were taken of the fresh ice sheets, it would not be known whether the sensors would be sensitive enough to track the ice sheets back to their source. The scientists were armed with an arsenal of detection equipment, including high-speed underwater robotic probes, thermal imaging cameras, ultrasensitive sonar and an array of classified sensors. The additional twenty-five scientists had been supplemented by ten military personnel from the US Navy. Their purpose and equipment was all classified and their findings and research was to be supplied to Wiley International before being released to the public and the scientific community.

The Chinese had requested the inclusion of two scientists who would arrive as the *Spirit of the Southern Ocean* approached the six hour delivery limit out of Fremantle. To avoid complications, Captain Delaney had insisted that the helicopter remain on board until the Chinese delegation cleared security.

A thorough risk analysis was conducted prior to the Chinese helicopter's arrival. The stern safety nets had been removed from the upper deck and foam cannons put in place to provide fire control if required. The final element of the risk strategy was to have a large forklift available at the edge of the helicopter deck.

The ship was put on high alert as the Chinese helicopter approached. The helicopter was to remain under total video surveillance while on deck, and the transport team was to be monitored every moment they were on board. The transfer of the Chinese crew on board and all the subsequent checks proved to be uneventful, as no firearms or bugs were found in the equipment. The crew did not deviate from the directions given and there was no hint that they had transferred anything while boarding.

At 7.00 pm, an hour after the crew had landed, the captain manoeuvred the vessel back to the rendezvous point and the helicopter lifted for departure.

Seconds after take-off, the Chinese helicopter crashed back onto the deck. It remained upright, smoke billowing from its engine exhausts. The crew rushed from the helicopter and were quickly ushered into a holding area. Within seconds the response team was mobilised.

The flight deck controller commenced his defensive drill. 'Foam blanket now, get the forklift rolling and get that heli off my deck. Do it now!' he screamed into his headset.

The helicopter deck was awash with foam cannons, their jets concentrated on the helicopter. The large forklift roared into life – it made contact with the helicopter on the rotor line and was able to easily push it to the edge of the helicopter deck. The forklift driver used a safety line connected to a deck crane to assist him in pulling free, as the forklift and the helicopter went over the edge of the deck. In the meantime, the vessel had accelerated to full speed. The captain's intent was to put as much distance between his vessel and the sinking helicopter as possible in the shortest time.

The team on the deck didn't have long to wait. An enormous explosion occurred less than 300 metres off their stern, sending water several hundred metres into the air.

As sound of the explosion dispersed, fresh commands here heard. 'Arrest the helicopter crew now.'

CHAPTER 37

A few minutes later, Captain Delaney appeared on the helicopter deck; with him were two armed guards carrying semi-automatic weapons. The captain addressed the Chinese crew and the scientists. 'Do any of you speak English?'

The helicopter's pilot stepped forward. 'I speak English.'

Captain Delaney addressed the pilot. 'I'm hereby arresting the four of you in relation to the explosion that just occurred. Based on the available information, it is my current belief that it was either your intent or the intent of others to detonate that explosion on my helicopter deck. There is a helicopter inbound that will transfer you to the brig on an American naval vessel.

'Sergeant, handcuff the prisoners and hold them on the flight deck until their transport arrives.'

In the background, Timothy's camera crew had been capturing all the action.

Captain Delaney then headed back to the bridge, where Timothy met him. 'I'm up to date, Captain.'

'Thanks Timothy, I have to avert a potential international crisis. Radio, get the Chinese vessel on the phone please.' When he confirmed a radio link he spoke directly to the Chinese ship. 'This is Captain Delaney of the *Spirit of the Southern Ocean*. I'm calling to inform you that your helicopter has been lost. From our observations, we believe the helicopter had been used in an attempt to sabotage our vessel. As a result, the helicopter's crew and the scientists they transported have been arrested and will be held subject to a trial to be held in Perth at a later date.

'Under no circumstances should you attempt to approach our vessel. Any such attempt will be taken as a sign of aggression and will be repelled. Is that clear?'

Captain Delaney heard commentary going on in the background for some time before he received an answer.

'I do not believe you have any legal right to detain my people,' said the Chinese captain. 'I'm sending a helicopter over to retrieve them. I must insist on this course of action.'

At that point, the Chinese cut off the radio communication.

Captain Delaney then ordered a link to the American support vessel and spoke directly to their captain. 'Captain, I believe we have incoming hostiles from the Chinese. They're insisting on retrieving their personnel that we have arrested on suspicion of attempted sabotage. Can you provide support please?'

'Sorry to hear that *Spirit*. Rest assured, help is on the way – one Black Hawk transport inbound for prisoners, two Viper assault helicopters being dispatched for security and support. Intend to leave one Viper on your helipad as a visual deterrent for the time being.'

'Thank you, Captain. We look forward to having your boys on board.' Captain Delaney turned to Timothy. 'Things are going to get tense around here.'

A report come through from the radar operator. 'Sir, we have two radar contacts, one each from the direction of the Chinese and the Americans.'

Captain Delaney picked up his binoculars and searched the horizon; he began talking to himself. 'I can see them both, I would say we can expect the Americans here first.'

'Sir, we have two more radar contacts coming from the direction of the Americans; they're moving much faster than the first two contacts.'

'Incoming message from the Americans, Sir.'

'*Spirit of the Southern Ocean*, the Royal Australian Air Force has scrambled two fighter jets; expected in your location within ten minutes.'

'Thanks Captain, we can see one bogey and your boys inbound.'

There was absolute silence on the bridge as they watched the incoming helicopters.

CHAPTER 37

The Viper helicopters arrived first. Captain Delaney had stopped the *Spirit of the Southern Ocean* and the helicopters hovered on either side of her bridge facing the stern. Two minutes later, the Black Hawk touched down on the deck. The prisoners were transferred unceremoniously and the helicopter lifted off the deck as the Chinese Harbin Z-20 approached from the stern.

A Viper positioned itself between the stern and the incoming helicopter as the Black Hawk settled back onto the deck. The Harbin appeared to have rocket launchers and machine guns fitted.

'Put the helicopter frequency on the speakers, operator,' commanded Captain Delaney. When that was done he boomed into the receiver. 'You are within the Australian economic zone and the people being transferred are suspected of a terrorist activity. Turn your craft around and return to your vessel.'

Two helicopters were getting so close to one another that the pilots were having trouble with flight stability. The tense stand-off continued just off their stern, then the second Viper issued a tense warning. 'Chinese Harbin helicopter, move away from the *Spirit of the Southern Ocean* or I will fire.' The Harbin didn't move. The pilot issued a further warning. 'Chinese Harbin helicopter, I have missile lock. You have five seconds to stand down.'

Several of the observers on the bridge crouched down below the window line. There was a deathly silence on the bridge.

The pilot of the second Viper gingerly moved his thumb to his missile controls and flipped the protective cover. All the time whispering to himself, 'Step-down, step-down, step-down, step-down …'

The Chinese pilot was staring straight ahead, his missile lock warning screaming. He held his ground.

The Viper pilot directly in front of him armed and locked his missiles. 'Chinese Harbin helicopter, we both now have missile lock. We will shoot you down; stand down now.'

Back on the deck, one of the camera crew had crept out to the very edge of the deck. He was able to zoom his camera in on the face of the Chinese pilot, catching the agonising tension of the moment.

The pilot caught sight of the cameraman; this was not what he expected. To be the first to fire now would condemn himself and China. He contacted the naval vessel. 'Sir, we are on live camera. Do I proceed?'

His captain showed no hesitation in his immediate reply. 'Break off immediately; that is a Wiley camera – it'll go worldwide.'

Just before the pilot committed himself to move, two Australian fighter jets roared by several hundred metres above his head in tight formation. He lowered his eyes, slowly waved his left hand at the Viper pilots and began what was at first a slow climb and then a very rapid exit from the scene.

The fighter jets reappeared and escorted him back over the horizon.

'Yes, yes, yes.' chanted the cameraman down on the deck, with a punch in the air and a loud scream.

One of the Viper pilot's voices was the first to be heard. 'Okay boys, party's over; let's get these prisoners back over to the ship.'

As the Black Hawk cleared the deck, a Viper landed facing the stern. The deck crew secured the helicopter and escorted the pilot below deck to resounding cheers and a lot of back slapping.

On the bridge there was total relief after the stand-down of the Chinese pilot. 'That was a close one,' said Captain Delaney.

Timothy was beaming. 'Captain, you won't believe it but it's all on camera for posterity. The take-off, the massive explosion, even of the Chinese pilot's face during the showdown.'

CHAPTER 37

'That will be handy ... can I have a copy of the footage please? I'll send it through with a report to the government. There will be an official complaint to the Chinese and I believe we should be able to get them to withdraw their Navy from the area.'

'The pleasure will be all mine.'

Back on the Chinese catamaran, the strategists were having a heated discussion about the situation. Chen Way, a senior tactical official, was pacing the floor as his analysts scrambled for a solution to the requests coming from Beijing.

'There must be a way to cut communications to and from the Wiley catamaran,' he growled. 'We must be able to sink the vessel without the American Navy or the Australian fighter aircraft stopping us.'

One of the junior analysts stood. She was very animated. 'With respect Sir, your vessel is a prototype with as yet untested stealth technology. If you were to deploy that technology with the cover of darkness, we may be able to get close enough to the other vessel to destroy it. It would be possible to use one of our attack helicopters as a drone to deliver an air blast bomb. It would be a high-risk manoeuvre, Sir – we would approach the bow of the other vessel at full speed, the helicopter cloaked by our vessel. You turn at the last moment and launch the helicopter. It would only be visible for a few seconds before destroying the vessel.'

The analyst sat at her desk, head bowed.

Chen Way paced the room two more times. 'Make it happen. There will be suspicion but we should have time to escape if our technology works.'

For the next four hours there was frantic activity on the Chinese vessel as they prepared the stealth technology, the helicopter and the air blast device. The bomb was the same device that failed to destroy the *Spirit of the Southern Ocean* earlier in the day; the team was concerned that they had no details of why that attempt failed.

At just after 9.00 pm, all the work for the stealth transformation was complete. The captain sent one of his helicopters out to check the stealth technology. Results were very pleasing to the captain; head-on, his vessel was invisible, and side on from the air, it was difficult for the helicopter to detect amongst the waves. It was only from directly above that he had some vulnerability at low altitude. The captain felt confident that unless he was unlucky and spotted by an aircraft flying under a kilometre directly overhead, he could accomplish his task and escape.

By 10:30 pm, the Chinese vessel was ahead of the *Spirit of the Southern Ocean*.

'Full speed ahead,' ordered the captain.

In the control room of the *Spirit of the Southern Ocean*, the radar operator noticed a distinct blip 4 kilometres out, then another a few seconds later.

The Chinese captain was concerned; at this speed, his vessel was breaching the waves, possibly causing a radar target from his underside. He was sixty seconds into his manoeuvre when he ordered a speed reduction to stop the breaching. 'All ahead half speed.'

By now the *Spirit of the Southern Ocean* radar operator had Captain Delaney and several other crewmembers crowded around his screen.

'Sir, the only other time I've seen this type of contact has been during manoeuvres that involve stealth technology. It's consistent yet inconsistent, if you know what I mean.'

'Sergeant-at-arms, get the Viper in the air,' ordered Captain Delaney. 'Radio, get me the Americans.' As soon as the radio link was made, Delaney wasted no time. 'Captain, permission to deploy your Viper on my deck; we have an inbound stealth bogie at under 4 kilometres. We are commencing communication attempts, but given the location, we can only assume the bogie is hostile. Can you also deploy additional aircraft for support?'

'Help is on the way Captain; please reduce your speed to half.'

'Reduced speed to half. The bogie is incoming, due southwest. No response to our communications; again, we can only assume the bogie is hostile.'

On the Chinese vessel, there was a burst of activity in response to their exposure. 'Captain, the Wiley vessel has reduced speed to half.'

'Captain, we're being hailed; they must have seen us coming.'

'Helm, keep us between the waves,' ordered the Chinese captain. 'Run with and between the waves – at 8 metres they should provide us with good coverage.'

Back on the *Spirit of the Southern Ocean*, the radar operator cursed. 'Captain, we've lost all radar contacted at around 3 kilometres.'

'Advise the Americans, include the comment that they either stopped, or are moving with the waves to reduce their profile.'

The second officer approached the captain. 'Captain, we have some pretty intense floodlights below including a couple of 11 kilowatt night sun spotlights. They're good for at least two or three kilometres.'

Captain Delaney was showing severe strain; he gave his second officer a brief smile and a tap on the shoulder. 'Brilliant son, just do it.'

Ten minutes later, the *Spirit of the Southern Ocean* was steaming forward in a floodlit circle of a kilometre and spotlights were beaming out to 2 to 3 kilometres.

'Pretty as a picture,' came the comment from one of the Viper pilots. 'That's a fantastic idea; gives us a great defence perimeter.'

The radar operator reported. 'One radar contact, a kilometre south of the previous contact. They're running with the waves, Sir.'

'Advise the Americans.'

All activity on the *Spirit of the Southern Ocean* focused on the bridge and radio room. Captain Delaney was surround by his officers on the bridge. 'Any ideas on what they will try and throw at us next?' he said.

His second officer was the first to respond. 'Sir, I believe they're going to launch a helicopter or drone to come at us. The pitch and height of these waves is almost enough to hide one.'

'The American ship is fading Sir,' came a new report from the radar room. 'It's getting close but its signal is getting weaker.'

Captain Delaney shook his head. 'Everybody has stealth technology except us. Relay our concern to the Americans, and also provide them with trajectories for launch sites for helicopters or drones by the bogie.'

A line of flares erupted to the south of the *Spirit of the Southern Ocean*.

The radio channel monitoring the American aircraft burst into life. 'We have a visual of the bogie. It is carrying no distinctive markings but it has what appears to be a Chinese assault helicopter on the pad. Baby, she is one mean looking stealth machine. In excess of 150 feet and staying well down in the waves. What are your orders? Hold that Captain, the helicopter's firing up. I believe we can now assume we have a hostile situation; no response to hailing on any frequency – do I go hot?'

There was no hesitation from the American captain. 'Go hot, son. God be with you.'

Within seconds, the Viper was in position, the target

acquired and rockets launched. What happened next, no-one had predicted. The Viper was no more than 500 metres away when it had fired at the Chinese helicopter which had been 20 metres above the deck height and at least 30 metres behind the vessel when the rockets hit it. The ensuing fireball that erupted engulfed everything within 250 metres. The Viper fell from the sky like a stone, totally disabled by the shockwave.

The *Spirit of the Southern Ocean* was 5 kilometres away when the bomb detonated. The explosion lit the control room with an intensity that exceeded daylight. 'My God, what was that?'

The captain of the American vessel came on the radio. '*Spirit of the Southern Ocean*, is everything okay over there?'

'All okay here Captain; how are your boys?'

'We have one Viper down; looks as though he was caught in the blast radius. That was one nasty bomb – I suspect it was the same device that detonated when you pushed the other chopper over the side. Looks like an air detonation device. One of the nastiest pieces in anybody's arsenal.' The American captain paused for a moment. 'My boys have changed channels – looks as though there's nothing left of the other vessel. Our Viper is down missing without a trace.'

'We're sorry for your loss Captain but we certainly appreciate your ongoing support.'

That night the dining room was crowded. Captain Delaney welcomed the sixty guests on board the vessel, made up of scientists, Timothy's media production personnel and his management team. The dinner was a jovial affair, with many of the scientists knowing one another from research papers or conferences. None of them had been made aware of the events of that evening and why the captain had been called away just after 10 pm.

The bar was busy until the early hours of the morning. Scientific arguments, assumptions and propositions were beginning to gel. Dr Mellows was expecting to have a brainstorming session with the scientists at midday the following day.

The next day at 4.00 pm, the scientists began to disband from the brainstorming. They were polarised in their beliefs and they were not prepared to look at alternative arguments. Dr Perry decided to leave the academic discussion until they had physical proof with which to challenge the various arguments.

In the meantime, Timothy, Caroline and the production crew continued the broadcasts, tracing over the developments with the Chinese, UK and UN, along with all the dramas in Perth. The team now had a social media crew that was busily adding content to YouTube and Twitter. The YouTube hits on the breaching ice sheets and the rooftop firefight in Perth were in the millions daily.

After the first brainstorming session, the tension on board began to grow within the scientific community. They were broken up into small groups, congregating at tables at different ends of the dining room. They were still forty hours from the target zone and tensions were running high. The American team was keeping very much to themselves and the other teams were suspicious of them as they didn't recognise any of them as being part of the climate change scientific community. They suspected them to be military liaison officers – spooks or spies not able to contribute very much to the overall scientific effort.

In the meantime, Dr Perry and Dr Mellows were the recipients of a constant barrage of scientific information from the global scientific community, with various theories about the cause of the ice sheets occurring in the Southern Ocean. Timothy and his team continued to send updates every twelve hours to a public audience that was now approaching two and a half billion viewers. The attempted murder of Timothy had caused a spike in viewers of almost half a billion people. The sinking of the mysterious stealth vessel and the horrific explosion that killed the pilot of the Viper helicopter was now overshadowing the earlier broadcasts, showing the tense stand-off between the Chinese and American helicopters. No nation was prepared to take responsibility for the stealth vessel and explosion – however, the suspicion that they were Chinese was almost irrefutable.

CHAPTER 38

Timothy took Caroline, Miles and Gary out of the process of preparing the broadcasts and got them to take a little time off. That evening, Timothy had planned for Caroline and himself to dine alone in his suite after drinks at the bar. It had been several days since they had spent much time alone together and in the meantime, Caroline had become a globally recognised news presenter, famous in her own right.

Timothy was feeling a little wicked, buoyed by the success with the UN and the massive overall audience of the venture. He felt on top of the world. He had ordered his broker to sell down his holding in the company by ten per cent, only to find bulk buyers waiting for twenty per cent or more. A deal was struck, selling Timothy's shares at a fifteen per cent premium to the market. Timothy now found himself financially secure, in charge of the biggest event in the media world, and with a gorgeous woman by his side. He now wanted the evening to slow down a little so he could enjoy these moments to the fullest.

Caroline entered the dining room looking absolutely radiant. Her short black dress accentuated her alabaster skin. The deep neckline of the dress drew all eyes down to her sensational long legs and elegant black stilettos. The dress was a work of sensual art, revealing enough to capture interest, then defying imagination as to how it remained in place. Timothy was spellbound.

Caroline appeared to be playing the game tonight as well – it should be a fun evening. Maybe they should skip the drinks. He remained motionless as Caroline walked towards him, standing at the last moment.

'Good evening Caroline, I've arranged for a private dinner in my stateroom. We have a lot to discuss tonight.'

Caroline look surprised, but did not resist as he took her by the arm and led her from the room.

Timothy's stateroom had a beautifully decorated dining table with candles and a dinner set for two. Caroline stood just out of reach, surveying the room. To her the room gave nothing away about the intention of the discussion they were going to have.

'What can I get you to drink?'

Timothy hadn't taken his eyes off Caroline for a moment. She sensed that the chase was on; her eyes flashed and she gave him a nonchalant look. 'I thought we might have a few drinks at the public bar and see what's going on.'

Timothy's excitement level rose rapidly. Caroline brushed her dress against him and he groaned as she moved just out of reach.

'Come on Timothy, let's go get that drink!'

Timothy felt as though he had been caught out. The last thing he felt like doing was sharing his time with Caroline with anyone else. How was he going to turn the situation around and still stay in the game?

'Could wreck a special night,' said Timothy. 'The things I have to say to you will just have to wait. I might even forget what I was going to say. That would be such a shame.'

Timothy watched Caroline carefully. He certainly had her attention; her gorgeous blue eyes were pensive. He sensed that he may have the upper hand again.

'You make it so hard on a lady when you put it like that. What are you suggesting?'

Timothy had to be very careful not to lose the game. He thought of a wicked approach then proceeded. 'Firstly, I suggest we start with champagne, and over canapés, we could discuss a proposal or two that I have to put to you.'

Caroline tried to suppress her excitement. Timothy having canapés – that was a first. This had to be something different. What could he mean? A proposal could mean …

Let's not think of that, she thought to herself. *Not yet anyway.* Possibly it had to be something to do with the news reading. Was he going to offer Caroline her own show? She was struggling to hide her feelings.

Timothy had been watching this gorgeous woman who looked so excited at what he was saying. He sensed the tension in her growing, her eyes so wide with expectation. Timothy began to lose concentration under Caroline's gorgeous gaze and felt he had to say something, otherwise he risked drowning in those big blue pools.

He broke her gaze. 'I'll get the champagne,' he said. *That should give me at least a minute to think*, he thought to himself. *Yes, then another minute while I get the canapés. This is great.*

Timothy returned with the champagne, then shrugged. 'The canapés, I will just grab them.' He turned away without looking at Caroline's eyes.

What is he up to? she wondered. *If he keeps this up I don't know what I'll do. If I can't get his attention soon, I'll go crazy!*

When Timothy returned with the canapés, Caroline seemed like a different person. Her blue eyes were flashing fiercely. The tension was electrifying. Timothy placed the canapés on the table and sat opposite Caroline. He raised his glass. Caroline held his gaze, stood with her glass in hand and walked around the table to Timothy. Without breaking his gaze she tipped the champagne down his shirt.

CHAPTER 38

'Oh, I'm so sorry! That is so clumsy of me!' She placed her glass on the table and leant over Timothy, her breasts popping forward in her dress. 'We'll just have to take that wet shirt off you.'

She straddled him and sat on his knees, then began to undo his shirt.

Timothy took a sip of his champagne without breaking Caroline's gaze. Both of them were now breathing heavily. Timothy continued to sip his champagne as Caroline pulled the tails of his shirt out of his trousers. She licked the remnants of the champagne from his chest. Timothy dropped his glass onto the carpet and rolled back onto the sofa with Caroline on top of him. The soft fabric of her dress created an electrifying feeling between the two of them. They paused for a moment, enjoying the amazing sensation. Then there was nothing but frantic action. The stilettos, dress and trousers were quickly discarded. They were now naked on the sofa, entwined and breathing heavily.

'You make it so hard for a lady,' moaned Caroline, as Timothy entered her.

When their breathless passionate lovemaking had concluded, Caroline pushed him back and asked, 'The first proposal is?'

'First,' Timothy captured Caroline's gaze, 'is what would you like for dinner?'

Caroline took a clump of Timothy's chest hair between her thumb and index finger and twisted viciously. Timothy grimaced with the pain, then held up his hands in surrender. 'No more, I give up!'

Caroline slowly released her grip.

'I think you might want to put on your dress for this,' he said.

Caroline released herself from their embrace, found her dress and slipped it on. She then returned and sat on Timothy's knees. She locked her fingers behind his neck. 'What?'

Timothy's eyelevel was at Caroline's breasts; he looked up at her, then back down.

'Keep your mind on what you're about to say Timothy. Otherwise remember the pain.'

Timothy looked down at the clump of hair that was surrounded by a red ring. The burning sensation was still there. 'Yes, I can still feel that. Down to business.' *Let's draw this out,* he thought. 'Caroline, I have been thinking. Things have been going so well between us – do you think we can take it to another level? You're so captivating that you even have a global audience of over two and a half billion. That has to mean something. How do you feel about … Look this is really difficult, I don't know how to say this …'

He looked with pleading eyes into Caroline's.

'Get on with it!' she hissed. 'I'm all dressed up with nowhere to go.'

Sensing that he had pushed the tension enough, Timothy began his delivery. 'Over the last few weeks, you've done so much to add value to the company that we've decided to offer you … a seat on the board. That means you will get a seven digit salary, stock options et cetera, as part of an overall remuneration package – but we can go into detail on that later.'

Caroline was looking for words, but all she could ask was, 'What does seven digits mean?'

'That's a number between one million and ten million pounds per year.'

Caroline was speechless. Those numbers were so big that they didn't make sense. She slumped forward onto Timothy, they embraced and sank back into the sofa. They spent an endless time whispering sweet nothings to each other until Timothy suggested that it was time for dinner. They felt like eating in the dining room rather than the suite after their intimate time together.

CHAPTER 39

A hush came over the room as Timothy and Caroline entered. The captain's table had two empty chairs at it and Caroline made a beeline for the chair beside the captain.

He rose and pulled out the chair for her. He found her stunning and very attractive. Her little black dress had him struggling to keep his eyes on hers. They sat and immediately began talking.

'Caroline, I think I have seen every one of your broadcasts. How are you finding the change in work style?'

Caroline was delighted by his distraction and uneasiness. 'Well, Captain, I haven't really had time to think about it. However it is very dynamic and exciting and different every day.'

Captain Delaney's conversation was mainly about Caroline's new career, and how different it was to her life in the UK a few weeks ago. Caroline was delighted to discuss the dramatic changes from being the communications coordinator on the Mercedes Around the World Ketch Race to now being the anchor of the Wiley International expedition into the Southern Ocean. She enjoyed the captain's interest.

'So what have you been doing while we were off the vessel?' she asked.

'I'm not sure if you were aware, but Timothy had re-hired us for an expedition to find the cause of the ice sheets before we got back to Fremantle.'

Caroline took the comment in her stride and gave nothing of her annoyance away. She was not aware that Timothy had chartered the vessel for a return expedition even before they had arrived in Fremantle. Was she overreacting? He had said 'additional equipment would be required' when Dr Perry gave her report – so they had had prior discussions about going back. She decided to let her annoyance go; it was around the time of Janice's disappearance and the assassination attempt; there was no room for suspicion in their relationship.

'We began resupplying the vessel and sourcing test equipment for Dr Perry while it was still three days away from Fremantle. This was the only way that we managed such a quick turnaround in going back out to sea.'

'That is amazing, Captain. Very organised of you and Timothy.'

The captain looked very pleased with himself. Timothy, meanwhile, was deep in conversation with Dr Perry.

'I'm astounded by the amount of attention this expedition has created,' said Dr Perry, 'and also the way the scientific community has become very defensive about their work. It appeared that the most defensive scientific theory groups were those associated with climate change, carbon emissions and government policy changes. Do you have any idea why these groups are so defensive?'

'Yes, those groups potentially see the expedition as a focal point that could allow other theories to challenge their own. The enormous media penetration created by the expedition had the ability to put an alternative in front of billions of viewers. Even the politicians were terrified of this sort of invasive scrutiny. The associated coverage has the ability to change governments, if their policies or actions were found to be wanting.'

'Goodness, I had no idea. This is even more exciting; we may change history with this expedition.'

'Yes, quite possibly.'

Later in the evening, Captain Delaney advised Timothy that he had invited the captain of the American Navy vessel to join them for dinner the following evening.

'Any particular topics you want to cover?' asked Timothy.

'I was thinking risks and issues that we could encounter over the next few weeks. Also, the weather is going to intensify as we head south. We need to plan as to how we can work effectively in those conditions.'

'We should have Dr Perry along. She'll be coordinating all the test work – she may have a better idea of restrictions and impacts than we do.'

'Great idea.'

The dining room was mostly empty by 11.00 pm; a small group of scientists remained at the bar. Timothy and Caroline called it an early night and headed back to their suite.

The next day was taken up with extensive preparation work for the planned testing scheduled for the following day. The US team had set up their satellite telemetry. They were running extensive tests in preparation for the research tests. They were planning to commence searching for ice sheets from 6.00 pm, hoping to have targets by midnight for the captain to steer towards.

The weather conditions in the target zone were continuing to deteriorate, with winds howling at 90 kilometres per hour, 15 metre waves, swells approaching 220 metres and a wind chill corrected temperature at around -50 degrees Celsius. Cranes had been erected at the stern of the vessel and the cables had been fitted with monitoring devices, in preparation for testing temperatures and flows to depths of up to 4000 metres.

A smart winged buoy, similar to a small submersible, was attached to the end of the cable to take readings while the vessel was travelling at speeds of up to 10 kilometres an hour. Sensors along the cable gave temperature readings at ten metre intervals. The daily broadcasts and planning were barely complete when Caroline and Timothy had to prepare for dinner with the captain and Dr Perry.

The dinner with the American captain turned out to be a formal affair. Captain Delaney's private dining suite was palatial with seating for twelve. There were formal pre-dinner drinks, a wonderful entrée, main and desserts. They then retired to the lounge room to discuss plans for safety and risk management.

They had barely sat down when at 9.45 pm, an officer entered the room with a message for Captain Delaney – they had detected ice sheets in the target zone and had a destination for the morning.

The meeting took on a new level of urgency and anticipation. They now had real targets to chase.

Dr Perry was the first to speak after the sailor left the room. 'The wind's expected to rise to 100 kilometres per hour in the target zone by the morning. The only safe work we would be able to do would be to calibrate the satellites to track the ice sheets on the ocean's surface and also to monitor temperatures over a wide area. Having done that, we would then focus on attempting to use the satellites to track the ice sheets beneath the water.'

Captain Delaney looked intrigued. 'How can the satellites track the ice underwater?'

'The Americans have an experimental system on their satellite that is supposed to be able to do that. It is very hush-hush though.'

'Impressive technology – I'll be curious to see if they can actually track the ice and how deep they can track it.'

CHAPTER 39

'I'll make sure I keep you informed, Captain.'

The following morning, there was a buzz of excitement throughout the ship. Targets had been detected and they were approaching them rapidly. Timothy addressed the scientific team at 7.00 am – a meeting that dampened the mood on the ship a little, as no scientific testing other than the preliminary work with the satellites could be conducted until the wind strength fell below 50 kilometres an hour. This wasn't likely to occur for at least twenty-four hours.

The telemetry from the satellites produced amazing feed footage for the morning news broadcast, showing ice sheets emerging from the ocean amongst towering 20 metre waves. The tops of the 300 metre swells were being lashed by 100 kilometre an hour winds. The images were of a very inhospitable, extremely cold environment. The captain was forced to circle the target zone to keep the vessel in motion and minimise the effect of the swells and wind upon the stability of the vessel. The telemetry feed had been patched into the ship's network, allowing access for every scientist on board. Scientists all over the ship were glued to their monitors, observing the data coming in on the ice sheets as they emerged. In the target zone, one or two new ice sheets were observed every ten minutes. They varied in weight from 5 to 100 tonnes.

By midday, the feed from the satellites had been stabilised and calibrated to show the ocean temperature over an area radiating out 25 kilometres from the centre of the target zone. Four calibration target zones were established, each due north, south, east and west of the primary target. As the data streamed in, it became obvious that there was a difference in temperature between the target zone and the four calibration points. At all four calibration points, the temperatures were significantly higher than the target. There was also a dramatic temperature profile across the target zone.

Shortly after midday, a request came in from the Kerguelen Islands. They wanted to be included in the expedition's studies. Timothy rejected the request; a diversion at that point would add another week or two to the overall schedule and he was not prepared to stretch the budget that far.

Unknown to the vessels on the surface, half a kilometre beneath them, a British Astute-class submarine had its own set of plans.

'Sir, we have a reasonable plan that can allow us to do what we have to do and getaway undetected. For the last twelve hours we've monitored the trajectory of the ice sheets as they've arisen from the depths. We believe it's possible to control one or more large ice sheets, changing their directories to intersect the target vessel.'

The submarine commander moved over to the simulation screen. 'Explain away son.'

Well, you see Sir, you've got this large object rising up through the water and it only takes a small force in the right position to change its direction. If we were to open our torpedo tubes and inject high-pressure water through them, by training that at exactly in the right position of one of these objects, we could manage its trajectory to hit a vessel above. At the moment, I believe the vessels above are simply maintaining a safety margin to avoid being hit. We can look at where these objects are rising, look at the safety margin and direct objects where we want them to go.'

CHAPTER 39

The commander nodded his agreement. 'Let's do the calculations and make it happen gentlemen.'

By 6.00 am, they were ready for their first trial. The submarine maintained its maximum depth of 500 metres. Five minutes passed before its sonar detected a rising ice sheet.

'Open torpedo tubes one and two. Fire up the water jets; pilot ahead standard. Controlled blow of ballast now.'

A sonar operator reported in. 'Sir, the object is moving with us and taking on the new trajectory.'

'Pilot, bring us to a stop.'

'It's working Sir; we're tracking right to the trajectory line.' The operator counted down the distance.

'Pilot, start backing us off gently, then take us to periscope depth.'

When they raised the periscope, the commander observed the ice sheet crashing up through the waves 500 metres away.

'Okay gentlemen, let's set the trap, locate the target and work out the trajectories. Let's see if we can line up one of the sheets to do our work for us.'

It took several hours for the submarine crew to identify the correct set of conditions. The commander was advised and his team began tracking the variables required to execute his plan.

The *Spirit of the Southern Ocean* had been stationary for some time as technicians attempted to track the underwater objects with the satellites.

One of the technicians on board the submarine became excited. 'We have a go sir, all ducks in a line.'

The commander acknowledged with a barked command. 'Let's make it happen – get to it sailors!'

The submarine dropped into position, waiting for the rising ice sheet. The commander surveyed his team; in less than forty-five minutes they would become unacknowledged heroes, the players in a classified operation to send the *Spirit of the Southern Ocean* and Timothy Wiley to the bottom of the ocean. The plan was brilliant, the analogy being to use a feather to redirect a massive moving object. The gentle force of the water jets would change the direction of the ice sheet, giving it a trajectory straight into the path of Timothy Wiley's catamaran.

Sonar detected a sheet at 2000 metres deep and rising. The team were totally focused on the activities needed to manage the rising sheet. The countdown began for engagement.

'Ten, nine, eight, seven, six, five, four …' There was silence from the crew until the sonar operator screamed, 'Blow all tanks! Brace for impact!'

The commander and the sonar operator made eye contact as the first large ice sheet smashed into the submarine amidships. It was only in the last second that the single sonar contact had split into no fewer than five individual contacts.

The impact was devastating. The hull ruptured with a deafening roar; there were cries of pain and terror along the length of the submarine. They were in total blackness. It only took seconds for the cold ocean water to engulf the ruptured shell.

At 1.30 pm, Timothy received a briefing from Dr Perry. 'Timothy, the satellite technicians are now working to calibrate their equipment to detect the ice sheets beneath the surface of the ocean.'

By 4.00 pm, the technicians had determined that their equipment would not be able to track the ice beneath the surface. Dr Parry reported the findings to Timothy.

'What now, Doctor?'

'It had been anticipated that the satellites may not be able to track the ice beneath the surface, so we have been working on a sonar solution to this problem. It involves towing sonar devices through the target zones to track the ice sheets.'

'Sounds pretty realistic to me. When will you be able to start?'

'As soon as the winds drop.'

At 4.36 pm, there was massive disruption amongst the scientists. The satellite team's appeared to be rushing in all directions. An alert siren sounded on the *Spirit of the Southern Ocean*, indicating that there was some form of emergency in progress.

Timothy took a call in his office; it was Captain Delaney. 'You need to be in the satellite monitoring room right now, Timothy.'

Timothy collected his team and moved to the satellite tracking room.

The scientists in the room were crowded around the large monitors, talking in highly agitated tones. On the large screen monitors, there was an area of massive turbulence in the middle of the target zone. Instead of large ice sheets merging in the ocean, there was now a field of ice fragments and other material in the water. No-one could explain what had just happened, to cause an ice sheet to be torn apart. The scientists were still struggling with the first event when a second occurred. This time the satellite detected some form of heat flash in the target zone, some twenty to thirty seconds before ice fragments began to surface. There was definitely other material in the water. The American vessel moved at full speed towards the centre of the target zone.

In the satellite monitoring room, Timothy and his team watched in silence, until Timothy addressed the scientists. 'Can someone tell me what we are looking at please?'

The captain came into the satellite tracking room. 'Timothy, we have sonar contacts and a massive amount of noise coming from the centre of the target zone. I'm in contact with the Americans.'

The Americans arrived in the zone of the fragments within

ten minutes, but due to rough seas, howling winds and ice in the water, they were forced back. The captain of the American vessel surmised that the heat signature contact indicated that a nuclear submarine may have experienced a fatal collision with an ice sheet. Their sonar contacts were now showing two objects sinking rapidly into the depths.

As the objects sank, there appeared to be one further collision with an ice sheet, with multiple fragments heading towards the surface. The collisions were punctuated by a massive amount of noise below the surface. Matters got worse rapidly, as the satellites reported a massive increase in temperature at the centre of the target field. Two minutes later, the satellites reported significant radiation in the target zone, streaming north. Both vessels were moved to 50 kilometres south of the centre of the target field to maintain safety.

The captains of both vessels had a telephone conference with Timothy. The American captain was adamant about what he had just witnessed. 'Timothy, what we have just witnessed, was the destruction of a stealth nuclear submarine, origin unknown. It generated both noise and a heat flash followed by an intense radiation signature. I must insist this was irrefutable proof of the nature of the incident that we just witnessed.'

Timothy addressed the captains. 'Can we launch a search mission?'

The American captain was quick to respond. 'It's much too hot in there at the moment. We're going to need to wait until the radiation dissipates and the swells reduce before we can send a chopper in.'

Captain Delaney added, 'Local conditions aren't suitable for a search and rescue operation, with wind speeds 90 to 120 kilometres an hour, wave height to 20 metres and a wind chill air temperature of -50 Celsius. We need those winds below 50 kilometres per hour for safe operations.'

His American counterpart came back in agreement. 'Couldn't agree more, Captain … anything above fifty and it's too risky. The maps are showing a bit of a wind reduction an hour after dawn tomorrow – that would be the time to go out and search. Unfortunately, it will be bodies only by then.'

'We need to ask the UN to advise all member nations that the identity of the vessel is still unknown,' said Timothy. 'We need urgent assistance in identifying the vessel and any information on potential pollutants and radiation levels that we may encounter.'

After issuing the communiqué, Timothy and his team swung into immediate action to get the latest news out to the world. The headline read: 'Intruder submarine destroyed by ice sheets in the Southern Ocean'.

'That's an eye-catching headline,' commented Timothy.

'How much information do we have to offer the public?' asked Miles.

'Not much I'm afraid,' said Timothy. 'We have sonar contacts, the flash, temperature and radiation detected from the satellites and sonar noise. Let's do the best we can with that. There may be some debris in the morning.'

They worked feverishly to put together the feed material from the satellites. At 5.30 pm, darkness descended across the target zone; the *Spirit of the Southern Ocean* and the Americans continued to circle. There had been no sign of a distress beacon flare or any other indicator that anybody was alive out there.

The story came together and two hours later, Caroline was on the air around the globe with the headline story.

The mood in the dining room that night was very subdued; the scant information about the event under the ocean, and the knowledge that a whole crew had potentially died beneath them, made for a lot of very glum conversations. The speculation was depressing and the implications – beyond human loss – was numbing. Fifty kilometres away, there was potentially an environmental disaster and only time would tell the extent of the damage done. Captain Delaney had flown to the American vessel for a detailed discussion with its captain. He was not expected back until late into the evening.

After dinner, Timothy and Caroline met with the doctors to plan the next day's schedule and Dr Perry outlined her plan. 'The buoy will be towed through the target zone without endangering the vessel or the occupants. It should be able to give us valuable information on the temperature profile in the target zone, depths and water velocity. If by chance it detects an ice sheet, it'll also tell us the velocity that the ice sheet is rising at. With the wind velocity dropping rapidly, we should be able to start testing as early as 6.00 am.'

Things moved quickly – Miles and Gary spent all their time coordinating between the production and satellite teams, Dr Perry, Captain Delaney, Timothy and Caroline. Their days stretched out to sixteen hours but there was no time to complain. The global reach had now extended to three billion people – almost half the planet was watching the developments in the Southern Ocean in all forms of media.

When dawn broke the next morning, the wind had dropped to a relatively calm 40 kilometres per hour and the wave height had eased to 8 metres but the temperature was still low, hovering at around 1 degree Celsius. The ocean looked majestic with the perfectly formed swells, rolling from west to east on 100 metre centres, like unbroken ranks of marching soldiers.

On board the *Spirit of the Southern Ocean*, there was a three-pronged attack on the target zone. The scientists were using the buoy to probe the target zone, while the satellites were searching

CHAPTER 39

for debris and survivors from the submarine. A naval helicopter was checking current and wind vectors to identify any debris from the previous night.

The naval helicopter made the first grim discovery. 'Body in the water,' came the call from the helicopter radio operator.

The next report from the helicopter proved their worst fears. 'The body's too hot to recover without safety gear and a net. We're tagging the body and returning for nets and safety equipment.'

One of the satellites was recalibrated off the tagged body in the water and detected seven others within a short period of time. The helicopter was kept busy well into the afternoon retrieving bodies.

In the meantime, the buoy was in place and towed through the target zone. The telemetry feedback was mind-boggling. Dr Perry called a briefing for Timothy and his team in the monitoring laboratory.

'Timothy, 1190 metres down, at the southern end of the zone, is a very tall mountain range. As the Antarctic currents of cold water heading towards the equator hit the mountain range, it is forced up towards the surface. After clearing the mountain range, the current continues to flow north and rises toward the surface as it moves north, getting to the surface some 30 kilometres from where it initially strikes the mountain range. If the ice sheets were in this flow and had struck the submarine some 15 kilometres from the mountain range, it would be 800 to 1000 metres below the surface.

'We have observed this morning that the intensity of the radiation plume has dropped to below safe levels, which tends to indicate the remains of the submarine are a very long way down.'

Timothy moved away from the screens he had been observing. 'Dr Perry, have any ice sheets been detected in the current yet?'

'Not at this stage – the satellites have not detected any at all this morning.'

'Okay, please let me know as soon as we have a sheet to track.'

Dr Perry was feeling a little pressured by Timothy's first appearance of impatience. 'As soon as we detect a sheet, you will know.'

Timothy motioned to his team. 'Back to the office team; show's over.'

The helicopter was able to recover several tonnes of debris by nightfall. Tracing through the debris and the sailor's uniforms and belongings, the US Navy was able to identify the origin of the stealth submarine by mid-evening.

The captain briefed Timothy on the origin of the submarine at 10.00 pm in his stateroom.

'Timothy, take a seat. I asked you to come alone due to the sensitivity of this matter.' He paused. 'The submarine's origin is now known. We don't have a vessel name but the crew was definitely British Navy.'

Timothy looked perplexed. 'That's hard to believe, after all that we have been through with the UN and Parliament. Knowing that these objects have a very vague sonar or radar image, why in god's name would you send a sub into harm's way?'

'It also has us baffled. It seems like a very risky, if not foolhardy, strategy that ended in disaster.'

'You know, from the moment the sub was detected, I assumed it was Chinese.'

'I would have agreed … I'm just as surprised as you about its identity. We do need to insist that you don't broadcast the identity of the sailors for at least two hours – that will give the navy time to brief their personnel and governments to be informed.'

'Obviously it will take us some time to prepare the story, Captain – two hours sounds about right. If that's all, we have a story to write.'

'That's all for now Timothy, good night.'

'Thanks Captain, good night.'

Timothy walked slowly back to his office, deep in thought about the repercussions of this story on parliament and the British nation.

Caroline went live at 1.00 am local time. Her headlines were about to bring a government down.

'Resign now!'

'All dead on-board stealth submarine in the Southern Ocean.'

'Government lies, sailors die.'

Within hours the British Government was under siege. The global and social media was baying for their demise. The Parliament had gone into lockdown in an attempt to find a position of unity to present to the world. Behind closed doors, both houses of parliament were locked in angry debate. The government was using the Official Secrets Act to control the information being provided to Parliament. This was occurring at a time of unprecedented pressure from within the parliament. With the media assault and now the added pressure of a relentless social media, there appeared to be a need for a new order. How could a government hide behind the Official Secrets Act at a time when the available public information rendered the act unusable? The opposition was relentless in their attack. Member after member demanded that the government stop hiding behind the act. Three hours into the debate, a division was called. The government's majority evaporated as members crossed the floor. The speaker tied the vote and the houses of parliament went into uproar.

The uproar ended abruptly as the Queen entered the parliament. She stood before both houses. Never before had the members experienced their monarch showing such passion or determination. She didn't ask or implore them to set their differences aside and work as one for god and country – she demanded it. She went on to paint a grim picture for them. This, for Britain, was a moment of extreme infamy. This was Britain's *Rainbow Warrior*. They needed a stiff upper lip and unflinching determination to win back the confidence of her people and the respect of the world.

The Queen surveyed the parliament as if challenging each and every member. 'Should we fail to act as one in this matter, and convince the world of our commitment to democracy and a rule of law, then we face the possibility of economic disaster. The wolves are at our door, ladies and gentlemen – now act as one to save our people.' The Queen then addressed the speaker. 'Mr Speaker, I suggest you and I meet privately.'

In that private discussion, the Queen requested that Mr Wiley be asked to join in, in solving the problems of the nation as soon as possible, 'to assist in cleaning up the mess'.

With that, the Queen was escorted out of parliament to a waiting convoy and whisked back to Buckingham Palace. There was a hushed silence in the house until the speaker returned and brought the house to order. 'You heard the demand of the Queen – I call for a division. This is for Queen and for country.'

The division was carried decisively in favour of the Queen's request. The speaker, now empowered by the joint houses, called for a balanced committee from both houses to immediately convene to prepare their response to the world.

The response included an understanding that the government would take responsibility and resign – a caretaker government would be sworn in immediately.

CHAPTER 39

Back in the Southern Ocean, the scientific research was continuing at fever pitch.

Several hours earlier they had detected their first ice sheet in the Antarctic current. They were now planning to follow the ice sheets and the current back to its source.

The buoy had been fitted with sonar, so it was now possible to avoid the ice sheets as they approached if needed. The buoy was played out gradually to a depth of 3500 metres as they moved away from the underwater mountain range. It was travelling 300 metres above the polar river containing the ice sheets. Ice sheets were observed travelling north as the buoy travelled south. Less than 100 kilometres from the target zone, the ice sheets began to thin out and disappear. The buoy was reeled in and over the course of the day, they made five more passes. They gathered an enormous amount of telemetry information that the scientists were busily studying. The last buoy run was made at 3.00 pm with the scientists planning to have a review at 6.00 pm.

Timothy met briefly with Dr Perry for an update. Dr Perry was able to provide him with sufficient information for the production team to start work on the next news broadcast. She anticipated that they would be able to table sufficient information during the evening for a midnight broadcast. For the first time since the expedition began, the scientists and the media were able to schedule their work for a twenty-four hour operation. The buoy was to be refitted with additional sensors, with runs to commence at 9.00 pm that evening. The new series of tests would continue until 9.00 am, when the buoy would be fitted with another new set of sensors.

The testing of this site would be completed within twenty-four hours. Timothy had authorised testing of two additional sites, should they be found within 100 kilometres of the current position.

CHAPTER 40

The world had become mesmerised by the eruption of events precipitated by Wiley International's expedition into the Southern Ocean.

On board the *Spirit of the Southern Ocean*, Timothy and the team assessed the impact. Miles read aloud the headlines from emails pouring in from around the world:

From their London office:

'Queen dictates the need of the people to Houses of Parliament'

'British Government resigns, caretaker government sworn in'

'Did the Queen push the Government or did it resign?'

'Law Council challenges the Official Secrets Act!'

From New York:

'World Criminal Court to investigate the assault on Timothy Wiley and his team.'

'British Defence and Environment Ministers "people of interest".'

From Brussels:

'EU distances itself from Britain.'

Timothy sat quietly at his desk, absorbing the enormity of what he and the team had unleashed on the world. 'How are China and India responding, Miles?'

Miles scanned his emails. From Beijing:

'Unrest grows in China; orders are cancelled for energy projects globally.'

'Chinese Government in lockdown for emergency measures meeting.'

From Delhi:

'Indian riot squads mobilised.'

'Riots in six cities as manufacturing giants close their doors.'

Miles shook his head. 'It's looking pretty grim Timothy – this is the makings of a massive global recession.'

Timothy had a grim look on his face. 'Let's take a break; I need to make a few phone calls.'

As soon as the room was clear, Timothy was on the phone to his broker. 'Hi Mark, how are the shares looking?'

'Couldn't be better – they went through $100 on the New York exchange thirty minutes ago, up 15 per cent today.'

'How many do I have left?'

'Fifty-six million.'

'How much in other shares?'

'Fifteen million at current values.'

'What can I get for our stock in large parcels?'

'In the current market, upward of $120.'

'Mark, sell all my other shares at best, then offload forty million of our stock at $120 and above. Then place a conditional order for fifty million of our stock at $20 in five days.'

'That's a real power play – any particular reason for it?'

'I don't think the rise is sustainable; the whole market is in freefall. Our stocks must eventually follow the market down.'

'Okay Timothy, sound plan. Was there anything else?'

'That's it – let me know when it is done.'

'Will do; text you soon.'

Timothy's attention slowly came back to the room. Caroline was seated on the sofa, absorbed in a magazine. He looked at her.

She probably had no idea that the deal he had just put in play would give him a net cash worth in excess of five billion dollars, possibly by the end of the day.

'Caroline, the stock went through $100. You have two million – I suggest you sell now and possibly buy some back later when they fall, which they must. Here's my broker's details. Please feel free to mention my name – he'll help you set up the sell-buy orders.'

Caroline looked stunned. 'That's …'

'Don't think about it Caroline, just do it now.'

Caroline, departed for her office still looking stunned. She returned five minutes later. 'All done at $120.'

Timothy received an SMS as she entered. 'All sold, got $120 for Caroline as well; market's at $105.'

'Let's drink a toast to that, Caroline,' said Timothy. 'You just had your bank account improve by $240 million, less commissions.'

Caroline had that stunned look again. She looked at Timothy. A month ago, she had a unit in London, with a large mortgage on it; today, she was independently wealthy. This relationship was a real life-changer. She had fallen for Timothy before all of this and she was having difficulties believing it was all really true.

Timothy poured the champagne. 'Here's to the rewards of very hard work.'

She responded quietly, watching Timothy the whole time. 'Thank you Timothy, I love you.'

Timothy hesitated, then for the first time was able to acknowledge how he felt about her without a twinge of remorse. 'I love you Caroline.'

They were moving toward one another when there was a knock and Miles entered the room.

Miles noted the champagne, ignored it and proceeded.

'Timothy, the UN is issuing a caution to us. They feel that parts of the world are on the brink of upheaval. They say they need our assistance in averting massive unrest and riots.'

'I'm not sure how we can meet that request without it being a response to media censorship!'

'They further claim it would be a humanitarian gesture, to avoid death and suffering. They're saying that we have broken new ground in global coverage and that a higher level of moral responsibility is required. They are suggesting self-regulation be applied and that we refer to the UN for acknowledgement, not approval.'

'What do the lawyers say?'

'They basically say the same as the UN – that we are in new unchartered territory, to take care.'

'Then let's proceed with caution, Miles. Tell the editors to take into consideration the possible humanitarian impact that the reports could have and to deal with it with caution.'

CHAPTER 41

Later that day on the *Spirit of the Southern Ocean*, Dr Perry was concluding the 6.00 pm scientific update.

'As we can see from the display on the screen, it appears that the cold Antarctic stream was gradually forced towards the surface by hitting the submerged mountain range. The stream is moving at approximately 2 kilometres an hour and it takes up to five hours to curve over the mountain range. At some stage during that climb, the ice sheets are formed, but at this stage we only have theories as to how. The buoy runs commencing at 9.00 pm, would have sensor packages aimed at testing out some of those theories. We anticipated having sufficient telemetry information by 3.00 am to start assessing some of the scientific theories.'

The production team was ecstatic as there was finally an outcome to report to the world. They had found the source of the ice sheets. An upbeat news broadcast was prepared and went to air at 10.00 pm local time.

At Halley station Ed Chew had spent the time during the communication blackout coming to terms with his impending fate. This morning, communication had been gradually restored with the outside world; his time of contemplation was at an end. He had systematically inspected the station modules ensuring that they were all locked and secure. Once back at the canteen, he retrieved a small backpack containing his dart pistol; he loaded a dart and placed the pistol in his parker pocket.

Ed had moved slowly through the airlock to the blizzard outside. When he reached the door, he had turned with a remorseful look on his face. Memories of the good times with his colleagues flooded back. He had enjoyed all of their company, from Andy's practical jokes to Sarah's warmth and compassion. They were all wonderful people. He had lived for very long time amongst them. In the last few days, he had begun to realise that his dedication to his political ideology was only strong because of the dependency of the welfare of his family back in China. They would not have been safe had he not carried out his orders. Without that dependency, he saw no reason for the terrible act he had committed here.

Ed had walked about 100 metres out into the blizzard before throwing his backpack away. He had planned his last minutes carefully. First, throw the backpack away, then walk another 100 metres or so. Then in one rapid action he shot a dart into his thigh and threw the pistol as far away from his body as possible. In the event that his body was found, it would look like all the other bodies – even killed by the same dart.

Ed felt relieved as the darkness of death closed in over him. He now no longer had to deal with his conscience.

Overnight there had been considerable political and military activity in London and Paris. The automatic telemetry at the Halley Station had come online two days ago. MI6 had placed secret monitoring equipment on the base just prior to the departure of the summer team. There had been some concern about security around data manipulation and the Defence Minister had requested that he have 'eyes on the base'. The new equipment had captured the deaths of three scientists in the canteen and the departure of Ed from the base into a blizzard soon after the cameras came online. There had been no sightings of anyone alive on the station for the past two days. No contact could be established with the other six scientists on the base for the six hours since the telemetry had been established. After that time, a vertical take-off and landing aircraft was dispatched from the Falklands with a tanker escort. The jet was expected to reach the base within three hours.

In the meantime MI6 had begun high level discussions with the French DPSD. It appeared more than coincidental that the Halley scientist and the maintenance engineer of the grounded French helicopter were both ex-Chinese nationals. Investigations were proceeding with both countries cooperating fully.

At 7.00 am the following morning, Dr Perry submitted her next scientific update. The telemetry from the second sensor package on the buoy had given inconclusive results. The scientists had found what appeared to be a series of complex eddies in the uplift region where the Antarctic stream rose to go over the mountain range. Other than having some temperature profiles and water velocities, the scientists didn't feel that they had come any closer to resolving how the ice sheets were formed from that set of readings. The next sensor package on the buoy would hopefully provide more information allowing some conclusive findings.

The telemetry from the third sensor package had just started coming in. The scientists began to develop a three-dimensional model showing the interaction between the Antarctic current, the eddy and the mountain range. By noon, they had sufficient information for Dr Perry to call another briefing.

In this briefing, Dr Perry was able to show in detail how the ice sheets were forming. 'Ladies and gentlemen, as the Antarctic flow approaches the mountain range, it's approximately 4 kilometres down. It appears that due to stratification and laminar flow, a thin ice layer has been able to form between the freshwater and saltwater layers. This is due to the salt water being at close to -2 degrees and fresh water freezes at zero degrees. This thin ice layer prevents intermixing of the salt and fresh water, allowing fresh water to exist in the ocean over 1500 kilometres from any known source. As the flow approaches the mountain range, it moves up the mountain slope and encounters the eddies, where the ice surrounding the freshwater breaks into segments and is trapped until it exits the eddy. The eddy velocity is higher than the approaching Antarctic flow because of the acceleration caused by a large volume of water trying to move through a reduced gap over the mountain range. This increased velocity, and the time the ice is trapped in the eddy, gives better heat transfer and a longer time to freeze the sheets.

'As the sheets are ejected from the eddy, they pass over the mountain range where they are breaking free of the slowing Antarctic stream and then take a separate trajectory to the surface with some of the stream, while the bulk of the stream heads down the other side of the mountain. These upwellings, as they are known globally, are well known around these types of structures in the ocean. But never before have ice sheet formations been associated with upwellings.

'The findings are irrefutable. The temperature of the Antarctic stream is lower than would have been expected but the existence of stratification and freshwater streams in the ocean more than 1500 kilometres from the nearest source is exciting for all of us.'

Dr Perry looked up at her audience and held a long silence.

'One question still remains – how does fresh water enter the ocean and remain in an intact stratification to get into the Antarctic flow?'

Timothy and the production team were stunned by the report.

While the production team worked on their latest broadcast, Timothy called a meeting with Dr Perry and Dr Mellows. Dr Perry was dreading the meeting, as she was already anticipating its content.

'Thanks for coming on such short notice,' said Timothy. 'I've called for this meeting to determine where we are up to with our research and findings. I guess what I'm looking for in particular is whether or not we have determined how and where the ice sheets are forming.'

'Yes, we can definitively say that we have determined how and where the ice sheets are forming.'

'Then I assume the next step is to determine how the fresh water got here?'

'Correct.'

'This is not what you want to hear,' said Timothy, 'but my job is done here. I have been summoned back to London and unfortunately, it's not a request I can refuse. Within twelve hours we will be packing up and heading back towards Perth. After this meeting, I will make an offer to the UN for them to take over searching for the source of the freshwater.'

'Of course we understand that; it's a business decision you have to make. Our next step in the research could take some weeks to determine. From the telemetry information that we have, it appears that the surface currents in the area and the wind chill temperature are considerably lower than expected. We need to test several other theories before we fully understand what is going on here.'

'So Dr Perry, if you were to summarise what you feel is going on here, what would you say?'

'I am confident in saying that carbon-related global warming has never been the only significant influence on the planet's weather. The findings here in the Southern Ocean conclusively show us that all the other climate-influencing factors need to be monitored very closely. What we have found could be the first sign that the competing influences of global warming, along with polar cap and glacial melting, as well as larger winter ice sheets, are causing substantially colder winters and changing the global thermal flux. In this hypothesis, I would include the impact of several other influencing theories, each driving lower Antarctic temperatures, higher wind speeds and more reflectivity in the clouds due to salt inclusion. Beyond that, we can't begin to fully understand the competing dynamics that we have seen here until we transpose our findings to the northern hemisphere and test the same dynamics there. If the summer melt doesn't keep the ice at bay, then we could easily fall into a cascade of events to produce an ice age, triggered in part by global warming itself.'

Dr Perry hesitated for a few moments as if capturing a fleeting thought.

'The east coast of Australia had upwellings recently with the presence of very large sharks, and massive schools of bait fish. I didn't think of it before but the documented cause was an upwelling of nutrient-rich cold water that impacted on the coast as far north as Sydney. In January and in late February, Lake Eyre received water again and there had only been a gap of a couple of years since the last water in the lake. This is unprecedented since white settlement. My god – Timothy, are we beyond the tipping point?'

AUTHOR'S NOTE

This work is the result of the author's ideas being skilfully arranged by a collaborative group of wonderful people.

Beyond Tipping Point, like all works of fiction, has invented characters. The themes and underlying scientific theories, however, do exist out there in news articles, technical journals and scientific publications. As an engineer, innovator and scientist, I used to dedicate one day a year to looking at world issues an example being global warming. That research proved to have enormous scope for producing material for a series of eco thrillers the first being *Beyond Tipping Point*.

My first editor, Tanya, skilfully introduced me to third person tense and the bite of correction, and criticism skilfully packaged as skill development.

Beau Hillier, my final editor, has guided the words and ideas – and skilfully culled, cajoled and teased them into an exciting novel that delivers the message.

Thank you Stephanie for the support in the form of self-learning, and the wonderful complex books on how to write.

Catherine delivered the wonderful photo for the 'About the Author'. 'He scrubs up well in the hands of a skilful professional photographer.'

And Lydia, thank you for the excitement you expressed after reading those first few chapters three years ago – you can't imagine how much that meant. As for reading the final edit cover-to-cover and uttering those magic words, 'I couldn't put it down' – absolutely priceless. Love you.

www.ingramcontent.com/pod-product-compliance
Lightning Source LLC
Chambersburg PA
CBHW060148050426
42446CB00013B/2718